WHY THE UNITED STATES DOES NOT HAVE A NATIONAL HEALTH PROGRAM

D0076128

Vicente Navarro, Editor

**POLICY,
POLITICS,
HEALTH AND
MEDICINE
Series**
Vicente Navarro, Series Editor

BAYWOOD PUBLISHING COMPANY, Inc.
Amityville, New York 11701

Library of Congress Catalog Card Number: 92-23584
ISBN: 0-89503-105-1

Library of Congress Cataloging-in-Publication Data
  Main entry under title:

Why the United States does not have a national health program   /   edited
  by Vicente Navarro.
        p.   cm. – – (Policy, politics, health and medicine series)
    Includes bibliographical references and index.
    ISBN 0-89503-105-1 (pbk.)
    1.   Medicine, State– –United States.   2.   Medical policy– –United
States.   3.   Insurance, Health– –Government policy– –United States.
I. Navarro, Vicente.   II. Series : Policy, politics, health and
medicine series (Unnumbered)
RA412.5 U6W52   1992
362. 1'0973– –dc20   92-23584
                                                                              CIP

TABLE OF CONTENTS

Introduction

The United States is the only major industrialized nation whose government does not guarantee the right of access to health care in time of need by providing universal and comprehensive health benefits coverage to its citizens. The majority of funding and administration of health services in the United States is private, and the market—a highly controlled market—allocates resources according to the consuming power of the U.S. population. Health care is rationed; its availability depends on the consumer's financial resources. As a consequence, the United States faces a unique set of problems in health care. One is the extremely high cost of care: 12 percent of the gross national product is spent in health care, the highest in the world today. Another is the lack of any form of health benefits coverage for 18 percent of the population and, equally important, insufficient health benefits coverage for the majority of the population. Eighty-seven percent of Americans, for example, do not have health benefits coverage for long-term care services, which on average cost $27,000 per year, way beyond the reach of the average family (median family income in the U.S. was $32,000 in 1991). Third is the extremely inefficient system of health services, in which 25 percent of every health dollar goes to administration and paper shuffling. In summary, this health care system is the most inefficient, costly, and inhumane attempt at health care in the Western industrialized world. Every day the press covers heartbreaking stories of people of every class, race, gender, and age facing the nightmare of not having access to life-saving medicine or treatment because they cannot pay for it. No other population in the industrialized world faces such a humiliating and painful situation.

Not surprisingly, poll after poll shows that the overwhelming majority of the U.S. population wants to see profound changes in the funding and organization of health care. But in spite of this popular desire, we do not see that change. Popular will is not realized through our political institutions. Why? The contributors to this book attempt to answer this question.

The book is divided into six sections. The chapters in Section I present analyses of the ideological positions put forward by the government, mainstream media, and academia in the United States to explain and justify the current situation. In the 1980s we witnessed federal health policies that included (*a*) a reduction of federal health expenditures, (*b*) a weakening of federal health and safety regulations to protect workers, consumers, and the environment, and (*c*) a further privatization and commodification of medical services. These policies, which have substantially hurt much of the U.S. population, have been justified by four major assumptions that have been reproduced by the nation's major value-generating systems, including the government and the media: first, the Reagan and Bush Administrations received an overwhelming popular mandate to reduce the federal role in the health sector; second, the size and growth of federal social (including health) expenditures are contributing to the current economic recession; third, the costs to business of federally imposed health and safety regulations have contributed to making the U.S. economy less competitive; and fourth, market interventions are intrinsically more efficient than government interventions in regulating the costs and distribution of health resources. All of these positions are heavily ideological and conflict with the evidence available to us. Vicente Navarro shows in Chapter 1 that, contrary to conventional wisdom, the evidence supports a different set of assumptions: the majority of Americans want an expansion of federal health expenditures and a strengthening of federal health regulations; U.S. government expenditures and regulations are much more limited than those of other countries whose economies are performing more satisfactorily; and those countries with larger government interventions have more efficient health care systems than does the United States, where "free market" forces are primarily responsible for the allocation of resources.

The enormous crisis in U.S. health care has led a growing number of voices to call for the establishment of a government funded and administered National Health Program (NHP) that—like the governments of all other major industrialized countries—would provide universal and comprehensive health benefits coverage to its population. Again, we have seen the entire ideological apparatus of the medical-industrial complex and its government mobilized to oppose this call. In that ideological avalanche, four positions are reproduced. They state that "Americans do not want a further expansion of government roles in their lives"; "a National Health Program would further increase the rate of growth of health expenditures"; "the federal deficit is too large and needs to be reduced before establishing a National Health Program"; and "people do not want to pay higher taxes." These arguments are being reproduced in most health policy forums in which establishment voices are dominant. In Chapter 2, Navarro questions each of these assumptions, presenting evidence that shows their ideological rather than scientific basis.

The lack of ideological diversity in the hegemonic media and the limited plurality of positions in academia explain the strength of conventional wisdom in the United States. Heavily ideological statements are presented as objective facts, in spite of the potent evidence to the contrary. One of these objective facts, reproduced in the 1980s and continuing into the 1990s, is that the Reagan policies of austerity responded to a popular mandate. People wanted the federal government to continue to follow the path it had taken. In a country that claims to be democratic, the legitimacy of government policies is based on the popular mandate. People had spoken in 1980, in 1984, and again in 1988: they wanted government off their backs. There was an almost universal agreement on this interpretation of the 1980s elections. Yet the facts show otherwise. Reagan and Bush were elected by minorities, not majorities, of the U.S. electorate (almost half stayed at home on election day). And polls showed that by large majorities people did not agree with the federal health policies created by the Republican Administration and supported by the Democratic Congress. In December 1982, Navarro published in the *New England Journal of Medicine* evidence to show that there was no popular mandate for the Reagan policies in the health sector. In August 1984, R. Blendon and D. E. Altman, leading figures of the Robert Wood Johnson Foundation, a most important molder of "acceptable" opinion, replied in an article in which they rather contemptuously referred to Americans as schizophrenic. Shortly after, in the fall of 1984, the main intellectual instrument of the U.S. corporate health establishment, the journal *Health Affairs,* published a whole set of positions put forward by the publisher, the editor, and several contributors, including an interview with the President of the Johnson Foundation, in which the popular mandate argument was again reproduced. Navarro wrote a letter to *Health Affairs* questioning these positions. A debate followed that was only partially published in that journal. Chapter 3 consists of this debate in its entirety.

The popular mandate argument assumes that the political institutions are representative of the U.S. population. This assumption is widely held not only in the major media but in academia as well. A representative work is one of the most acclaimed explanations of U.S. Medicine, Paul Starr's *The Social Transformation of American Medicine.* In this book, which received the Pulitzer Prize, Starr explains the evolution of U.S. medicine as the result of the wishes of the U.S. population expressed through its political institutions. Different interest groups interact in the medical sector, of course, and this conflict influences the evolution of the medical institutions. But these conflicts and their resolution take place within a set of parameters defined by the majority of Americans, whose beliefs and wants eventually determine what occurs in medicine. In Chapter 4, Navarro criticizes this idealization of U.S. political institutions. The voice of the people is only one voice, competing with other, more influential voices in the shaping of health policy. Many powerful forces have a stronger influence in the determination of health policy than does the voice of the popular majority. U.S. medicine is not the form of medicine chosen by most Americans. Actually, the evidence indicates that Americans have for quite some time wanted significant changes in medicine. The large abstentionism of the U.S. electorate (unmatched in any other society) and the majority's suspicion of the political institutions and their instruments, both Republican and Democrat, have been a longstanding characteristic of the U.S. political scene.

This degree of political alienation from both parties and from political institutions has reached its peak in the 1980s and 1990s, while the government has been following, according to Starr, the popular mandate. The 1992 election campaign has illustrated the mass alienation in the United States, a political alienation that a perceptive observer, less influenced by hegemonic ideology, could have seen building up for several decades. Starr's position justifies rather than explains a current political order in which the few rather than the many control the nation's destiny. The U.S. constitution opens with the inspiring and moving phrase "We the People." But, given the lack of an NHP in a country where the majority of the people support one, "We the People" should be amended to add the insurance companies, the medical-industrial complex, and many other interest groups whose influence in the corridors of power is much greater than that of the American people. The analysis of these key interest groups is the subject of Section II of this volume.

In Chapter 5, Thomas Bodenheimer, one of the most articulate critics of the U.S. health insurance industry, analyzes the behavior of this industry showing how the principle of insurance, as practiced by the industry, is in conflict with the principle of health care as a human right. Combining theoretical with empirical information, Bodenheimer debunks each of the arguments put forward by the U.S. insurance industry to sustain its dominance in the funding of health care. He shows how the industry has contributed to health care inflation: it wastes billions in administrative and marketing costs, it is unfair to many groups in society, it has undermined the positive features of health maintenance reforms, and it has far too much economic and political power.

A frequently heard argument against the possibility of establishing an NHP in the United States is that we cannot afford it, it is too expensive. Yet this country already spends more on health services than does any other nation, in both absolute and percentage terms. In spite of this, U.S. society faces problems in the health sector unmatched in any other society. The problem is not the money but the channels through which the money flows. The United States is not just the only major industrialized country without an NHP, it is also the only such country where most health care funding and administration is private rather than public. This is the root of the problems of costs, limited coverage, and waste. Robert Brandon, Michael Podhorzer, and Thomas Pollak show how wasteful and inefficient the U.S. health insurance industry is (Chapter 6). For every dollar the commercial health insurance industry paid in claims in 1988, the industry spent 33.5 cents for administration, marketing, and other overhead expenses. Thus, not including profits, the industry spent 14 times as much on administration, overhead, and marketing per dollar of claims as did the Medicare system and 11 times as much per dollar of claims paid as Canada's National Health System. The authors document the sources of waste in the health insurance industry, including excessive marketing costs and administrative costs bloated by discriminatory underwriting practices that segregate the profitable groups and individuals—people who are healthy, young, and in "safe" professions—from everyone else.

The crisis of costs and coverage of health benefits has triggered the appearance of a number of proposals for health insurance reform at the state governmental level. These include Medicaid expansion for the below-poverty or near-poverty uninsured, state subsidies to industry and/or business for the medically uninsurable, insurance industry-initiated reforms within the small group market, the promotion of "stripped down" insurance plans to reduce premium costs, and state mandating of employer-sponsored health insurance for the employed uninsured. In Chapter 7 Bodenheimer carefully analyzes these state-based proposals and shows that all have serious limitations. First, they fail to address the inequities of the underwriting by which older and sicker people pay more for health insurance than the young and healthy population. Second, they extend the illogical linkage of employment and health insurance. Third, they do not slow the rate of health cost inflation nor do they contain a mechanism to finance broader health coverage through savings within the health sector. An alternative to insurance reform, Bodenheimer writes, is the establishment of a social insurance program that brings the entire population into a single risk pool.

The insurance industry, of course, is one of the major opponents of the establishment of an NHP. Another opponent is the American Medical Association (AMA), which, consistent with its long tradition of putting its economic interests above the interests of patients and of the population, has used all means available to stop the establishment of an NHP. Navarro criticizes the assumptions behind the AMA's explanations of U.S. realities and the AMA's recommendations on how to solve the current crisis (Chapter 8). He also critically reviews some of the major proposals—such as employer-mandated coverage—that are being put forward by several forces in the United States, including the AMA, for resolving the twin problems of high costs and limited health benefits coverage. The political context in which the AMA's calls for reforms are being made is also discussed.

The power of the insurance industry, the AMA, and other components of the medical-industrial complex is enormous and expresses itself in many different ways. Among these is the buying of influence in the U.S. Congress, through PAC (Political Action Committee) money that goes to members of the health-related committees of the Senate and of the House. Tim Brightbill documents how the influence of the health- related PACs continued to grow during the 1990 elections (Chapter 9). He presents data showing that, during the first 18 months of the election cycle, contributions from medical care PACs to congressional candidates reached a total of $7.7 million. As Senator Mikulski once indicated, "we have the best Congress money can buy." Brightbill documents this phenomenon, which substantially hinders the democratic process. Most of the financial support for members of the health-related congressional committees flows from the coffers of the medical-industrial complex.

As powerful as these interest groups are, their power has larger resonance than their impressive size alone entitles them to; they are parts of an even larger category of power. Civil rights leaders may accuse the medical-industrial complex of being predominantly "WASP," and feminists may denounce these establishments as male, but besides race and gender power these establishments have class power, rarely mentioned in the United States since the whole category of class is perceived as un-American. Yet, class is the most important category for an understanding of why the country does not have an NHP.

The corporate and professional groups constituting the medical-industrial complex belong to the corporate class and upper middle class that hold enormous power in U.S. economic, political, and social life. Classes are not uniform, and a diversity of interests does exist. Most of the current proposals for health care reform are put forward by representatives of the different components of these classes. Large employers, for example (the top Fortune 500 companies), may have different interests from the AMA or the insurance companies, but their commonality of interests is larger than their differences. For example, the top Fortune 500 companies, the insurance companies, the AMA, and the pharmaceutical and hospital industries are all against a single-payer system such as the Canadian system, in which the government funds and administers the health services (the proposal, incidentally, supported by the majority of Americans).

Power is a relational concept. While the corporate class and the upper middle class hold enormous economic, political, and social power, the lower middle and working classes—the majority of the U.S. population—are relatively powerless. This is why the majority of the U.S. working class does not vote. The working people in this country are poorly organized with little access to instruments that could respond to their interests. This is the primary reason why the United States does not have an NHP. In Section III, Navarro shows how the different forms of funding and organization of health services, structured according to the corporate model or to the liberal-welfare market capitalism model, have responded to the different correlation of class forces in various societies. Navarro shows how in all Western societies, the major social force behind the establishment of an NHP has been the labor movement (and its political instruments— the labor, social democratic, and socialist parties) in its pursuit of the welfare state. Again, the absence of such instruments and parties explains the absence of an NHP in the United States.

The Democratic Party was the instrument of the labor movement during the New Deal era. Indeed, this great historical period and its social achievements owe much to the labor movement and its alliance with President Roosevelt's Administration. This type of alliance has been weakened considerably as corporate capital and the professional and technical strata have gained influence in the Democratic Party apparatuses and Democratic Party congressional delegations. This shifting of influence has also meant the distancing of the Democratic Party from the New Deal project and from the labor movement. Given the current influences discussed thus far, it is unlikely that the Democratic Party, as currently constituted and funded, is the appropriate instrument to call for a major reform in U.S. health care.

The struggle to establish an NHP is at one with the struggle to democratize U.S. political institutions, accurately perceived by most Americans as having been captured by specific corporate interests alien to their own interests. The road to democratization will require a most important struggle. Section IV begins with Navarro's description of one such struggle: the Jesse Jackson 1988 Presidential campaign (Chapter 11). Navarro was the senior health advisor in that campaign, defined by the *New York Times* as a political earthquake. He shows how the struggle for an NHP is part and parcel of a larger project to democratize the United States. Jesse Jackson called not only on race but primarily on class mobilization to confront "the barracudas that eat the little fish," in the health care sector as elsewhere. Navarro gives a personal account of the politics of health policy in one of the most politically important periods in recent U.S. history. Chapter 12 presents the Jesse Jackson NHP proposal, as prepared by Navarro with David Himmelstein and Steffie Woolhandler, also advisors to the Jesse Jackson 1988 campaign. This was the first detailed health proposal put forward in the 1980s by any major political force. It was also the proposal that enjoyed the most popular support.

The overwhelming insufficiency of the U.S. health care system has stimulated a growing interest in this country about the experience of other countries with their NHPs. The health care debate in the United States has until recently been quite paradoxical and chauvinistic: we could not learn from other countries. This attitude has changed, and many international points of reference have appeared in the debate. Section V consists of two chapters that look at the international experience and its relevance to the establishment of an NHP in the United States. First, Navarro analyzes the relevance of the U.S. experience in general and health maintenance organizations (HMOs) in particular to the reforms advocated by the Thatcher government for the British National Health Service (NHS) (Chapter 13). Navarro provides empirical information that questions the basic assumptions of the Thatcher and Major reforms that (*a*) the HMO type of practice is better able to respond to people's needs than are current general practitioner arrangements; (*b*) entrepreneurship in medicine is good for patients; (*c*) market-based primary care is more efficient than the nonmarket system in the United Kingdom; and (*d*) the expansion and strengthening of the private sector is an efficient and equitable means of encouraging competition and raising revenues. The British NHS is a much more efficient, equitable, and humane health care system than the U.S. system. The introduction of U.S.-style practices into the NHS will negatively affect it. But despite its superiority over the U.S. system, the British NHS is not a useful point of reference for the current U.S. health policy debate. The public funding and public ownership of the health care institutions are only remote possibilities in the heavily ideological academic and political culture of the United States. Indeed, contrary to prevalent belief, U.S. culture is not pragmatic but heavily ideological. It is enough to introduce certain words or concepts into a discourse to immediately trigger a heavily ideological and aggressive response. The idea of socialized medicine with the public funding and ownership of health institutions is such a concept. There is far more openness and tolerance, however, toward the socialization of funding, retaining the delivery of services in the private sector. In this regard, the Canadian experience, with government acting as the single payer for services contracted with the private sector, has become a very powerful point of reference in the U.S. health policy debate.

Until 1972, Canada and the United States had the same type of funding and organization of health services. Since the establishment of an NHP in Canada, with government as the primary source of funding of health services, Canadians have been able both to expand the comprehensiveness of coverage at a much lower cost and to improve their health indicators much faster than the United States. A critical requirement for this success was the elimination of the health insurance industry. This explains the ferocious resistance of the U.S. insurance industry to a Canadian-style system. A more acceptable model for the industry is the German model, in which the insurance industry continues to play an important role as intermediary. A continuing role for the insurance industry has been one of the concerns of those forces that want to reduce insurance opposition to the establishment of an NHP. Among these forces are important unions in the current leadership of the AFL-CIO, the U.S. trade union federation. The leadership is currently split into those who favor a single-payer system like the Canadian model and those who prefer, for tactical reasons, the German model. Chapter 14 is a detailed report on the weakness of the German model, prepared by Navarro (a member of Physicians for a National Health Program) for the AFL-CIO committee on health policy.

The volume concludes in Section VI with proposals for the solution of the U.S. health care crisis. In Chapter 15 Woolhandler and Himmelstein show how an NHP with single-payer funding and administration would save between 47,000 and 106,000 lives annually by providing comprehensive and universal coverage, while saving $10.2 billion. They also show that the problems of the U.S. health care sector can be resolved at even lower costs than are currently incurred. The problem is not economic but political.

The final chapter, also by Himmelstein and Woolhandler, expands on these points. The authors demonstrate the administrative savings that could be realized from instituting a Canadian-style NHP or an NHS similar to that in Britain, and the potential savings from additional reforms to curtail profits, marketing, and litigation. Calculations based on 1983 data suggest that Canadian-style national health insurance would save $42.6 billion annually; $29.2 billion on health administration and insurance overhead, $4.9 billion on profits, $3.9 billion on marketing, and $4.6 billion on physicians' incomes. An NHS would save $65.8 billion: $38.4 billion on health administration and insurance overhead, $4.9 billion on profits, $3.9 billion on marketing, and $18.6 billion on physicians' incomes. Complete nationalization of all health-related industries and reform of the malpractice system would save at least $87.2 billion per year. The authors conclude that an NHP, in addition to improving access to health care for the population, could achieve cost containment without rationing of care. It is of more than passing interest that when this article was first published in the *New England Journal of*

Medicine, the editor of that journal dropped the part of the article that referred to savings that could result from reducing the extravagant incomes of many medical specialists. The *International Journal of Health Services* published the original article in its entirety.

We hope that the publication of this volume will help to shift the focus of the current debate toward the politics of establishing a National Health Program, and to demonstrate the urgent need to democratize the political institutions that are hindering the establishment of such a program. All of these chapters were published as articles in the *International Journal of Health Services* and have been kept as originally published, since the relevance of their subject matter continues undiminished. Differences exist among the authors, primarily in terms of emphasis. But all share the felt need—as does the majority of the U.S. population—to have an NHP that can assure access to health care as a human right.

The proposals for an NHP put forward in this volume have been tested in other countries, have worked, and enjoy great popular support. Popular will alone is not enough to establish such a program. There is a need for a popular mobilization that will force U.S. political institutions to respond to popular wishes, rather than to the wishes of the powerful economic interests that control the health care system and constrain the full development of human rights, including health care rights and democratic rights. The two are clearly interrelated. We hope that this book provides a useful theoretical tool for that purpose.

Vicente Navarro
The Johns Hopkins University
June 1992

SECTION I

The Myths: Their Reproduction in the Political, Media, and Academic Spheres

CHAPTER 1

Selected Myths Guiding the Reagan Administration's Health Policies

Vicente Navarro

The Presidential and Congressional elections of 1984 are likely to have great relevance for the health and health services of the American people. Therefore, it is important to analyze some of the assumptions that guide the Reagan Administration's health policies and look at the evidence that is used to support each of these assumptions. These assumptions are as follows:

Assumption 1—President Reagan was elected with a popular mandate to cut federal expenditures, including health expenditures for the poor, elderly, and disabled, and to decrease federal government regulations in the areas of health and safety protection of workers and consumers and protection of the environment.

Reagan won the 1980 presidential election by a narrow margin—no greater than Carter's in 1976. Over 116 million of the 160 million eligible voters did not come out to support him (1). Post-election polls showed that Reagan won not because of his stand against big government and social and health expenditures, but rather because of popular discontent with the Carter Administration's policies, especially Carter's seeming inability to reverse the increasing rate of unemployment (2). Contrary to widely held belief among policy makers and medical establishment leaders (3), Reagan did not receive a popular mandate to cut federal health expenditures nor to weaken federal regulation in the health sector. As I have shown elsewhere (4, 5), all published evidence of popular opinion as expressed in major nationwide polls from 1976 to 1983 shows that (a) American public opinion is not as volatile as it is assumed to be, and (b) there has been strong and undiminished support by the majority of the American people throughout this period for federal government health expenditures for the elderly, poor, and the handicapped and for federal regulations to protect the safety and health of the worker, the consumer, and the environment. Moreover, while agreeing that federal government expenditures may need to be cut to balance the budget, the overwhelming majority of Americans believe (according to George Martin of Yankelovich, Skelly, and White Surveys) that "balancing the budget should be done by cutting down defense and increasing corporate taxes, not by cutting social

Originally published in the International Journal of Health Services, 14(2): 321–328, 1984.

3

(including health and medical) services" (6). In summary, if by "popular mandate" is meant "what people want," then all evidence shows that the popular mandate is for national health policies that include not cuts but rather expansions of government health expenditures for the aged, handicapped, and the poor and strengthen rather than weaken government regulations to protect workers, consumers, and the environment. Indeed, there is no evidence to support the first assumption, which is based on myth rather than reality.

Assumption 2—Federal social (including health) expenditures have grown too large, contributing to the current economic recession. Thus, there is a need to reduce these expenditures.

According to the Reagan Administration, federal social expenditures are major contributors to the current crises faced by the U.S. economy. It is assumed that these supposedly too large expenditures are partially financed by credit, contributing to the federal budget deficit, perceived to be one of the major causes of our economic difficulties. It is worth clarifying, however, that the United States has lower federal budget deficits (as a percentage of the GDP) than Japan, West Germany, and Sweden, all of which have faster economic growth and healthier economies than the U.S. (7).[1] Moreover, these countries have larger government outlays for non-defense expenditures than the U.S. Sweden allocates 56.5 percent, West Germany 42.2 percent, and Japan 28 percent of its GDP in general government outlays for non-defense expenditures, compared with just 26 percent in the U.S. (7). All these countries have larger social (including health) government expenditures than the U.S. Sweden spends 33.8 percent, West Germany 30.6 percent, and Japan 17 percent of its GNP on social welfare expenditures (which include unemployment benefits; workman's compensation; social assistance to children, handicapped people, and others; health care; and old age and disability insurance) compared with only 14 percent in the U.S. (8).

The U.S. government is indeed one of the governments in the industrialized (developed) world that allocates the least to government health expenditures, with lesser benefits provided in government programs. Government expenditures represent 91.7 percent of all health care expenditures in Sweden and 77.1 percent in West Germany, while they represent only 42.7 percent in the U.S. (9, p. 61). In terms of benefits and coverage, the U.S. federal government programs are less comprehensive than those in most other countries at a similar level of economic development. Contrary to formal pronouncements by top U.S. federal health officials that "Americans have the world's best medical care" (10), the reality is that the U.S. health system is the only one among developed countries that leaves large sectors of its population unprotected. Eleven percent of the U.S. population still does not have any form of health care coverage (11). And this figure does not include the unemployed who have recently lost their health insurance.

In summary, other countries with better economic performance than the United States have larger government expenditures and broader coverage for health than the U.S. Based on this international comparison, it is difficult to conclude that the U.S. government spends too much in health and that the rather limited U.S. government

---

[1] These comparisons are made taking into account indicators of "total deficit of general government," "unemployment," "inflation," and "economic growth" for the period 1975-1978.

health expenditures are a major contributor to its economic problem. Again, evidence available from international comparisons shows that the second assumption is also based on myth rather than reality.

Assumption 3—U.S. government regulation of the workplace (to assure the health and safety of the worker and of the environment) has interfered with management prerogatives and has meant higher costs for management, thus contributing to the slowing down of the competitiveness of the U.S. economy.

U.S. workers, however, have less—not more—government protection than workers in other developed countries. Table 1, for example, compares the health rights guaranteed by national legislation to the majority of workers in Sweden with workers' health rights guaranteed by national legislation or collective agreement in the United States.

Regarding U.S. government regulation of the environment, also claimed to hinder the competitiveness of the U.S. economy by adding unbearable social costs to industry, two points need to be made. The first is that, as shown in Table 2, many important environmental conditions are worse in the U.S. than in other developed countries with better economic performance. As indicated in a report of the U.S. Senate (12), all available evidence "does not convict U.S. regulation of decreasing competitiveness with other nations. The U.S., for example, has less stringent air quality objectives than a number of major competitors." The second point that needs to be made is that industry investments in pollution control are lower rather than higher in the U.S. than in other countries. For example, an argument put forward by the U.S. steel industry to justify a lowering of government environmental regulations has been that those environmental controls are raising the price of steel to noncompetitive levels. Table 3, however, shows that during the period from 1972 to 1976 when the U.S. steel industry was asking for a weakening of those regulations, it was actually investing far less on pollution controls than the Japanese steel industry.

Table 1

Rights of safety delegates and safety committees in Sweden and the United States[a]

Right	Sweden	United States
Right to be consulted prior to changes in the work process	+	–
Right to bring in consultant paid by management	+	–
Right to mandatory health and safety training for all new workers	+	–
Right to be trained for monitoring	+	–
Hiring and firing of occupational physicians and engineers	+	–
Right of workers' safety delegates to stop work	+	–
Right of inspectors to stop work	+	–

[a]Source: V. Navarro. The determinants of occupational health policy. A case study: Sweden. *Journal of Health Politics, Policy and Law*, in press.

Table 2

Pollution levels in selected countries, 1975[a]

Country	Carbon monoxide	Hydrocarbons	Nitrogen oxides
A. Emissions per capita (kg)			
United States	402	122	103
Sweden	171	52	38
West Germany	–	30	31
Japan	–	–	20
Austria	129	6	15
B. Emissions per unit of energy consumed (tons/103 tons of energy)			
United States	51	69	13
Sweden	29	15	6
West Germany	–	8	8
Japan	–	–	7
Austria	42	2	3

[a]Source: *The States of the Environment in OECD Member Countries (1979)*. OECD, Paris, 1980.

Here again, based on international evidence, the third assumption that U.S. government regulations to protect workers' and consumers' health and safety and to protect the environment are contributing to the noncompetitiveness of the U.S. economy is based more on myth than on reality.

Assumption 4—Market intervention is intrinsically more efficient than government intervention in regulating the costs and distribution of health resources. It is important to give priority to the former over the latter in order to solve our major health care problems. The privatization and commodification of medical and health services is therefore a key element in Reagan's health policies.

Roemer and Roemer (13) have already shown the fallacy of the argument that the market forces are the best and most efficient forces to allocate resources in the health care sector. They have detailed the failures, distortions, wastages, and human inequities of the "free market" in the U.S. Its failure to achieve effective allocation of resources for meeting the needs of populations has been gigantic. In the absence of any national health planning system and practice, the market forces have been the primary determinants of the allocation of private and public funds. Waste on the one side and insufficient coverage on the other are the major trademarks of the medical care system in the U.S. According to a British observer (14), "A U.S. Senate committee has said that between a quarter and a half of the 8,500 million pounds spent on Medicaid is being wasted each year—a sum not far short *of the total costs of the British National Health Service*" (emphasis added). Meanwhile, "nearly six million children in families with incomes below the poverty level are without Medicaid coverage and less than 40 percent of children in poverty are covered by Medicaid"

Table 3

Pollution control investments at steel mills, United States and Japan, 1971-1977[a]

Year	United States			Japan		
	Total investment (millions of dollars)	Pollution control investments (millions of dollars)	Pollution control as % of total investment	Total investment (millions of dollars)	Pollution control investments (millions of dollars)	Pollution control as % of total investment
1971	1,473	162	11	2,433	219	9
1972	1,188	202	17	2,185	284	13
1973	1,428	100	7	2,165	368	17
1974	2,211	199	9	2,926	556	19
1975	3,236	453	14	3,806	685	18
1976	3,260	489	15	4,381	920	21
1977	2,267	408	18	3,700	555	15
Total	15,063	1,913	12.7	21,596	3,587	16.6

[a]Source: Technology and Steel Industry Competitiveness. Office of Technology Assessments, U.S. Congress, Washington, D.C., 1980.

7

(15). Waste plus insufficient coverage is indeed the outcome of the "free market" forces. Evidence from international comparisons shows that the problem is not too much government intervention and regulation, but rather too little. Regarding hospital costs, for example, Detsky, Stally, and Bombardier (16) have recently shown that active government regulation has been able to control these costs in Ontario, Canada, far better than the market forces have in the largely unregulated hospital sector of the U.S.

Another argument put forward by the current Administration in favor of the market as the allocator of resources is the need to avoid higher administrative costs and large bureaucracies. It is worth clarifying, however, that most evidence shows precisely the opposite. The medical care sector of the U.S.—where market forces are the primary allocator of resources and where private institutions are the most numerous ones—has far larger administrative costs and structures than other countries where government expenditures and institutions dominate the medical sector. No less than 4.7 percent of all medical expenditures in the U.S. goes toward administrative expenses compared with 0.9 percent in the U.K., 0.4 percent in Sweden, and 1.7 percent in Canada—all countries with medical sectors in which government plays the major role in the allocation of resources (9, p. 83). Here again, we find that the evidence for the fourth assumption is lacking. It, too, is more a myth than a reality.

CONCLUSION

The evidence presented in this article shows that the national health policies carried out by the current U.S. Administration—which include (a) a reduction of government health expenditures for the poor, elderly, and handicapped; (b) a weakening of government regulations for the protection of the health and safety of workers and consumers and for the protection of the environment; and (c) the privatization and commodification of medical services—are based on myth rather than reality. Contrary to what is indicated by the Reagan Administration, there is not a popular mandate for these policies. The mandate is for precisely the opposite: for an *expansion* of those expenditures and a *strengthening* of those regulations. Moreover, the evidence presented here also challenges the assumption that government health expenditures and regulations are hurting the competitiveness of the U.S. economy. This article has shown that U.S. government expenditures and regulations are much more limited than those of other countries whose economies are performing far more satisfactorily. The justifications put forward by the current Administration for cutting or reducing these government interventions are neither empirically proven nor politically justified. The majority's wants and needs are in contradiction with current national health policies. Last but not least, the myth of higher efficiency of the market is also questioned. The market private-oriented medical care system, dominant in the U.S., is not more but less efficient than the government-run and regulated health care systems in other countries.

In summary, the policies currently being implemented by the Reagan Administration are based on ideological positions that are not supported by any evidence. Quite to the contrary, the wishes of the majority of the U.S. population, as well as the factual evidence that has been accumulated from this and other countries, suggest policies quite the opposite of the ones now being pursued by the Reagan Administration.

REFERENCES

1. Ferguson, T., and Rogers, T. *The Hidden Election: Politics and Economics in the 1980 Presidential Election.* Pantheon Books, New York, 1981.
2. Markus, G. B. Political attitudes during an election year: A report on the 1980 NES Panel Study. *Am. Polit. Sci. Rev.* 76: 538-560, Sept. 1982.
3. Iglehart, T. K. Special report: Report on the Duke University Medical Center Private Sector Conference. *N. Engl. J. Med.* 307(1): 68, 1982.
4. Navarro, V. Where is the popular mandate? *N. Engl. J. Med.* 307: 1576, 1982.
5. Navarro, V. A reply to conventional wisdom. *Int. J. Health Serv.* 13(1): 169, 1983.
6. Lipset, S. M. Poll after poll after poll after poll warns President on programs. *New York Times*, January 13, 1982, p. 23.
7. *National Accounts, OECD. Statistics 1961-1978,* Vo. II. OECD, Paris, June 1980.
8. Table 5: Public collectivized expenditures on social welfare as percentage of GNP for selected countries, 1977. In Magaziner, I. C. and Reich, R. B. *Minding America's Business.* Harcourt, Brace, Jovanovich, New York, 1982.
9. Maxwell, R. T. *Health and Wealth. An International Study of Health Care Spending.* Lexington Books, Lexington, Mass., 1981.
10. Rubin, R. An Rx for costs. *New York Times*, May 12, 1983, p. A-23.
11. Table 9: Persons with and without health insurance coverage. In U.S. President's Commission for the Study of Ethical Problems in Medicine and Biomedical and Behavioral Research. Vol. 1. Report on Securing Access to Health Care. 1983.
12. Committee on Finance, U.S. Senate, Conferences on U.S. Competitiveness: Can the U.S. Remain Competitive? U.S. Government Printing Office, Washington, D.C., 1980.
13. Roemer, M. I., and Roemer, T. E. The social consequences of free trade in health care: A public health response to orthodox economics. *Int. J. Health Serv.* 12(1): 111-129, 1982.
14. Steele, T. How U.S. doctors bleed the government. *Guardian*, August 30, 1976.
15. Six million children without Medicaid coverage. *The Nation's Health.* American Public Health Association, August 1983, p. 3.
16. Detsky, A. S., Stacey, S. R., and Bombardier, C. The effectiveness of a regulatory strategy in containing hospital costs. The Ontario experience 1967-1981. *N. Engl. J. Med.* 309(3): 151-159, 1983.

CHAPTER 2

The Arguments against
a National Health Program:
Science or Ideology?

Vicente Navarro

One of the most dramatic changes in national health policy debates in this country during the last 15 years has been the shift of focus from discussing the expansion of the federal role in the health sector through a National Health Program (the theme of the 1970s) toward debating and implementing ways and means to reduce that federal role (the theme of the 1980s). As the editor of one of the major U.S. health policy forums wrote in the early 1980s, we have witnessed during these years "the demise of any real constituency of national health insurance" (1). While the use of the word "demise" is hyperbolic, since many groups, including the American Public Health Association (APHA), kept the issue of the need for a National Health Program (NHP) alive, still it was true then and continues to be true now that during the 1980s there has been a deafening legislative silence in this area, not only in our Congressional chambers but also in the main political, academic, and media establishments. Moreover, when some solitary forces such as the APHA have raised their voices in support of a NHP, those voices have been silenced by a huge avalanche of messages and counterarguments (all of them presented, of course, as scientific and reasonable) against the advisability and/or feasibility of such a program.

In this article, I will list some of those arguments against a National Health Program in the United States and analyze the evidence that supports them. In such an important area, we need to apply our rigorous scientific lenses to the analysis of such arguments and see whether they are (as they claim) scientific or are just plain ideological. By National Health Program I mean—as the APHA clearly states—a nation-wide federal health program that is universal and comprehensive and is funded primarily with general revenues (2). Let us look at the anti-NHP arguments.

Originally published in the International Journal of Health Services, 18(2): 179–189, 1988. Some of this material was first published in Health/PAC Bulletin, Spring 1988.

1. *The majority of Americans, as expressed in the 1980 and 1984 elections, do not want a further expansion of the federal government role in their lives.*

The mandate expressed in these two elections was loud and clear, i.e., people wanted government off their backs. In the light of this popular mandate, to continue asking for a NHP goes against what people want. I could cite a huge list of quotations from prominent and not so prominent figures in political, media, and academic establishments in which those messages are reproduced over and over again, ad nauseam.

But let us look at this argument and, most importantly, the assumptions that sustain it. The first assumption is that the majority of Americans voted for an administration—the Reagan Administration—clearly committed to reducing the federal role in the health and many other social sectors. I do not doubt that the second part of the assumption—that the Reagan Administration wanted to reduce federal health expenditures and interventions—is correct. The experience has shown it. Health expenditures as a percentage of the federal budget have declined, and federal interventions to protect workers, the environment, and consumers have diminished during the Reagan years (3). The evidence is indeed extensive that the second part of the assumption is correct. But the evidence is also abundant that the first part of the assumption—that the majority of Americans voted for that Administration and its "austerity" policies—is wrong. First, only 26.6 percent of the electorate (by electorate I mean people who could have voted if they chose to) in 1980 and 32 percent in 1984 voted for Reagan. This means that 73 percent of the electorate in 1980 and 68 percent in 1984 did not vote for Reagan and his policies (4). *In both elections the majority of Americans did not vote for Reagan.* Unless one is willing to accept that those who did not vote for Reagan are non-Americans—a position that comes remarkably close to some of the beliefs of this Administration—one cannot keep repeating that the majority of Americans chose Reagan and his anti-government positions.

There is yet another assumption that is made in the argument of the popular mandate: that electoral behavior and popular opinion or mandate are the same. I quite understand that those who win elections like everyone else to believe that the voters are actually in full agreement with all of their policies. Reality is likely to show otherwise. Our democratic system is such that we are not given the possibility to vote for specific policies, such as the health policies of Party A, the educational policies of Party B, and so on. As Walter Lippman once mentioned, we are forced to vote for totalities, i.e., everything or nothing (5). We may disagree with many and even the majority of the policies of the candidate we choose, but we still may vote for that candidate because we agree with a policy or component of a policy that we feel is specially important or because, for that specific issue or issues, we feel that the alternatives are worse. And that is what happened in 1980 and 1984. The minority of the electorate voted for Reagan because they identified Carter with the growing inflation and unemployment that was taking place at election time. One week before the 1980 Presidential election, 43 percent of Reagan adherents among registered voters "were more interested in voting against Carter than for Reagan" (6); 1980 was the year of the defeat of Carter rather than the year of victory for Reagan. Actually, at the time of the election Reagan was the least popular of all elected presidents since 1952, when Gallup Polls started surveying the popularity of elected Presidents (Gallup Poll release for October 18, 1980, cited in reference 7). And on election day, Reagan's share of the total potential vote (26.6 percent) was the third lowest of any winning candidate since 1921 (7, p. 169). A similar mechanism operated in 1984. The minority that voted for Reagan did so because it identified the low inflation with him, and disliked Mondale's call for higher taxes to reduce the federal deficit, an abstract objective for the average American (8). But in both elections, in exit polls, the majority of voters expressed their disagreements with Reagan's social (including health) policies. (For an analysis of polls on election days and on other dates in 1980 and 1984 see reference 4.) Actually, poll after poll shows that by overwhelming majorities, people want the federal government to have more rather than less of a role in assuring coverage of health benefits for all the population, in protecting the health and safety of workers and consumers, and in protecting the environment (4). Even ex-Senator Laxalt, close friend of Reagan and Chairman of the Republican Party, noted "the strange phenomenon that most Americans . . . are opposed to much of what the President supports" including his health policies (quoted in reference 9). In brief, electoral behavior and population opinion are not the same.

The evidence is overwhelming that popular mandate is for expanding rather than reducing the federal role in the health sector (4, 10). The latest poll in which people were asked their feelings about government's role in the health sector confirms the findings of all previous polls. Sixty percent of Americans feel that government is spending too little in improving and protecting the nation's health and in improving and protecting the environment (with only 6 and 7 percent, respectively, feeling that we are spending too much in each area) (11, p. 28). Also, 50 percent think that the government should ensure that everyone has access to health care and can pay for it (with only 18 percent opposing this) (11, p. 23). And this extensive support for a larger government role in the health sector includes support for a NHP (12). This support, incidentally, has existed since 1943, the first time that Americans were asked whether they supported a National Health Program (administered by the Social Security Administration) (13, p. 77).

The overwhelming evidence of a large popular support for a NHP has been ignored by large sectors of the political, media, and academic establishments, which keep reproducing the idealized version of our political system as one in which it is we the people who decide what occurs or does not occur in the legislative chambers of our government. They keep parroting the position that the United States does not have a NHP because we do not want it. To the contrary, the majority of Americans do want it but they do not get it.

Others have finally admitted that yes, people may want a larger government role in the health sector (including a NHP) but are not willing to pay the higher taxes that may be needed to pay for such a government expansion. I will not discuss at this point whether the extension of government's role in assuring, for example, comprehensiveness and universality of health care in this country will indeed require higher taxation for the majority of our population. Let us assume for the moment that yes, it will require higher taxes, and now see what people are saying. In popular opinion polls, when the question has been phrased in such a way as to ask whether people will be supportive of such an expansion even at the cost of higher taxes, their reply is equally clear: *yes, they will still be supportive*. The most recent poll on this subject also confirms the findings of previous polls: 66 percent of Americans said that if necessary they would support a small earmarked federal tax with the money going for health care (cited in reference 14). And here again there was a similar willingness the first time people were asked a similar question, i.e., in 1943 they were willing to pay higher taxes if those extra revenues went to the establishment of a NHP (13, p. 77).

More recently, some powerful voices have tried to dismiss this accumulated evidence of people's support for a NHP by referring to an assumed "schizophrenia" of the American people. Two leaders of the influential Johnson Foundation, for example, recently wrote an article entitled, "Public Attitudes about Health Care Costs: A Lesson in National Schizophrenia" (15), in which they refer to the assumed schizophrenia shown by the U.S. public, which, while supporting government expansion in the health sector, also shows hostility to government and to welfare (terms that include health and other social services). As I have shown elsewhere, however, Americans are not schizophrenic (16). Their opinions are consistent. When the questions are presented in highly ideological terms (e.g., are you in favor of government or welfare?) the answers are overwhelmingly negative. However, if the questions are asked referring to specific government interventions in resolving people's needs, the answers are overwhelmingly positive. For example, more Americans (34 percent) believe that the government spends too much in welfare expenditures than believe the government spends too little (30 percent). If, however, Americans are asked their opinion without using the term welfare (with the negative connotations of the welfare cheater put forward by the media evening after evening) but rather government's assisting the poor, then 71 percent of Americans feel that the government spends too little (with only 6 percent feeling that it spends too much) (11, p. 28). Similarly, the majority of Americans respond differently if they are asked about the government in general or the government as provider and defender of people's needs: their answers are quite opposite. These differences in response are not due to schizophrenia but rather to the heavily ideological nature of the political discourse, in which terms and definitions are abstracted from specific realities and redefined in heavily ideological terms.

Similarly, there is nothing paradoxical or even contradictory about some people being against raising taxes in general (particularly when they do not have much of a voice in how they are allocated) while supporting increase in taxes if they are assured that these higher taxes will go to a specific approved purpose such as health services.

In brief, the evidence presented here shows that the argument of lack of popular support as an explanation for the absence of a NHP is more ideological than scientific. More than an explanation, it is a justification for the serious limitations that our democratic institutions face. Vox populi (i.e., We the people . . .) is not the only or even the most important voice in the determination of national health policies. The popular wants compete with many monied, powerful interests that exercise enormous influence in shaping anti-NHP policies. As Senator Barbara Mikulski (17) has recently indicated "Our Congress is becoming like a coin operated machine. Whatever you get out depends on how much money you put in it."

2. The growth of health expenditures in this country is getting out of control. A National Health Program would further increase the growth of these health expenditures.

The United States spends more than any other country in health services: nearly 11 percent of the gross national product (GNP). And this percentage is expected to increase to 14 percent by the year 2000. In spite of these huge health expenditures, we still face problems that no other country faces. In 1986, 16 percent of our population (38 million people) did not have any form of coverage whatsoever, and 6 percent (13.5 million people) reported not receiving medical care for financial reasons. This percentage was even higher among the uninsured: 13 percent of people who did not have any form of coverage did not receive care that they needed because they could not pay for it (18, p. 13).

Also, in no other developed industrialized nation do people still pay such a high percentage of the health bill directly out of their own pockets. Twenty-seven percent of expenditures are still paid directly by the patients in the United States, compared with 5 percent in Great Britain, 8 percent in Sweden, 12 percent in West Germany, 19 percent in France, and 20 percent in Canada (19, p. 61).

In summary, we pay a lot of money for health services but still the health benefits coverage for the majority of our people is rather limited, and for a substantial minority of our population is nil. This situation is getting worse rather than better. Indeed, we are witnessing a paradox: while the health expenditures have continued to grow unabated (both in absolute figures and as percentage of the GNP) during the 1980s, the health benefits coverage of our population and utilization of health services by our people (for both the majority of our population and the minorities) have been declining. The percentage of our population that is uninsured has grown; the physician and hospital utilization has declined; the percentage of people without a physician's visit during the past year has increased; and the percentage of our population without a usual source of care has also increased (Table 1).

In the light of this reality, it is not surprising that 75 percent of our people want to see profound changes in the health sector (12). In brief, we see how our health

Table 1

Changes in the number of insured and the utilization of physicians and hospitals in the United States, 1982–86[a]

	1982	1986
Percentage of population uninsured	14	17
Mean number of physician's visits per person per year		
Insured	3.8	3.2
Uninsured	4.7	4.4
Percentage hospitalized		
Insured	5.2	4.6
Uninsured	8.5	5.7
Percentage without a physician's visit in the past year	19	33
Percentage without a usual source of care	11	18

[a]Source: reference 18.

expenditures continue to grow while our people get less rather than more services. Why? A look at the international picture will give us the answer. The United States is the only major industrialized nation (besides South Africa) in which most of the health revenues come from the private sector and most expenditures are made through the private sector. The overwhelming majority of Western industrialized nations fund their health services with public revenues. No other country spends less public funds in the health sector than the United States. In 1983, only 4.5 percent of the GNP went to health, a very small figure compared with other western industrialized nations: Sweden spent 8.8 percent of its GNP on health, the United Kingdom 5.5 percent, West Germany 6.6 percent, France 6.6 percent, Italy 6.2 percent, and Canada 6.2 percent (20). The other side of the coin is that no other country has a larger for-profit sector than the United States: 44 percent of all expenditures went to private for-profit institutions and contractors, compared with 17 percent in Sweden, 26 percent in the United Kingdom, and 42 percent in Canada (19, p. 68). Actually, the figures for profits and administrative costs in the United States are rather staggering. In 1983, the expenditures for profits of several institutions were as follows: health institutions, $2.8 billion; financial institutions, $2.1 billion; hospital institutions, $0.2 billion; medical equipment and supplies, $2.8 billion; and pharmaceutical industries, $5.6 billion. Administrative costs were as follows: program administration and insurance overhead, $15.6 billion; hospital administration, $26.9 billion; nursing home administration, $4.1 billion; and physicians' overhead, $31.1 billion (21). No other country spends, either in absolute numbers or in percentages of all health expenditures, such a huge amount in profits and administration.

And these types of expenditures have increased rather than declined during the Reagan years. Profit (in absolute and in percentage terms) has increased rather than declined during this period. For example, profit margin in the hospital sector has increased 19 percent, far larger, incidentally, than the overall rate of growth (7 percent) of profits for the whole economy (22). This growth of profit has been particularly accentuated in hospitals with large Medicare populations (23).

In summary, during the Reagan years the further unleashing of market forces and profit interests in the health sector (characteristic of the current political regime) has been accompanied by a diminution of health care coverage and health care utilization for all of our population. The former (the growth of market forces) is the cause of the latter (the diminution of coverage and utilization). During this period, we have seen how the competitiveness strategy has shown its inability to reduce costs, to broaden coverage, or to increase people's satisfaction. The rate of growth of health expenditures has not diminished; the level of coverage has been reduced rather than increased; and in 1986 there was an all-time high of 75 percent of people asking for major changes in the system of funding and delivery of health services. The only area in which the competitiveness strategy has been successful is in increasing the profits of the interest groups that dominate the health sector. The strengthening of market forces of the profit-oriented system has made matters worse not better. The solution to these problems of growing costs and limited coverage resides in larger government role in the funding and organization of health services, with reduction of the profit sector in these services.

In this regard it is worth looking at the experience of our neighbor to the north. The rate of growth of national health expenditures in both countries was quite similar until 1968, when Canada established a NHP. Since then the percentage of the GNP going to health expenditures has continued to increase in the United States while it has remained almost constant in Canada. Moreover, this control of expenditures in Canada has occurred while the health care coverage (comprehensiveness and universality of health benefits) has increased (24). Whereas 100 percent of the Canadian population has hospital and ambulatory care covered by public programs, in the United States only 40 percent and 25 percent of the population has hospital care and ambulatory care, respectively, covered by public programs. And the Canadians have this at a much lower cost (20).

In the light of this evidence, it is clear that the first part of the argument—that health expenditures are getting out of control—is indeed valid, but the second part of the argument—that a National Health Program would make things worse—is wrong. Quite to the contrary, the figures presented here show that it may be a condition for things to get better.

3. *The federal deficit is too large, and is one of the major reasons for the poor performance of the economy. A National Health Program and the larger health expenditures that it would require would make the deficit situation worse.*

This is one of the most frequently used arguments against the establishment of a National Health Program. It has also been put forward by U.S. Labor—the AFL-CIO national leadership—and Senator Kennedy to explain their backing away from supporting a NHP and their shift toward the coverage of the uncovered population by mandating employer-paid coverage (25). The size of the deficit, it is said, needs to be reduced before we can think of enlarging the federal role in the health sector. Otherwise our economy is going to get worse and all of us will suffer. Here again there are dozens and dozens of quotations from leading figures in the political and medical establishments that reproduce this widely held belief.

In presenting evidence that questions this argument let me clarify several points. First, the deficit—as we know it today—was created by the current Administration with the support of the U.S. Congress, at least until the 99th Congress. It was created by the federal tax cuts of 1981 that benefited primarily the upper income brackets, and by the unprecedented growth (in peace time) of military expenditures (26).

Second, this deficit was *deliberately* created to force a reduction of social (including health) expenditures now and in the future. As David Stockman, one of the main architects of Reaganomics, put it, "the plan was to have a strategic deficit that would give us an argument for cutting back the programs that weren't desired" (quoted in reference 27). The 1981-84 proposed budget cuts show clearly what those undesired programs were: the Reagan Administration proposal included reductions of 60 percent in non-income tests programs for low-income individuals, 27.7 percent in means-tested programs, and 11.4 percent in social insurance entitlements (28). Actually, health programs were among those federal programs that suffered the most reductions. Medicare, for example, which represents 7 percent of all federal health expenditures, during this period has received 12 percent of all the cuts. In the 1987 Reagan budget, 36 percent of total proposed federal budget cuts were supposed to take place in health programs (29). The purpose of the deficit was indeed to reduce social expenditures; the huge campaign orchestrated by this Administration to reduce the deficit has been a campaign to reduce social expenditures. As J. Peter Grace and other top business supporters and directors of the Reagan Administration-backed anti-deficit advertising campaign recognized, "we are not concerned about the deficit [rather] we are concerned about the level of government spending" (quoted in reference 30). Government spending is the code name for social expenditures.

Third, the roots of our economic problems cannot be reduced to the federal deficit. The U.S. federal deficit in 1986 represented 4.8 percent of the GNP. Sweden in the late 1970s had a federal deficit three times higher than this (15 percent of the GNP). Even today its deficit is higher (7 percent of the GNP). And the rate of growth of social (including health) expenditures in Sweden during the period 1975-82 (4.4 percent) was higher than that in the United States (3.67 percent) (31). During all these years, Sweden has had lower unemployment, lower inflation, and faster economic growth than the United States. Similarly, Japan, Austria, and Norway have government deficits that are not too dissimilar to those in the United States—between 4 and 5 percent of the GNP (32). And the rate of growth of their social expenditures has been larger than that in the United States (Japan 8.6 percent, Austria 4.6 percent, and Norway 6.2 percent) (32). All these countries have better economic performance (with lower unemployment, higher economic growth, and lower inflation) than the United States, and all, incidentally, have well established and growing National Health Programs. All three countries have higher public expenditures in the health sector and a higher rate of growth of these expenditures than the United States.

In summary, if it is true that the government deficit and the rapidly growing public social expenditures (including health) are at the root of our economic problems, then we would expect those countries with higher deficits, higher public expenditures in social areas (including health), and a higher rate of growth of these expenditures to do worse economically than the United States. They do not. As I have shown, they do much better. Actually, the evidence shows that unless the working population has social supports (such as health and social services) to cushion the impact of changes in the economic structure, this population is unlikely to cooperate with those technological and other changes that may be required for the successful development of the economy. No other country has as many robots per capita (a sign of technological advantage) and more labor flexibility than Sweden. This situation is related to the job, social, and health security of the labor force. In the United States, one of the major reasons for resistance to labor mobility and flexibility is workers' fear of losing their health benefits. The expansion of coverage, comprehensiveness, and universality of social and health support is a condition, rather than a handicap, for the successful economic performance in our country.

5. People do not want to pay higher taxes. Consequently, they will not be willing to pay the higher taxes needed to establish a National Health Program.

Before answering this argument in toto let me disaggregate it into its different components. First, paying taxes is no more unpopular now than before. Paying taxes has always been unpopular. It is interesting to note, incidentally, that social security taxes are less unpopular than other types of taxes, because people know they will benefit from the program paid directly with these taxes.

Second, in the last 10 years we have seen a further shift of taxes from corporate to income and social security taxes. In 1960, corporate taxes represented 23.2 percent of all federal revenues, while income taxes represented 44 percent and social insurance taxes 15.9 percent. In 1984, the percentages had changed quite dramatically: corporate taxes represented only 7.8 percent while income taxes and social insurance taxes represented 44.8 percent and 36.8 percent, respectively (33). Here again it is important to indicate that U.S. employers pay less in corporate taxes and fringe benefits than employers in other Western industrialized nations. The overall payroll taxes and premiums (including health premiums) for fringe benefits in the United States in the late 1970s were only 26 percent of total wages, compared with 51 percent in Italy, 43.7 percent in France, and 40.7 percent in West Germany. Our employers do not pay much compared with the employers in other countries. This point merits emphasis in the light of current voices raised against Senator Kennedy's proposal of employer-mandated benefits for the current working population that remains uncovered. Recently, the editor of the American Hospital Association journal, *Inquiry*, warned against mandating higher payments from employers since these proposals would weaken our economy by making our employers less competitive (34). What these voices ignore is that other countries with higher employer contributions have performed better economically than the United States. The rate of economic growth and employment in the late 1970s was better in Italy, France, and West Germany than in the United States (35).

Third, while it is true that the overall level of taxation is lower in the United States than in the majority of Western industrialized nations, some sectors of the population are already paying a lot of taxes. Let me explain. In 1974, the U.S. tax level was 27.5 percent of the gross domestic product, placing this country 14th of 17 major industrialized countries. However, if instead of looking at overall levels of taxation we look at levels of taxation by occupational groups, we find that average production workers in the United States ranked 8th highest in the tax burden (36). In other words, the difference in the level of taxation of U.S. workers and workers in the other top industrialized nations is not so large. But enormous differences are evident in the government benefits that the U.S. production worker receives compared with his or her European counterpart. For the most part, European workers (and other citizens) get free or almost free health care, family allowances, and better unemployment insurance, pension, and disability, as well as many other social benefits that increase individual income. The U.S. worker, however, gets comparatively little from his or her taxes. The majority of workers and citizens do not receive government health benefits or social benefits comparable with those that European workers receive. This situation is largely explained by the huge percentages of U.S. taxes that go to defense expenditures: 67 percent of the federal budget goes to military expenses (37). This type of expenditure does not benefit, for the most part, the average citizen. Let me add that during the Reagan Administration (in which military expenditures have increased enormously, social expenditures have declined, social security taxes have increased, and tax reforms favorable to upper-income groups have been implemented), the average citizen has got even less from his or her taxes.

It is because of the highly regressive nature of our taxes that the average citizen feels under a heavy tax burden and opposes increasing taxes. People are against increasing taxes and rightly so—they are not getting much in return. But they are willing to pay higher taxes if they are assured that they will benefit from them. This explains both why social security taxes are the least unpopular taxes, and why the majority of Americans would be willing to pay higher taxes if these revenues were used to establish a universal and comprehensive health program.

Here let me clarify that I refer to people's willingness to pay higher taxes for a NHP as an expression of their desire for such a program, not because I believe that a NHP would require the average citizen to pay higher taxes. I do not believe so. It may or may not, depending on the type of NHP that is established. The NHP could indeed be established based on (a) corporate taxes, which would not necessarily be higher than the amount that the majority of corporations pay in employees' health benefits; (b) higher income taxes for the top 20 percent of the income population; and/or (c) transfer of funds from military to health expenditures.

With the revenues obtained in this way, we could provide universal and comprehensive care to our entire population if the federal government, assisted by the state and local governments, were willing to face—as the APHA recommends—the major interest groups in the health sector and say, enough is enough. Which leads me to my last point. The great success of the ideological conservative avalanche has been in transforming political issues into economic ones. The issue, however, is clearly political. This year we are celebrating the 200th anniversary of our Constitution, which starts with the famous sentence, "We, the people. . . ." No other intervention could better prove that it is we the people (the majority in the United States) who govern this country than the passing of a National Health Program. I have already shown that the American people want this program, and have wanted it for quite a long time. Will it occur? This still depends on who governs this country. We shall indeed see who governs this country, either "We, the monied interests . . ." or "We, the people . . ." We shall see.

REFERENCES

1. Walsh, W. B. Publisher's letter. *Health Forum*, Winter 1983, p. i.
2. American Public Health Association. *Criteria for Assessing National Health Proposals.* American Public Health Association Public Policy Statements, 7734 (P.P.). APHA, Washington, D.C., 1986.
3. Navarro, V. Federal health policies in the United States: An alternative explanation. *Milbank Mem. Fund Q.* 65(1): 81-111, 1987.
4. Navarro, V. The 1980 and 1984 U.S. Presidential elections and the New Deal. *Int. J. Health Serv.* 15(3): 359-394, 1985.
5. Lippman, W. *The Phantom Public*, pp. 56-57. Harcourt, Brace Publications, New York, 1925.
6. *Time*, November 3, 1980.
7. Kelley, S. *Interpreting Elections*. Princeton University Press, Princeton, 1983.
8. Nelson, M. *The Elections of 1984*. Congressional Quarterly, Washington, D.C., 1985.
9. Lipset, S. M. Feeling better: Measuring the doctor's confidence. *Public Opinion* 8(2): 6, 1985.
10. Navarro, V. Where is the popular mandate? *N. Engl. J. Med.* 307: 1516-1518, 1982.
11. What Americans want. *Public Opinion*, May/June, 1987.
12. Schneider, W. Public ready for change in health care. *National J.* 3(3): 664-665, 1985.
13. Coughlin, R. M. *Ideology, Public Opinion and Welfare Policy*. University of California Press, Berkeley, 1980.

14. Blendon, R. T., and Altman, D. E. Public opinion and health care costs. In *Health Care and Its Costs*, edited by C. Schramm, p. 55. W. W. Norton, New York, 1987.
15. Blendon, R. T., and Altman, D. E. Special report: Public attitudes about health care costs: A lesson in national schizophrenia. *N. Engl. J. Med.* 311(9): 613-616, 1984.
16. Navarro, V. In defense of the American people: Americans are not schizophrenic. *Int. J. Health Serv.* 15(3): 515-519, 1985.
17. Mikulski, B. Making our electoral system truly democratic. *Common Cause Newsletter*, May/June, 1987.
18. Freeman, H. E. et al. Americans report on their access to health care. *Health Forum*, Spring 1987, pp. 6-18.
19. Maxwell, R. T. *Health and Wealth: An International Study of Health Care Spending*. Lexington Books, Lexington, Mass., 1981.
20. Organization for Economic Cooperation and Development. Measuring health care, 1960-1983: Expenditures, costs and performance. *OECD Social Policy Studies*, No. 2, Table 2, p. 12. OECD, Paris, 1985.
21. Himmelstein, D. U., and Woolhandler, S. Socialized medicine: A solution to the cost crisis in the health care of the United States. *Int. J. Health Serv.* 16(3): 339-354, 1986.
22. Profits in hospitals. *New York Times*, March 29, 1987.
23. Hospital profit under projecting payment system. *Health Care Financing Rev.* 8(1): 7, 1986.
24. Evans, R. G. Lessons from cost containment in North America. *J. Health Polit. Policy Law* 11(4): 588, 589, 1986.
25. Kosterlitaz, J. Kennedy's new task. *National J.*, March 14, 1987, p. 608.
26. Center for Popular Economics. Strategic deficit. *Economic Report of the People*, p. 140. South End Press, Boston, 1986.
27. Wicker, T. A deliberate deficit. *National J.*, July 19, 1985.
28. Heclo, H. The political foundations of anti-poverty policy. In *Fighting Poverty*, edited by S. Danziger and D. H. Weinberg, p. 339. Harvard University Press, Cambridge, Mass., 1986.
29. The Reagan budget. *The Economist*, June 10-16, 1987, p. 20.
30. Ferguson, T., and Rogers, J. *The Decline of the Democrats and the Future of American Politics*, p. 193. Hill and Wang, New York, 1987.
31. Therborn, G., and Roebroek, J. The irreversible welfare state. *Int. J. Health Serv.* 16(3): 319-338, 1986.
32. Therborn, G. *Why Some Peoples Are More Unemployed Than Others*, p. 122. Verso Books, London, 1987.
33. Edsall, T. B. *The New Politics of Inequality*, p. 212. W. W. Norton, New York, 1984.
34. Cohodes, D. R. Taking a wrong turn: Mandated employment based health insurance. *Inquiry* 24(1): 5, 1987.
35. Navarro, V. The welfare state and its distributive effects: Part of the problem or part of the solution? *Int. J. Health Serv.* 17(4): 543-566, 1987.
36. Kuttner, R. *The Economic Illusion*, p. 189. Houghton Mifflin, Boston, 1984.
37. Analysis of military expenditures. *Labor Economic Notes*, July/August, 1986.

CHAPTER 3

Debate on Popular Opinion and
U.S. Health Policy:
Are Americans Schizophrenic?

A RESPONSE TO CONVENTIONAL WISDOM

Letter From Professor Navarro to Health Affairs
To the Editor:

Several contributors, the editor, and the publisher of the journal, have, on several occasions, repeated statements I believe need to be questioned. One is that there has been a *popular mandate since 1980 to cut government health expenditures, including expenditures for the poor, elderly, and handicapped.* (See "An Interview with Dr. David E. Rogers" by J. K. Iglehart, Fall 1983). In those statements it is indicated that while Americans supported those government health programs in the sixties and seventies, they weakened their support at the end of the seventies and beginning of the eighties. All available evidence, however, shows otherwise. A survey of all major polls, including the Harris and Gallup polls, from 1976 to 1983, shows that (*a*) American public opinion is not so volatile as it is assumed to be, and (*b*) there has been strong and undiminished support by the majority of the American people throughout this period for federal government health expenditures for the elderly, poor, and handicapped. Moreover, while agreeing that the federal government expenditures may need to be cut to balance the budget, the overwhelming majority of Americans believe (according to George Martin of Yankelovich, Skelly, and White Surveys) that "balancing the budget should be done by cutting down defense and increasing corporate taxes, not by cutting social (including health) expenditures." In brief, any detailed analysis of people's opinion shows that there is not a popular mandate for current federal health policies which include cutting of expenditures for those vulnerable populations.[1] Quite to the contrary. According to Pollster Harris (2):

> . . . people all over the country have been profoundly shocked to find that the people running the country seem to want to abandon the poor and the elderly and the minorities . . . and that American people [think] that America could be systematically stripped of all its compassion for decency and humanity . . . but they are just beginning to get fighting mad about it. . . .

[1] For a review of all the polls on federal health programs since 1976 to 1983 see Navarro (1).

Originally published in the International Journal of Health Services, 15(3): 511–519, 1985.

Actually, it is usually forgotten that the majority of the electorate did not vote for Reagan in 1980. They voted for someone else or did not vote. And even among those who voted for him, there is evidence that many did not support his social policies. The current policies of cuts of federal health expenditures do not respond to a popular mandate.

Another position that frequently appears in the pages of the journal is that *those cuts in federal health programs were a consequence of the taxpayers' revolt that began in California and spread the country.* (See Introduction to article "The Role of State and Social Government" by Altman and Morgan, Winter 1983.) It is repeatedly said that Proposition 13 in California was an indicator of a revolt that appeared in the late seventies in this country against increased taxation and that this revolt has forced tax and spending cuts. By definition, however, a revolt assumes a heightening of protest that creates a new situation different from the previous one. An analysis of the popular mood toward taxes, however, does not show evidence of such a revolt. Taxes have been, for the most part, unpopular since they were established. The major changes have been on variations of which of the many (federal, state income and sales, and property taxes) is the worst. Since 1968, the percentage of those who feel taxes are too high (by type of tax) has not changed much, as shown in Table 1.

In spite of popular awareness of the inequities of the tax structure and its unpopularity, tax reform has not been considered to be a popular top priority. When we look at the open-ended Gallup question (asked since 1939) as to what is the most important issue facing the nation, we find fewer people mentioning taxes in the seventies than in the fifties. In the 1970–1980 period, less than 3 percent named taxes, and these respondents were often more concerned with the relative incidence of taxes than with their level. This confirmed the finding of many polls that the concern with taxes seems to focus not on their level but on equity and incidence questions, with the fairness of the tax system rather than the amount of taxes being the major concern (3).

It was not a heightening of popular discontent about taxes that triggered the passage in California of Proposition 13. The changes in popular mood happened after, not before, Proposition 13. Peretz has convincingly shown how the debate that followed the passage of Proposition 13 (due in large part to the rapid growth of property taxes in a state that had a state budget surplus) raised the level of unpopularity of paying taxes, a

Table 1

Percentages of Harris Poll respondents who felt taxes were too high,
by type of tax, 1969–1978

Type of Tax	July 1969	Feb. 1973	June 1974	Jan. 1975	Aug. 1976	March 1977	June 1978
Federal income	73	67	73	77	77	73	74
Federal corporate	44	40	25	21	25	45	48
Federal capital gains	55	54	47	48	59	57	—
State income	58	60	52	52	57	56	52
State sales	65	58	62	55	58	53	47
Local property	73	75	67	65	71	73	70

level that fell back afterwards to approximately the same level as that of one year earlier. Just two years after the passage of Proposition 13, Proposition 9 (which would have cut state income taxes) failed by a decisive margin of 62 percent to 32 percent (3).

It is worth stressing that even at the time of highest dissatisfaction with taxes (immediately after Proposition 13), the June 1978 Harris Poll found that the majority of respondents opposed tax cuts if they thought they would lead to cuts in aid to the elderly, disabled, and poor (71 percent opposed), and cuts in services in public hospitals and health care (62 percent).

Another position frequently put forward in your journal is that *national health insurance has lost its way because of lack of supporters.* In the introduction of the Winter issue of 1983 (Publishers' Letter, W. B. Walsh), your publisher indicates that "there has been a demise of any real constituency of national health insurance." This position seems to ignore that, since the early seventies, all major polls that have asked people's opinions about a comprehensive universal health program show that either large pluralities or the majority of Americans favor it (1, 4). One would hope that in a democratic society a plurality or majority of people (depending on the year) count as a major constituency after all.

In light of all the already published evidence that contradicts those positions it is clear that the uncritical acceptance of large segments of the medical and academic establishments of the existence of a popular mandate to reduce rather than expand federal health expenditures and related statements cannot be seen as a mere reflection of reality in the United States but, rather, as an advocacy statement rationalizing and justifying those policies.

Vicente Navarro, Professor of Health Policy
School of Hygiene and Public Health
The Johns Hopkins University

REFERENCES

1. Navarro, V. Where is the popular mandate. *N. Engl. J. Med.* 307: 1516–1518, December 9, 1982.
2. Pollster says opposition to Reagan mounting. *Nation's Health* 12(7): 1–2, 1982.
3. Peretz, P. There was no tax revolt. *Politics and Society* 11(2): 231, 1982.
4. Schneider, W. "Public Ready for Real Change in Health Care." *National J.* 3(23), 1985, p. 664.

WHAT DO AMERICANS REALLY WANT?

A Reply by Dr. D. E. Altman

To the Editor:

I am happy to comment on Vicente Navarro's "Response to the Conventional Wisdom." Since the sad fate of most articles is to go unread, I am even more pleased that the interview with David Rogers (Fall 1983) and my own article ("The Role of State and Local Government in Health," Winter 1983), may have helped stimulate him to write.

The crux of Professor Navarro's argument is that Americans want more health spending, not less, particularly for the poor and the elderly. He seems easily upset whenever it is suggested that Americans might want government health spending reduced, and especially bothered whenever anyone mentions Proposition 13, which he regards as an isolated event signifying basically nothing.

It seems fruitless to quibble with Professor Navarro about what was said in the article and interview. Rather, the compelling question is what do Americans really want? It seems important to answer this question, since the views of the public are likely to play a major role in setting the political and practical boundaries around what policymakers can do to affect change.

My colleagues and I have recently had occasion to examine what the public really thinks (R. Blendon, and D. Altman, "Public Attitudes about Health Care Costs: A Lesson in National Schizophrenia," *The New England Journal of Medicine*, 30 August 1984, Vol. 311, No. 9), and the fact is that Professor Navarro is about half right. Americans do favor more spending for health, not less. Public opinion polls tell us that only 14 percent of the public thinks that our society is spending too much for health care, while 53 percent think we are not spending enough. Two out of three Americans still believe that federal spending for health should be increased, and 59 percent still favor some form of national health insurance, even if coupled with a tax increase to pay for it. On the other hand, of course, he is also half wrong. In 1983, approximately two out of three Americans saw the high cost of medical care as the major problem facing the nation's health care system. Seventy-eight percent recognize that health care costs have been rising at a faster rate than inflation. Seventy-six percent of the public see our escalating federal deficit as a threat to the economy. Seventy-one percent want no additional spending on welfare (to which Medicaid is obviously closely tied). Most impressive of all, a recent Roper poll found that controlling health care costs ranked third (tied with inflation and behind crime and drugs and unemployment), as the most important priority for the nation as a whole.

Is there, perhaps, a poll to support virtually any position? Having analyzed all of the recent polls, I think not. They are remarkably consistent. Rather, what appears to be much closer to the truth is that Americans are highly ambivalent about health care costs and health spending and about what to do about the problem. Professor Navarro had decided to tell only one part of the story.

What is the nature of their ambivalence? The polls show that Americans are most concerned about the sharply rising prices of their health care and what they pay out of pocket; (68 percent believe the costs of their own medical care are unreasonable). However, in contrast to government officials, many business leaders, and many economists, Americans are not particularly troubled by the increasing share of our nation's resources devoted to health according to the polls. Perhaps more fundamental, most Americans are reasonably satisfied with their own medical care arrangements (72 percent of those hospitalized last year and 78 percent of those seeing a physician were "completely satisfied") and are unwilling to support cost reduction strategies that would change those arrangements to any significant degree. This fact—the public's reluctance to alter their current medical arrangements—much more than the public's complex and somewhat ambivalent feelings about spending for health, will influence what government and business can accomplish in the coming years to reduce health spending and affect change. The perception in Washington of the need for change in our health system, and the insistence of the proregulation and procompetition "camps" on their favorite solutions, will ultimately have to come to grips with this reality. Otherwise, we will do less than we must to control our mounting expenditures for health. (The views expressed in this letter are those of the author and no official endorsement by The Robert Wood Johnson Foundation is intended or should be inferred).

Drew E. Altman, Vice-President
The Robert Wood Johnson Foundation

IN DEFENSE OF AMERICAN PEOPLE: AMERICANS ARE NOT SCHIZOPHRENIC

A Further Reply From Professor V. Navarro

In my letter to the editor, published in the Fall 1984 issue of *Health Affairs,* I criticized some key positions put forward in the pages of the journal by its publisher, its editor, and several of its contributors (1). Specifically, I provided evidence that questioned the statements that there has been a demise of any real constituency for a national health insurance (W. B. Walsh), and that there has also been a popular mandate for cutting government health expenditures, including expenditures for the poor, elderly, and hand-icapped (D. E. Rogers and J. K. Iglehart). I also questioned that that "popular mandate" was in response to a taxpayers' revolt that began in California and spread through the country (Altman and Morgan). Altman, in his reply in the same issue, grants that: (*a*) there is indeed a national constituency for a national health program; (*b*) there is not a tax revolt in the health sector (59 percent of Americans are willing to pay higher taxes if those taxes are spent in establishing such a nationwide program); and (*c*) there is not a popular mandate for cutting health expenditures, including those for the poor, elderly and the handicapped; rather, the majority of people are asking for an expansion (2). I am glad that my letter triggered all those corrections and recognitions. Altman, however, does not stop with these recognitions. He moves on and criticizes me for telling the reader only half of the story. Americans also hold a series of views that, according to him, are in contradiction with the previous positions (*a–c*). Americans, for example, are also concerned about the rising costs of health services, the need to reduce the federal deficit, the rising expenditures for "welfare," and changing the personal health care arrangements that they like. Thus, he repeats what he and his colleagues have stated somewhere else, i.e., that Americans are schizophrenic in their views on health care and that that schizophrenia is the reason for the political inability to make substantial changes in American Medicine (3).

A more detailed and rigorous reading of American popular opinion, however, does not show any contradiction in those views. Quite to the contrary. Those views are logical, reasonable and consequent with the experience of the majority of Americans. Let me expand on each one of the assumed contradictions by referring both to Altman's letter, as well as to the article that he and Blendon wrote in *The New England Journal of Medicine* on popular opinions on health care, that he refers to extensively.

Blendon and Altman see a contradiction between the public being disturbed by the sharp rising prices of their health care on the one hand, and their apparent lack of concern with the growing share of the nation's economy that is devoted to health care on the other. They lament that most Americans believe that our society spends too little rather than too much on medical care services. They also refer to the apparently contradictory view that, in spite of public concern about health care costs, Americans are still willing to pay even higher taxes for health services (3). A more thorough reading and analysis of these views show, however, that there is nothing contradictory in them. Quite to the contrary—one is a logical extension of the other. Americans are rightly concerned that they still pay a very large percentage of their health care bill directly and out of their own pockets, with major health benefits still uncovered. An international analysis of health expenditures shows that that concern is, indeed, a very legitimate one. Not less than 27 percent of all health expenditures in the U.S. are still covered by direct payment, compared, for example, with only 5 percent in the United Kingdom, 8 percent in Sweden, and 12 percent in West Germany (4). This percentage is even higher among some groups in the population. For example, almost two decades after Medicaid and Medicare, our elderly still pay 40 percent of all their expenditures directly and out of their own pockets (5). The other side of the coin is that the U.S. is the Western developed country where for the majority of Americans, health benefits are more limited and large percentages of the population have major problems with insurance coverage (public or private). Here are just a few examples: 32 million Americans do not have public or private insurance coverage (6, 7); 100 million do not have any form of catastrophic insurance coverage (8); and one million American families have been refused medical care because of lack of financial means (9).

Because of these problems of coverage, and because (a) health is perceived by the public as an important condition for enjoying life, and (b) health care is considered to be useful and important for improving the public's health, we find a logical and conse- quent—rather than contradictory—response from the majority of Americans. They want an expansion rather than a reduction of health expenditures, to the point of being willing to pay even higher taxes if those tax revenues are spent in health care. It is indeed a sign of collective wisdom and solidarity that people are willing to pay less in direct payment (the reason for their concern about costs) and more in taxes (the indication of collective responsibility and solidarity). Actually, it is not only a more equitable way of funding health services, but also a more efficient one. Countries where the majority of health services are paid with public funds, have better coverage of benefits and of the popula- tion (e.g., United Kingdom, Sweden, Canada) than those, like the U.S., which still rely on private funding. And they spend less than we do (4).

The other public demand is for major changes in the medical care system. Here the authors see another major, schizophrenic contradiction between the public's desire to keep their own doctors and their personal health care arrangements, and the need for major changes in the health sector (3, p. 614). Here, again, there is nothing schizophrenic about this set of beliefs. The public can, indeed, be satisfied with many of the elements of the system but still be dissatisfied with how those elements relate together in their structurally defined, institutional settings. The medical profession is more than the aggregate of individual doctors and the medical care system is more than the mere aggregate of its individual components. Thus, there is nothing contradictory between liking one's doctor and disliking elements of the corporativist behavior of the medical profession, nor between liking elements of the medical care system and disliking how those elements are organizationally and financially related.

The polls show that the majority of Americans have supported, for quite a number of years now, (*a*) the establishment of a tax based comprehensive and universal health program, and (*b*) the federal control of doctors' fees, hospital costs, and prescription drugs (10–12). The implementation of these proposals would, indeed, mean major changes in medicine. The fact that the first proposal has never been implemented in the U.S. and only very few elements of the second, has nothing to do with a non-existent public schizophrenia, but rather with the power relations within America and its institutions of medicine, which continuously hinder the expression of the public's will. It is quite remarkable that in spite of the limited number of alternatives that are reasonably presented to the public by a highly conservative lay and professional media, the American public is farther ahead than their leaders in terms of needed changes. Contrary to widely held belief, the American media does not only reflect reality but creates and reproduces the dominant vision of reality. And this vision tends to be heavily ideological. The use of certain terms is consistently identified with negative ones aimed at triggering a predetermined public response. When the public is asked whether they would like to see "welfare" expenditures reduced, they answer in the affirmative. It is wrong to conclude, however, as Blendon and Altman seem to do, that Americans are not sensitive towards the poor and that they are tolerant of reductions in programs aimed at them (such as Medicaid), as a way of controlling costs. The term "welfare" has been transformed by the media (with the constant image of the welfare cheater) into a heavily ideological one. But, if instead of "welfare," the question is broken down into the different components of welfare expenditures, the responses are dramatically different. The public supports them by large majorities (10). Indeed, the cutting of social (including health) federal expenditures is one of the areas where Americans are expressing major concern (13). Here, again, there is not a contradiction between the public's concern about the federal deficit and the perceived need to reduce it on the one hand, and public willingness to increase federal spending for health and other major expenditures on the other. The major reason for the high rise of the deficit since 1980 has been the largest economic recession since the Depression, occurring during the current administration, as well as the huge growth in military expenditures and the tax cut that has benefited, for the most part, the top 15 percent of the population (14). Thus, it is quite reasonable that the majority of Americans believe that the way of reducing the deficit is by cutting military defense expenditures and raising the taxes of the corporations and high-income individuals, rather than reducing social expenditures (15). The international experience shows that the U.S. could indeed afford larger federal health expenditures without necessarily enlarging the federal deficit. For example, the United Kingdom, Sweden, West Germany, and Canada have far larger percentages for health expenditures covered by public funds and all have lower government budget deficits than the U.S. (16).

In summary, the fact that the U.S. is the only developed, industrialized society— besides South Africa—that does not guarantee efficient and effective health care to the whole population, is not due to the schizophrenia of the American public but, rather, to the unresponsiveness of American institutions to the public wishes, which are consistent, reasonable, and clear. The majority of Americans—although not their leaders—want to see major expansions of federal health expenditures side-by-side with major changes in the organization and funding of health care. The possibility and probability of those changes occurring does not depend on the development of consensus but on changes in the power relations within and outside American institutions—making them more responsive to the wishes of the majority of Americans.

Vicente Navarro, Professor of Health Policy
School of Hygiene and Public Health
The Johns Hopkins University

REFERENCES

1. Navarro, V. A response to conventional wisdom. *Health Affairs* 3(3): 137–139, Fall 1984.
2. Altman, D. F. What do Americans really want? *Health Affairs* 3(3): 139–141, Fall 1984.
3. Blendon, R. J., and Altman, D. E. Special Report. Public attitudes about health care costs: a lesson in national schizophrenia. *N. Engl. J. Med.* 311(1), 1984.
4. Direct payment for consumers. In *Health and Wealth: An International Study of Health Care Expenditures,* edited by R. J. Maxwell, p. 65, figure 4-4. Lexington Books, 1981.
5. Gibson, R. M., Waldo, R., and Lairt, K. R. The national health expenditures 1982. *Health Care Financing Review* 5(2): 1–31, 1983.
6. President's Commission for the Study of Ethical Problems in Medicine and Biomedical and Behavioral Research. *Securing Access to Medical Care,* Vols. 1–3. Government Printing Office, Washington, D.C., 1983.
7. Davis, K. and Rowland, D. Uninsured and underserved: inequities in health care in the United States. *Health and Society* 61: 149, 1983.
8. Califano, J. Secretary of HEW. Memorandum to the President of the United States on national health insurance, May 22, 1978.
9. Harris Poll survey. Updated report on access to health care for the American people. Robert Wood Johnson Foundation, Princeton, New Jersey, 1983.
10. Navarro, V. Where is the popular mandate? *N. Engl. J. Med.* 307: 1516, 1982.
11. Schneider, W. Public Ready for Real Change in Health Care. *National J.* 3(23): 1985, p. 664.
12. Equitable Health Care Survey by Harris, May–June, 1983.
13. Shriver, J. (ed.). The most important problem. Gallup Report 220–221: 28–29, 1984.
14. Ackerman, F. *Reaganomics, Rhetoric and Reality.* South End Press, Boston, 1983.
15. Lipset, S. M. Poll after poll after poll warns President on programs. *New York Times,* January 13, 1982, p. 23.
16. Navarro, V. Selected myths guiding the Reagan Administration's health policies. *J. Public Health Policy* 5(1): 65, March 1984.

CHAPTER 4

Medical History as Justification Rather Than Explanation: A Critique of Starr's *The Social Transformation of American Medicine*

Vicente Navarro

STARR'S MAJOR POSITION: AMERICANS' BELIEFS AS THE MOTOR OF HISTORY

Very few books on medical history have received so much acclaim as Paul Starr's *The Social Transformation of American Medicine* (1). Not only professional journals, but also the lay press have defined this publication—which received the Pulitzer Prize just a few weeks ago—as an indispensable reference to understanding the evolution of the institutions of medicine in the United States, referred to as the institutions of "American medicine."[1] Starr, in no less than 154 pages, explains why American medicine has evolved the way that it has. His explanation covers many subjects, including why American medicine was born at the time that it was, why there is no national health insurance in this country, why there is a large involvement of corporate interests in the field of medicine, why we are witnessing a retrenchment of the expansion of government intervention in American medicine, and many other important questions. We all should agree that the answers to these questions have enormous importance for the resolution of many health policy issues that the United States faces today. History is, after all, a much needed element in the explanation of today's realities.

Before answering these questions, Starr criticizes and dismisses previous explanations which have emerged from different ideological poles. One, defined by him (1, p. 16) as

---

[1] It is an indicator of cultural imperialism that U.S. institutions are referred to as American institutions, disregarding the enormous varieties of peoples and nations that exist on the American continent, north and south of the Rio Grande.

Originally published in the International Journal of Health Services, 14(4): 511–528, 1984.

the "most influential explanation of the structure of American medicine," traces the evolution of medicine to forces within medicine, and very much in particular to the scientific and technological advances that have acted as the primary motors in the evolution of medicine. While Starr agrees that these forces are important, he maintains that they cannot by themselves explain the evolution of American medicine. Scientists need to be reminded of the need for humility, after all.

The other explanation of American medicine is the instrumentalist interpretation that Starr attributes to Marxist authors. According to him (1, p. 17), Marxists view the development of American medicine as an "outcome of the objective interests of the capitalist class or the capitalist system." In this theoretical scenario, American medicine is what the capitalist class wants it to be. That class uses and shapes medicine in the way that best serves its class interests. Starr dismisses this interpretation, which he defines as *the* Marxist interpretation, as erroneous, i.e. it does not actually explain the evolution of American medicine. A proof that Marxists are wrong is that the capitalist class has attempted to rationalize medicine many times and has failed miserably. For example, Starr observes (1, p. 17), "The [capitalist] foundations have made repeated efforts to rationalize medical care [and] it is impressive how little these efforts have succeeded." Marxists and the Marxist historical method are thus plain wrong.

Starr's book represents in large degree an intent of offering an alternative explanation of American medicine to the ones recently presented by radicals and Marxist scholars. Thus, after dismissing these types of explanations of American medicine, he provides his own answer to the key question of why American medicine has evolved in the way it has. His explanation is remarkably simple: *American medicine has evolved as it has because Americans have wanted it that way.* American beliefs, concerns and wants have been the determinants of what has taken place in America's medicine, from its birth to the present. Needless to say, an interaction exists between forces within medicine (such as the power of physicians and other interest groups) and forces outside of medicine (such as Americans' beliefs). But of these forces, Starr maintains, the ones that determine the parameters of what happens or does not happen within medicine are the forces outside of medicine, of which the most important ones are the values and beliefs of Americans, by which it must be assumed Starr means the values and beliefs of the majority of Americans.

For example, the birth of what became known as scientific medicine is presented as an outcome of the power of persuasion of the physicians who convinced a responsive American public of the value of their tools and skills. Starr writes (1, p. 142) that "professional medicine drew its authority in part from the changing beliefs people held about their own abilities and understanding." At the time when medicine started, "there were profound changes in Americans' way of life and forms of consciousness that made them more dependent upon professional authority and more willing to accept it as legitimate" (1, p. 18). Also, "towards the end of the nineteenth century . . . Americans became more accustomed to relying on the specialized skills of strangers . . . Bolstered by genuine advances in science and technology, the claims of the professions to competent authority became more plausible, even when they were not yet objectively true; for science worked even greater changes on the imagination than it worked on the processes of disease" (1, p. 15). Consequently, Americans were convinced and persuaded that they needed the medical profession to solve their health problems: "Rather than trusting one's own skills and knowledge or those of competing sects or groups, Americans were persuaded to rely on the skills of the nascent medical profession; the less one could believe 'one's own eyes' . . . the more receptive one became to seeing the world through the eyes of those who claimed specialized, technical knowledge validated by a community of their peers" (1, p. 19).

In summary, Starr sees the rise of the medical profession as an outcome of Americans' beliefs, a result of their being persuaded by the medical profession's claims of the value of their skills. Once again, he castigates Marxists for believing that the monopolization of medical practice by regular physicians was accompanied by the repression of competing systems of medicine. He indicates (1, p. 229) that "to see the rise of the [medical] profession as coercive is to underestimate how deeply its authority penetrated the beliefs of ordinary people and how firmly it had seized the imagination even of its rivals."

Thus, Starr sees persuasion of the majority of Americans by a minority as the primary intellectual force behind social change in America. Several pages after having explained the birth of medicine as the result of the medical profession's powers of persuasion, Starr goes on to interpret the failure to establish a national health insurance, on the eve of World War I, as a result of the failure of social reformers to persuade Americans of the merits of that program. To the same degree that Americans have been "persuaded to adopt compulsory insurance against industrial accident, Americans could have been persuaded to adopt compulsory insurance against sickness" (1,p.236). Social reformers, however, failed to do so. In conclusion, America did not get national health insurance at that time because Americans did not want it.

American beliefs, wants and values appear again as the primary explanation of the events that took place in American medicine after World War II. This period is presented by Starr as characterized by the efforts of different interest groups to win the hearts and minds of the American people. Thus, one of the most conflictive periods in the history of the United States — which included the nightmare of McCarthyism, with brutal repression against radical and Marxist forces—is presented by Starr (in a chapter meaningfully entitled the "Triumph of Accommodation") as merely an outcome of U.S. labor's decision to change its image, style and strategy. Labor decided to change from radical to moderate in order to accommodate its interests to business interests and, in doing so, avoid antagonizing the majority of Americans, now redefined as the middle class public (1, p. 312). Indeed, Starr writes (1, p. 313), "The unions' struggle for influence in welfare programs was one of their few political successes during the post war period. Strikes during and immediately after the war antagonized much of the middle class public, and in the backlash against the unions, employers took the opportunity to get back some of the control they had lost." According to Starr, moderation as a tactic for persuasion was successful. Americans, via Senator Taft and the Supreme Court, included the right to bargain health care benefits in the Taft-Hartley Act. In this way, "unions have won the right to a say in health care" (1, p. 313).

American beliefs, values and wants are also perceived to be responsible for what happened in American medicine in the 1960s, with the establishment of new programs such as Medicare and Medicaid that were not allowed to interfere with the power relationships in existence in the institutions of medicine. According to Starr (1, p. 364), Americans "in the early 60s wanted to change, but did not want *to be changed.*

This was very much the case with regard to medical care. Americans wanted medicine to bring them change (new advances, more services), but they were not yet prepared for the sake of health to make changes in their way of life or their institutions." Needless to say, the final shape of those government programs also depended on the interplay of the different interest groups that operated within the institutions of medicine. Starr (1, p. 367) quickly adds, however, that American beliefs and public concern were the main forces responsible for the establishment and development of these programs.

Rolling along with time and moving on to the next historical period, American beliefs appear once again as the main force behind changes in American medicine in the 1970s and 80s. Thus, the expansion of government health interventions (expenditures and regulations) at the beginning and middle of the 70s and their reduction in the early 80s is explained as an outcome of a particular change in American beliefs. At the beginning of this period, Americans believed in government; at the end of the period, they did not. Starr summarizes this development as follows (1, p. 380); "Like American politics more generally, the politics of health care passed through three phases in the 1970's: (*a*) a period of agitation and reform in the first half of the decade when broader entitlements in social welfare and stricter regulation of industry gained ground in public opinion and law, (*b*) a prolonged stalemate, beginning around 1975 . . . and (*c*) a growing reaction against liberalism and government, culminating in the election of President Reagan in 1980 and the reversal of many earlier regulatory programs." While at the beginning of the 70s the majority of Americans favored government expansion, by 1980 "the majority of Americans clearly shared a general antipathy to government" (1, p. 418). According to Starr (1, p. 416), when the decade began, reformers were criticizing the inefficiency of the health care industry and they were able to persuade Americans of the need for government intervention; when the decade ended, the industry was criticizing the inefficiency of reform and was able to persuade Americans of the need to curtail government intervention. As a result of this situation and effective persuasion, "the public seems to be expressing a desire to return to older and simpler ways" (1, p. 419). Thus, Reagan's current drastic policies of cutting health expenditures for the elderly, poor, disabled and children, and of weakening government interventions, are perceived as responding to a popular mandate; these policies are the ones that Americans want.

Starr's interpretation of current events is a logical extension of his historical interpretation of American medicine. In his history, the social transformation of medicine is reduced to the ideological transformation of American beliefs and wants expressed either through the market or through their representative public institutions. In this theoretical scenario, the history of American medicine becomes the history of how interest groups have or have not been successful in persuading Americans of the merits of their proposals and ideas and how these groups have interacted among themselves to define the probable within the parameters of what Americans have already defined as possible. It is therefore not surprising that Starr concludes his explanations of the past and present of American medicine by predicting that the future of American medicine will depend primarily on what Americans want to happen. The last sentence of the book (1, p. 449) summarizes it well: The future of American medicine depends on "choices that Americans have still to make." History is, after all, a way of reading our own future.

STARR'S IDEOLOGICAL AND POLITICAL ASSUMPTIONS

I have gone to great lengths to summarize Starr's explanation of American medicine and to quote extensively from his acclaimed work because his views are highly representative of the view toward the workings of health policy upheld by large sectors of U.S. academia, government and media. His view sustains the ideological position that whatever has happened and will happen in America and its institutions is very much the result of what Americans want and believe.

Starr's interpretation of America sees the past and present structure of power in the United States as reflecting the wishes of the majority of Americans. To see the structure of power in America as the outcome of what Americans want, however, is to beg the question of which Americans. If by Americans it is meant the majority of Americans, then two assumptions are being made. One is that the majority of Americans share a set of beliefs, values and wants that provide an ideological cohesiveness to the totality of the unit called America. The other assumption is that that majority of Americans have had and continue to have the power to determine what happens both in the private sector of America (through the market forces) and in the public sector (through the representative public institutions). To these two assumptions Starr adds a third one: the dominant ideologies and positions become dominant through their powers of persuasion rather than through coercion and repression of alternative ideologies and positions.

These are the assumptions that sustain Starr's theoretical position and discourse. Needless to say, this interpretation of America is the one favored by those who benefit from current power relations in the U.S. It rationalizes the power of the establishment. They are there, on the top, because people want them there. Moreover, theirs is the power of persuasion rather than the power of coercion and repression. This legitimization function, incidentally, is what explains the "popularity" of Starr's book in the establishment's media and academia. Indeed, that acclaim cannot be attributed to the book's explanatory value of our realities (which is limited) but rather to its propagandizing function within that reality (which is large).

AN ALTERNATIVE EXPLANATION OF OUR REALITIES

A historical analysis of U.S. realities in general and of American medicine in particular shows that none of Starr's assumptions is correct. The historical analysis of the United States shows that Americans have been and continue to be divided into classes, races, genders and other power groupings, each with its own interests, set of beliefs and wants that are in continuous conflict and struggle. And these conflicts appear because, given the economic, social and political structure of the United States, certain classes, races, gender, and other groups have more power than others. Moreover, these power differentials are structural rather than conjunctural; they are built into the fabric of American society. In terms of classes, corporate America, for example, has far more power than working class America. This power differential results from the dominant position that the capitalist class—Corporate America—has over the means of production, consumption and exchange. And the hegemony of that class in the ideological and cultural sphere is due to its overwhelming influence over the means of value formation and legitimation. Needless to say, dominance and hegemony do not mean absolute control. The working class can also win victories. Power competition does exist after all. However, this competition is consistently and unavoidably unequal, skewed, and biased in favor of the dominant classes (and races and gender). As Miliband (2, p. 278) has indicated:

> There is competition, and defeat for powerful capitalist interests as well as victories. After all, David did overcome Goliath. But the point of the story is that David was smaller than Goliath and that the odds were heavily against him.

To believe that some classes, races and a gender are dominant does not mean that they alone determine the nature of what happens in the United States and its institutions, including the institutions of medicine. Indeed, to have a dominant class, race and gender means that there are dominated classes, races and a gender who do not necessarily accept the formers' domination in a passive way. Conflict and struggle continuously take place; and it is this struggle and conflict (rather than merely what one class wants) that determines changes in U.S. society and in American medicine. Starr is unaware of this reality. He indulges in facile stereotyping of Marxist positions by defining them as instrumentalist, i.e. they see the evolution of government and medicine as the outcome of the wishes of the capitalist class, which in a rather omnipotent fashion, shapes government and medicine to optimize its own interests. Starr's acquaintance with Marxist scholarship is characteristically limited. He would have benefited from a more rigorous reading and familiarity with that branch of scholarship before dismissing it so quickly. To reduce the large body of historical scholarship rooted in Marx to instrumentalism is abusive to an extreme. (For a critique of instrumentalism, see reference 3.) Actually, it was neither Marx nor any of his followers, but rather President Woodrow Wilson, who said that "the masters of the government of the United States are the combined capitalists and manufacturers of the United States" (quoted in 4). Although I find this instrumentalist vision of government too simplistic, I consider it equally simplistic to believe, as Starr does, that it is not the capitalist class but rather the will of the American people which defines government policies.[2]

American institutions, including the institutions of government and medicine, are the results of conflicts and struggles, of which class conflict is a key one. And by key I do not mean that class conflict is the only one. Other types of conflict do exist, of course, but class conflict is the one that explains the parameters within which all other conflicts unfold. And that conflict appears and has consequences in all societal institutions, including medicine. Moreover, that conflict emerges within a set of class (as well as race, gender, and other) forms of dominant/dominated power relations which *are reproduced not only by persuasion* (as Starr believes) *but, more importantly, by coercion and repression.*

---

[2] Starr refers only once (1, p. 315) to class struggle as a possible explanation for change in medicine. In a section borrowed heavily from Ploss' work (5), he explains the establishment of the United Mine Workers' health plan as an outcome of what he tactfully calls "a process of class conflict and accommodation." Otherwise, classes do not see the light of print in Starr's book. Instead, the capitalist and working classes are recycled as "interest groups" existing side by side with doctors, hospitals, and the drug industry, and other groups—all competing for the hearts and minds of middle-class Americans, assumedly the majority of Americans.

In summary, and as I have shown elsewhere (6), to understand the evolution of the United States and of American medicine, one has to understand the economic, social, and political structure of the U.S. and how it is reproduced through conflicts and tension among different groups and classes, conflicts that appear in all realms of society, including medicine. What happens in medicine is not the outcome of the conflicts between the different interest groups that exist within medicine, interacting within the parameters defined by the majority of Americans whose beliefs and wants eventually define what does or does not occur in medicine. These interest groups are, in reality, segments of classes (and other power categories) which, when considered in a systemic and not just sectoral fashion, are found to possess a degree of cohesion far transcending their specific differences and tactical disagreements. Thus, to understand the behavior and dynamics of the visible, and equally important, nonvisible actors in the medical sector, we have to understand their position within the overall economic and political scheme of the United States, i.e. their class and power position. Their position within a matrix of class, as well as sex, race and other types of power relations, explains why certain possibilities are being reproduced and others are being inhibited and repressed.

Let me illustrate this point by referring to an example: the historical evolution of occupational and other branches of medicine.

REPRESSION, BESIDES PERSUASION:
THE ESTABLISHMENT OF DOMINANCE

From its inception, the occupational branch of medicine was very close to management. As indicated in 1919 by one of the founders of occupational medicine, Dr. C. D. Relby (quoted in 7, p. 26), "industrial medicine is a specialty in the service of management." Forty-two years later, the head of the Council for Occupational Medicine of the American Medical Association, Dr. W. Shepard, put it equally well (7, p. 26): "The physicians' place in industrial medicine ... is auxiliary to the main purpose of the business: production and profit." This closeness of industrial medicine to the corporate class explains the sharing of views and beliefs among most industrial health professionals and that class. Both social groups believe that (a) most work-related accidents are caused by workers' carelessness, (b) there is a need for voluntary cooperation between management and labor and for voluntary enforcement of services and standards rather than compulsory government enforcement, (c) occupational health and safety professionals are scientists and therefore neutral, (d) most interventions need to be aimed at personal preventive devices and, (e) workers need to change their behavior and life styles.

These positions were and still are the dominant positions within industrial medicine and within the business establishment. However, this dominance was not, as Starr would have us believe, a result of the medical profession's persuasiveness. Rather, the rise of this position to dominance was based on a most brutal repression against alternate views of industrial medicine that saw most industrial accidents as caused by management's prioritization of productivity and profits over workers' lives, by faulty planning and equipment design, and by the use of toxic and hazardous materials that should either not be used or should be better controlled (8). This alternate view remained a repressed minority view because it conflicted with the interests of the employers who did not want to accept responsibility for the workplace damage, nor were they willing to change working conditions if this implied a reduction of their rights, privileges and benefits. The class of employers offered (*a*) rewards to those who favored the ideological position that reproduced their power, and (*b*) sanctions and repression against those who offered alternate explanations and solutions that challenged their power. The overwhelming influence of the class of employers in the funding of scientific endeavors, in the employment of occupational physicians, and on the agencies of the state explains why "the individual workers' responsibility" thesis became the dominant one in industrial medicine. The dominance of this position was based not on the power of persuasion of the industrial physicians but rather on the power of coercion and repression held by the dominant class whom those professions served and whose ideology they accommodated to.

The rewarding of those medical positions that reproduced the dominant ideology and the repression and exclusion of those that conflicted with these positions *appeared in all areas of medicine.* In summary, dominant professional positions become dominant not because of the persuasiveness of their upholders but rather because of their articulation within the dominant/dominated power relations. Interpretations that conflict with the dominant relations are likely to be repressed while those that strengthen dominant explanations of reality are likely to be rewarded. Needless to say, and like the David-Goliath conflict, the dominated positions can occasionally win. Moreover, the dominant positions cannot just ignore the dominated ones. There is a continuous need to repress them and recycle those elements of the dominated positions that can be absorbed within the dominant ones. But here again, the point of the story is that most of the time, one position becomes dominant or not depending on how it articulates itself with the overall power relations in society.

I suspect that some would argue that occupational medicine is not representative of what happened with medicine in general; that most of the institutions of medicine did not have such a close relationship with the corporate class as the occupational medical institutions did. While it is true that the other branches of medicine did not have as close a relationship with the corporate class, the differences involve degree rather than substance. The reality is that, from its birth, the dominant medical ideology and position became hegemonic because it complemented and reproduced the dominant class ideology. For example, American medicine as we know it—Flexnerian medicine— was established in Germany in the 19th century with the active support of the German bourgeoisie whose dominant ideology was compatible and in accordance with what was later to be called scientific medicine. Positivism was the ideology of the nascent bourgeoisie, and positivism appeared in the interpretation of health and disease that became the dominant one within medicine (9). Consequently, disease came to be perceived as a biological phenomenon caused by one or several factors which were always associated and observed in the existence of that disease.

We have to realize, however, that side by side with this interpretation was an alternate one that saw disease as a result of the oppressive nature of the existent power relations of society at that time. The intervention was viewed as one modifying (Virchow) or smashing (Engels) those power relations. This version of medicine did not prevail. Rather, it was repressed by the dominant classes who, of course, felt threatened by those alternative explanations of disease and the operational proposals for its resolution. These classes preferred to support the biological and individual interpretation of disease which has since been reproduced in curative and preventive medicine. Thus, medical interventions were aimed at eliminating, eradicating and controlling the outside microagents—bacteria or viruses—that created the disease.

This interpretation of disease and of medicine was also the one that became dominant in the United States. And it became dominant for the same reasons. The established centers of power favored that interpretation of disease and medicine, repressing other interpretations that represented a potential threat to their power and privileges. Starr dismisses this explanation of the birth of American medicine. He actually belittles the explanation that the dominance of Flexnerian medicine also meant the repression of its alternative. He denies, for example, that capitalist ideology favored medicine over public health. He writes (1, p. 228), "It is difficult to see why capitalism as a system, would have benefited by favoring medical care over public health. . . . To be sure, many companies resisted public health measures that would have increased their production costs or limited their markets. On the other hand, for equally self-interested reasons, life insurance companies actively stimulated public health measures." By posing the question the way he does, however, he already provides the answers. The question that needs to be asked, however, is not so much why the capitalist class favored curative medicine over public health, but rather, why the dominant ideology of disease was the same in both (medicine and public health), i.e. the positivist biological one which led to medical and public health interventions focusing for the most part on individual interventions that minimized conflict with the power relations within and outside medicine. A clear example of this is the approach that both public health spokespersons and the life insurance industry took toward prevention. C.E.A. Winslow (one of the founders of what became the established public health position) included in his report prepared for the Metropolitan Life Insurance Company (10) the following analysis of what was wrong at the workplace and what should be done:

> *Do you know* that a great many men and women die every year on account of the conditions under which they work? *Do you know* that if a man goes into certain trades it means he will have five, ten or fifteen years less of life than if he earned his living in some other way?
>
> It is true. The death rate among cutlery grinders in Sheffield, England, for instance, is just about twice as high as it is for other men of the same age. Half the men who die in this trade die of *industrial disease* (chiefly tuberculosis), due, largely, to breathing in sharp particles of dust.
>
> Most industrial diseases are preventable. The bad conditions that exist in factories and other industrial establishments are due mainly to ignorance. They keep the worker uncomfortable, they hinder his work, and they make him an easy prey to sicknesses that come along. They are likewise harmful to the employer's interests, for he is a constant loser from poor and careless work, spoiled stock, absences and the breaking in of green hands. *Dangerous conditions continue to exist because neither employer nor employee knows what is going on.* They do not understand that dust and fumes, bad air, poor lighting and dirt make sick men and a poor product. This book is written to help its readers to think of these things? for conditions will be made better as soon as people begin to think about them. You cannot keep your shop healthful unless your employer does his part. Neither can he unless you do yours.

"Ignorance" was presented in that report as the primary source of the problem. Winslow's examination of the "dangerous trades," however, did not lead him to ask Metropolitan's subscribers to force their employers to clean up their factories. It is a rather hyperbolic statement to present, as Starr does, that call for information and health education as examples of "active" public health interventions. The reality is that the meaning of "active" is dramatically reduced within the parameters of non-conflictive solutions. A more updated version of this interpretation of public health is reflected in current Reagan health policies that focus on individual health education as the best measure of prevention, while weakening government regulations and other collective interventions.

It is important to understand that side by side with the dominant interpretation of public health focused on the individual, there has always been another interpretation which views public health as a set of interventions that frequently conflict with the dominant capitalist relations existent in the areas of work, consumption, environment, and residence. This latter interpretation has more often than not been repressed. The power of this alternative interpretation has primarily depended not on its power of persuasion but rather on its articulation with an alternate source of power, such as militant sectors of labor or other rebellious forces capable of facilitating its expression. Thus, the periods in which this alternate view has opened up new spaces have been those where militant sectors of the working class and related rebellious forces have been able to press for these types of interventions. As I will show later on, expansion of government public health interventions has occurred in periods when labor and allied rebellious forces have been in a relatively strong position.

AN ALTERNATIVE EXPLANATION: CLASS INTEREST AS THE DETERMINANT OF CHANGE

Another example of Starr's erroneous interpretation of history appears in his rather idyllic explanation of how workers' compensation laws were passed in the United States. Not uncharacteristically, Starr explains this event as a result of the powers of persuasion of the social reformers who were able to convince Americans of the merits of their specific legislation. Reality, however, was quite different. The passage of these laws had little to do with social reformers' persuasive powers, nor with the will or wants of Americans. These laws were passed because of the interest of American corporations. The latter had enormous power and influence over the legislatures of several states that passed workers' compensation laws after 1910. At that time, there was widespread worker unrest centered around poor working conditions and the large number of workers injured at the workplace. Consequently, large sections of labor were demanding an end to management prerogatives, including management's right to control the workplace. Moreover, many workers were suing management for damages, with the courts ordering settlements that proved to be quite costly for management. Because of these pressures, the voice of the major corporations, the National Civic Federation, actively supported workers' compensation legislation. Among other consequences, that law eliminated the workers' right to sue for damages (8). Today we are witnessing a similar type of response to the current individual workers' litigation against Johns-Manville and other asbestos producers. Johns-Manville, one of the most offensive corporations to the health of American workers, is in the forefront of the campaign for government compensation laws for asbestos workers which will shift the social costs of the corporations' criminal behavior to the government. It requires an overgenerous reading of corporate America, indeed, to define Johns-Manville or the earlier National Civil Corporation as "social reformers" and their political muscle and influence over the state legislatures as "persuasion." The implementation of those laws had little to do with "social reforms" or with persuasion. It had to do with the threat that workers' demands posed to American corporations and the enormous political muscle they have over the state legislatures. It is Starr's unawareness of these social and political conflicts that makes his explanations so erroneous.

Similarly, to see—as Starr does—the victory of the corporativist view within labor, which occurred after World War II, as representing labor's desire to change its image in order not to antagonize the middle classes is to ignore the enormous conflicts that took place in the 1940s and 50s, including a most brutal attack by the corporate class against the most militant section of the working class. McCarthyism represented brutal repression against any class threat to corporate class dominance. The Taft-Hartley Act, a result of that attack, was not a victory for labor, as Starr seems to believe, but rather a defeat. It forced labor to act as an interest group rather than as a class. Because of it, the United States is the only country in the Western developed world where labor cannot act as a class. For example, steel workers cannot strike in solidarity with a coal miners' strike. By law, each section of labor has to act as an interest group. Consequently, this piece of legislation weakened labor most dramatically; each fraction of labor has to act on its own (11, 12). Thus, some sectors of labor did achieve great advances through private collective agreements; however, for the working class as a whole, their level of benefits remained far more limited than that of their counterparts in Western Europe where the working class could still operate as a class. As a consequence, the United States has an underdeveloped welfare state. In terms of health benefits, the U.S. population has less coverage (in their private and public programs) than the majority of the populations in developed countries (13).

STARR'S INTERPRETATION OF RECENT EVENTS

The ideological and apologetic function of Starr's interpretation comes through most clearly in his interpretation of the current Reagan policies as the outcome of a popular mandate. He uncritically reproduces prevalent conventional wisdom that Americans' opinion follows a pendular swing, oscillating from pro- to anti-government. It speaks of the overwhelming influence that corporate America has on the means of information in the United States (including academia) that this interpretation is so widespread and reproduced in spite of overwhelming evidence to the contrary. Indeed, as I have shown elsewhere (14), popular opinion is not as volatile as it is assumed to be. For the years that I have analyzed popular opinion polls—1976-1983—the evidence is overwhelming: by large margins, the majority of Americans are in favor of increased rather than decreased health and social expenditures and strengthening rather than weakening government intervention to protect workers, consumers and the environment. Reagan's health policies do not follow a popular mandate.

Starr is also empirically wrong when he explains Reagan's 1980 electoral victory as the "outcome of the wishes of the majority of Americans and a general antipathy to government." The opinion polls for 1980 show a similar result as previous and subsequent polls: the majority of Americans were in favor of the same government programs that Reagan soon started cutting. Moreover, the majority of Americans did not vote or voted for candidates other than Reagan. Starr should get his facts straight and be less willing to join the chorus, following the establishment's tune. Moreover, even among the minority of the electorate who did vote for Reagan, many indicated that they had voted *against* Carter because of his perceived inability to reduce unemployment rather than *for* Reagan.

To believe that Carter was defeated in 1980 because he was too progressive is to uncritically reproduce what the establishment wants people to believe and to ignore all evidence to the contrary. Carter was elected in 1976 with a program that included an expansion of social consumption (including establishment of national health insurance) and a reduction of military expenditures—policies that he reversed in 1978, alienating large sectors of the population and, most importantly, large sectors of the grassroots element of the Democratic Party. This change of policies explains why his job rating in the opinion polls fell more precipitously from 1977 to mid-summer 1979 than had been the case for any other president since polling on the subject began in 1945 (15). In brief, there was not a popular mandate in 1980 for cutting social consumption and weakening government health regulations.

What we are witnessing in the 1980s is not the outcome of American wishes, if by Americans we mean the majority of Americans. What we are witnessing today is a most brutal class warfare, carried out by the most aggressive sector of corporate America against the advances that workers, women, blacks and other minorities, and environmentalists achieved in the 1960s and middle-1970s. Even Lane Kirkland, the head of the AFL-CIO and a person not known for radicalism, has expressed alarm that big business in this country is involved "in an unprecedented class warfare" (16).

Why this response? Because of labor shortages in the 1960s, we witnessed the strengthening of labor's power, responsible in large degree for the passage of social and health federal legislation. In addition, other rebellious movements, such as civil rights, black liberation, women's and ecological movements, pressed for government intervention. Contrary to conventional wisdom, the 1960s and 70s proved the effectiveness of government intervention in the social arena. By the second half of the 1970s, only 7–8 percent of the American public remained beneath the poverty level compared with about 18 percent in 1960. As Schwartz (17) has shown, this reduction of poverty was accomplished primarily through government transfer programs.

In the health care sector we witnessed a similar progress. In 1963, before the implementation of Medicare and Medicaid, fully one in five of those Americans living beneath the poverty level had never been examined by a physician. By 1970, the percentage of people living in poverty who had never been examined by a physician was reduced from its 1963 level of 19 percent to 8 percent. From 1965 to 1975, the overall infant mortality rate among the poor fell by 33 percent. Gains among blacks were particularly evident. Between 1950 and 1965, before the great expansion in federal medical and nutritional programs, the infant mortality rate among blacks barely fell, from 44.5 per 1000 births in 1950 to 40.3 in 1965. Following the expansion of the programs, the rate of black infant mortality declined quickly, from 40.3 in 1965 to 30.9 in 1970 and to 24.2 in 1975. There thus occurred an approximately fivefold increase in the speed of decline in the black infant mortality rate after 1965.

Other social groups also improved their living conditions because of that growth of social consumption. In summary, the growth of social expenditures was an outcome of the relative strength of labor and other social movements. At the same time, that growth also strengthened the working class vis à vis the corporate class. Working families received collective and social wages that made them less vulnerable to the cyclical fluctuations of employment and thus less receptive to employers' pressures.

Government interventions took place not only by expanding expenditures but also by regulating the protection of workers, consumers, and of the environment. Regarding the environment, government interventions, in the Clean Air Act of 1970 and the Water Pollution Control Act in 1972, had a positive impact on improving water and air conditions in the United States. By 1979, the level of sulfur dioxide in the air had declined by about an additional 40 percent from its level in 1970, and concentrations of suspended particulate matter in the air in 1979 had declined by an additional 17 percent from their 1970 level. For carbon monoxide (from automobile exhaust), the decline was about 40 percent for the same period (17). Regarding water, the National Wildlife Federation indicates that fifty major bodies of water showed considerable improvement over the decade of the 70s (17).

Here again, the evidence is overwhelmingly clear that the growth of government health expenditures and of government regulations did improve the conditions of the majority of Americans and that the majority of Americans favor an expansion and strengthening of such interventions (14, 17). The fact that they were cut in 1978 and further cut in the 1980s was not because the majority of Americans changed their minds. The evidence is clear that they did not. The government social and health expenditure cuts and the weakening of government occupational and environmental regulations were an outcome of a most brutal repression from the most aggressive sectors of the U.S. capitalist class who saw those advances by the working population as threats to their privileges and interests (18).

To see those policies as aimed at "getting government off people's backs" is to indulge in the realm of apologetics, not rigorous analysis. The Reagan Administration is not anti-government. Actually, the percentage of public expenditures in the GNP has increased, not declined, under this administration. Primary characteristics of this administration have been 1) a dramatic transfer of federal funds from the social and health sectors to the military sectors, and 2) an enormous increase of the agencies of intervention and control, with a reduction of trade union, civil, women's, and ecological rights for the majority of the population. These interventions respond to a specific vision of the government role in today's United States, well defined by H. Salvatori (quoted in 19), a key member of the Reagan transitional team:

> In the history of man everyone has talked about expanding rights, having more and more freedom. But we have found that if you let people do what they want to do you have chaos ... what we have to do is to re-structure society. Frankly, we need a *more authoritarian state*. (emphasis added)

This is what we are witnessing today. In brief, the issue is not to be pro or anti-government. At issue, rather, is whose government and for what purpose. The overwhelming influence that those corporate class interests have over the media and political and academic institutions explains why a "new conventional wisdom" has been developed in which those government policies that are creating enormous pain and suffering are presented as responding to the wishes of the majority of Americans.

It is Starr's willingness to reproduce these ideological images that explains his popularity in the corridors of power. Here again, his "success" is not due to his persuasiveness but rather to his articulation with the dominant/dominated power relations in the United States. This fact also explains his repression of alternative antiestablishment views, repression that appears in his book by stereotyping (to the point of ridiculing) or silencing all positions that clearly threaten the ideological reproduction of established class relations.

This deafening silence is not without costs, however. For example, in his chapter on the increased involvement of corporations in American medicine, Starr (1, p. 428) characterizes the creation of a medical-industrial complex as an "entirely unexpected" consequence of government interventions in the 60s. A better reading of U.S. realities would have led him to conclude that there was nothing "unexpected" in that development. Other authors (nowhere mentioned in this chapter) had predicted and explained this growth of corporate involvement in medicine. Actually, contrary to what Starr indicates, Arnold Relman, the editor of the *New England Journal of Medicine*, was not the first author to introduce the concept of the medical-industrial complex. Kelman (20), Salmon (21–23) and myself (6), among others, have explained how the rationale of the capitalist system and the enormous influence of corporate America in the organizations and agencies of the state determines that even when government, as a result of popular pressures, intervenes in the health and social spheres to improve the health and well-being of Americans, those interventions are limited and compromised by the need to respond to corporate interests as well, which in turn diminishes the initial intent of those interventions. All those authors predicted the establishment and enlargement of the medical-industrial complex (both in the financing and in the delivery of health services) before Relman and Starr.

The fact that Starr does not acknowledge or refer to these previous works is characteristic of the discrimination and repression against Marxist scholarship in the U.S. academia and media.[3] By ignoring these previous works, however, he remains stuck in the same trenches with other "interest group" analysts. Indeed, this new version of the "corporatization of medicine," by ignoring the socio-economic-political context in which it takes place, and by seeing corporate America as one more interest group competing for government favors, is incapable of explaining why that corporatization is taking place now. It is not surprising that Starr finds that corporatization an unexpected event.[4] That event, however, is expected and predictable. As those authors explained, this corporatization of medicine is the logical outcome of the dynamics of U.S. capitalism within a process of class struggle in which the dominant capitalist class continues to have an overwhelming influence over the organs of the state. This overwhelming dominance explains that even when government responds to popular demands from working America, that response takes place within the parameters and

---

[3]It is interesting to note that the *New York Times* deleted the sections of an otherwise extremely favorable review of Starr's book in which the reviewer criticized the book for its discrimination and abuse of Marxists (personal communication from H.J. Geiger, author of the review). For a valuable discussion of repression against Marxist positions in U.S. academia, see reference 24.

[4]Starr finds this corporatization of medicine to be, besides unexpected, a worrisome development. This position partially explains the book's favorable review among liberals and even some radical reviewers.

conditions defined by the hegemonic elements within that capitalist or corporate class. The very limited power of the working class in the United States (a situation unparalled among developed capitalist societies) explains not only the underdevelopment of the U.S. welfare state but also the corporatization of its medicine.

In summary, government-as a branch of the state-is subjected to a matrix of influences, some of which are structurally more dominant than others. Dominant influences are not tantamount to absolute control. And the majority of Americans can have a voice after all. However, contrary to what Starr and the establishment would like us to believe, that voice is not the definitive one to explain our past, present or future. Other voices exist which limit, restrain and frequently even silence those majority voices. For example, the majority of Americans have desired for many years that the government assure that all persons in need of health care should receive it, or that whomever needs a job should have it (14, 25, 26). Neither popular wish has been fulfilled. The list of responsibilities that the majority of Americans feel their government should have and fails to take on is enormous. Whether government undertakes these responsibilities or not does not depend only or even primarily on what the majority of Americans feel or want. It depends on the sets of influences and dominances that shape government interventions, of which corporate American is a major one. And the majority of Americans know it. They believe, for example, that the major political parties are in favor of big business and that major American corporations tend to dominante and determine the behavior of our public officials in Washington (27, 28). It would be wrong to see corporate America as the only influence, with absolute control over government. But in a matrix of influences, theirs is a very powerful one indeed. And its power appears not only in political but also in civil, social and economic institutions. It is this overwhelming influence that compromises most significantly the meaning of democracy. Indeed, the public debate takes place within the parameters already defined by the dominant corporate class which influences, through its enormous varieties of communication agencies (academia, media, political institutions, etc.), the terms of the discourse and debate, through which that majority voice is supposed to appear. As an observer of the American scene has indicated (29), "The flaw in the pluralistic heaven is that the heavenly chorus sings with a very special accent. The system is askew, loaded, and unbalanced in favor of a fraction of a minority."

Thus, when government has to respond due to strong popular pressure (as in the 1960s and 70s), that response always takes place in a way that corporate class interests shape the nature of that response, continuing to be in a dominant position in those interventions. What alternatives are to be considered, and which ones are to be chosen depend not only on the majority of Americans but on many other forces as well, of which corporate class forces continue to be the dominant ones. Examples in the health sector are many. Witness the debate in the 1970s in the U.S. Congress about the type of national health insurance. The power of financial capital, the commercial insurance companies, forced a change in the Kennedy-Griffith proposal—the only proposal that excluded the insurance companies—and brought about the Kennedy-Mills proposal which accepted their role (6). As an editorial of the *New York Times* indicated (30):

> To retain the insurance companies' role was based on recognition of that industry's power to kill any legislation it considers unacceptable. The Bill's sponsors

thus had to choose between appeasing the insurance industry and obtaining no
national health insurance at all.

Even with these changes, the combined resistance of the dominant sectors of corporate
America, side by side with the opposition of the major medical and hospital interest
groups, defeated and silenced that alternative, in spite of the fact that the majority of
Americans wanted then, and continue to want now, a tax-based program that could
assure comprehensive and universal health coverage for the whole population.[5]

Also, witness today's discussion of federal health policies. The discourse focuses on
"consumer choice," "competitiveness," "rate of return" and the like, all heavily
ideological terms that characterize the acceptable intellectual exchange. Anti-corporate
positions are excluded by a most brutal force of repression from most of the communication agencies, including academia. Harvard University's Department of Sociology, incidentally the academic institution in which Paul Starr teaches, has not even
one token tenured Marxist professor. Repression, not persuasion, explains this reality.
The presentation of alternative explanations of reality and alternate socialist solutions
to the population is dramatically reduced in the institutions of ideological reproduction—like the media and academia—by unhindered repression.

In brief, the element of "choice" that Starr assumes when he writes that the past,
present, and future is what the majority of Americans have and will choose, assumes
that there is no control of information, no limitation of the agenda for change, no
predetermination of interest choices, and no limitation of instruments for change.
The past and present of America deny these assumptions, however. Actually, what we
are witnessing today is the increased alienation of people not from the values that (at
least in theory) their government institutions should uphold (e.g. responding to the
health needs of all people), but rather from the actual practice of those institutions
that operate on their behalf.

The available evidence shows that the majority of Americans are dissatisfied with
the major political, social and economic institutions of our country and the order of
things that they sustain.[6] They acquiesce to the existing order because they do not see
the possibility of change, or do not see what alternatives exist or how the rules of the
game can be changed. Indeed, the future of American medicine within the corporate
order will not be the one that the majority of Americans would choose. Rather, it will
be the outcome of enormous, heartbreaking struggle between the dominated and
dominant classes, races, gender and other power categories, in which the corporate
class will continue to have the major voice in defining the parameters, alternatives and
discourses of that future. The future of the United States and its system of medicine
will depend on the resolution of this struggle.

---

[5] During the 1970s and 80s, the majority, or a plurality of Americans (depending on the year),
have favored establishing a tax-based universal and comprehensive health program (reference 14;
New York Times, March 29, 1982, p. D11).

[6] In 1982, popular confidence in the leaders of ten leading institutions had reached 21 percent,
the lowest level recorded in any survey (30).

REFERENCES

1. Starr, P. *The Social Transformation of American Medicine*. Basic Books, New York, 1983.
2. Miliband, R. Marx and the state. In *The Socialist Register, 1965*, edited by R. Miliband and J. Saville. Merlin Press, London, 1966.
3. Navarro, V. Radicalism, Marxism, and medicine. *Int. J. Health Serv.* 13(2): 179–202, 1983.
4. Hunt, E.K. and Sherman, H.J. *Economics: An Introduction to Traditional and Radical Views.* Harper and Row, New York, 1972.
5. Ploss, J. A History of the Medical Care Program of the United Mine Workers of America's Welfare and Retirement Fund. Master's thesis, Johns Hopkins School of Hygiene and Public Health, 1980.
6. Navarro, V. *Medicine Under Capitalism*. Prodist, New York, 1977.
7. Berman, D. *Death on the Job*. Monthly Review Press, New York, 1979.
8. Navarro, V. The determinants of occupational health and safety policies in the United States. *Int. J. Health Serv.*, in press.
9. Navarro, V. Work, ideology and science: The case of medicine. *Int. J. Health Serv.* 10(4): 523–550, 1980.
10. Winslow, C.E.A. The Health of the Worker: Dangers to Health in the Factory and Shop and How To Avoid Them. Metropolitan Life Insurance Company, New York, 1913.
11. Davis, M. Labour in American politics. *New Left Review* 123: 3–46, 1980.
12. Davis, M. The legacy of the CIO. *New Left Review* 124: 43–84, 1980.
13. Maxwell, R. *Health and Wealth: An International Study of Health Care Spending*. Lexington Books, Lexington, 1981.
14. Navarro, V. Where is the popular mandate? *New Engl. J. Med.*, Dec. 9, 1982; *Int. J. Health Serv.* 13(1): 169–174, 1983; Navarro, V. An International Perspective on Health Care: Learning from Other Nations. Document prepared for the Select Committee on Aging of the U.S. House of Representatives, May 1, 1984 (in press).
15. Faux, J. Lessons for Democrats: Don't be conservative. *New York Times*, Jan. 6, 1984, p. A23; Countdown to Election: Presidential popularity. *National Journal* 11: 1729, 1979.
16. Raskin, A.H. Lane Kirkland: A new style for labor. *New York Times Magazine*, Oct. 28, 1979, p. 91.
17. Schwartz, J.E. *America's Hidden Success: A Reassessment of Twenty Years of Public Policy*. W.W. Norton, New York, 1983.
18. Navarro, V. The crisis of the international capitalist order and its implications for the welfare state. *Int. J. Health Serv.* 12(2): 169–190, 1982.
19. Reagan policy in crisis. *NACLA Report* 15(4): 10, 1981.
20. Kelman, S. Toward the political economy of medical care. *Inquiry* 8: 30–38, 1971.
21. Salmon, J.W. The health maintenance organizational strategy: A corporate takeover of health services delivery. *Int. J. Health Serv.* 5(4): 609–623, 1975.
22. Salmon, J.W. Monopoly capital and the reorganization of the health sector. *Review of Radical Political Economy* 9: 125–133, 1977.
23. Salmon, J.W. Corporate Attempts to Reorganize the American Health Care System. Doctoral dissertation, Cornell University, 1978.
24. Ollman, B. Academic freedom in America. *Monthly Review*, March 1984, p. 24.
25. Katznelson, I. and Kesselman, M. *The Politics of Power*. Harcourt, Brace, Jovanovich, New York, 1975.
26. Smith, K.M. and Spinard, W. The popular political mood. *Social Policy*, March–April 1981, p. 38.
27. Complete Hart Poll results. *Common Sense*, Sept. 1, 1975, pp. 16–17.
28. Bender, M. Will the bicentennial see the death of free enterprise? *New York Times*, Jan. 4, 1976, p. 27.
29. Schattschneider, E.E. *The Semi-sovereign People: A Realistic View of Democracy in America*. Holt, Rinehart and Winston, New York, 1960.
30. Health plan progress (editorial). *New York Times*, Apr. 7, 1974, p. E16.
31. Lipset, S.M. and Schneider, W. *The Confidence Gap: Business, Labor and Government in the Public Mind*. Free Press, New York, 1983.

SECTION II

The Reality: The Problems in U.S. Health Care

CHAPTER 5

Should We Abolish the Private Health Insurance Industry?

Thomas Bodenheimer

During 1989, U.S. health policy debate has experienced an important shift. For the first time in over 15 years, health analysts are giving consideration to the development of a publicly run single-payer health financing mechanism that would replace the current privately dominated multiple-payer health system. The attractiveness of the single-payer mechanism is its ability to solve simultaneously the growing problems of uninsurance and health care inflation. In particular, debate over the merits of the Canadian single-payer model, initiated by Physicians for a National Health Program in its January 1989 proposal (1), has intensified in medical staff meetings at diverse hospitals, in conferences of professional organizations, in board rooms of major U.S. corporations, in Congressional committee hearings, and in the media.

A central feature of the single-payer model developed by the Physicians for a National Health Program is the abolition of the private health insurance industry and the concentration of all health care payments in the hands of a publicly run health fund that pays hospitals, physicians, and other health providers. The health insurance industry is a $150 billion business employing tens of thousands of people, a central feature of the U.S. health care landscape over the past 40 years. It is no small matter to propose the extinction of such an important enterprise. This article proposes to address the question: should the private health insurance industry be abolished?

HEALTH CARE AS A RIGHT VERSUS THE INSURANCE PRINCIPLE

In seeking a method to finance health care, societies can choose between two fundamentally different conceptions: (*a*) the principle of health care as a right, and

Originally published in the International Journal of Health Services, 20(2): 199–220, 1990. This was first presented as a paper at the American Public Health Association convention, October 1989.

(*b*) the insurance principle that people get what they pay for. These principles are in conflict.

The Right to Health Care

Legally, health care is not a right in the United States (2, 3). But in constructing a conception of health and society, the current legal status of health care as a right is irrelevant. The important question becomes: *should* there be a right to health care in the United States?

Philosophers, ethicists, medical professionals, and health policy experts have written hundreds of pages on this question (4-8). Utilizing a variety of theories of justice, many conclude that health care should be a right while others disagree. Hundreds more pages are spent searching for the meaning of the right to health care. Does it mean universal entitlement to every available medical therapy, or does society set limits? Do people (e.g., smokers) who damage their own health have the same rights as others? How should payment for health services relate to amount of use or to personal income? Rather than summarizing these matters here, I refer the reader to Victor Sidel's concise discussion of "The Right to Health Care: An International Perspective" (9).

Among those who search for the meaning of health care as a right, a consensus formulation reads something like this: the right to health care means that society has a duty to allocate an adequate share of its total resources to health-related needs, and that each person is entitled to a fair share of such services as determined by medical need rather than by income, political power, or social status (10, p. 194; 11). A simpler formulation would be: all people should have equal access to a reasonable level of health services regardless of income.

Physicians, philosophers, or lawyers aside, whether or not health care should be a right in the United States is not primarily a medical, ethical, or legal issue; it is a *political* issue. Few would disagree that in a democracy, the majority should decide.

In fact, the majority has spoken. Our modern opinion-expressing mechanism, the public opinion poll, strongly indicates that the American people believe that health care should be a right. Polls conducted in 1968, 1975, and 1978 asked: is adequate medical care "a privilege that a person should have to earn, or a right to which he [*sic*] is entitled as a citizen?" In all three surveys, over 75 percent said health care should be a right (12). A 1986 poll asked: in general, do you think all Americans should have access to the same quality of care regardless of ability to pay for it? Eighty-six percent answered yes (13). In a 1988 Harris poll, 90 percent of the public felt that everyone is entitled to health care "as good as a millionaire could get." Sixty-eight percent of physicians agreed (14). It is true that people will not always back up their surveyed sentiments with political support if the monetary cost is too high. But in fact, several polls show that people would be willing to pay more for health care (15). Considering evidence from many years of public opinion polling, it is undeniable that Americans show overwhelming sentiment for the proposition that health care is a right.

Moreover, the United States is surrounded by nations that have enacted entitlement to health care into their legal systems. A recent survey shows that a large number of nations in the Western Hemisphere include the right to health services in their constitutions (3). In a *New England Journal of Medicine* editorial, Drs. Berwick and Hiatt observe: "Americans have no right to health care. In this respect, we stand almost alone among the industrialized nations of the world" (16). The Universal Declaration of Human Rights, passed by the United Nations General Assembly, affirms a right to medical care (17). Not only has the United States ignored the opinions of the great majority of its own citizens on this issue, it also stands apart from the community of nations.

How does one translate the principle of health care as a right into a health care financing mechanism? Recall the consensus formulation of health care as a right: all people should have equal access to a reasonable level of health services regardless of income. This principle has two major implications for the financing of health care: (*a*) financial barriers to health care should not be greater for people who need more care than for those who need less care, and (*b*) financial barriers to health care should not be greater for people of lower income than for people of higher income.

The Insurance Principle

An alternative principle for financing health care is the insurance principle. The elements of the insurance principle are clearly spelled out in Robert Holtom's book *Underwriting Principles and Practices* (18), published by the National Underwriter Company, a prestigious organization representing the insurance industry.

According to Holtom, the principles of insurance are embodied in the science of underwriting. Underwriting is a systematic technique for evaluating, selecting (or rejecting), classifying, and rating risks. (The term "risk" refers to the object of the insurance: a home, a car, or in the case of health insurance, a person.) Underwriters also establish the standards of coverage and amount of protection to be offered to each acceptable risk and the amount of premium to be charged. Holtom affirms that "The principal responsibility of an underwriter is to make a profit for his company" (18, p. 12).

Profit is best ensured through the system of classifying risks—separating people into homogeneous groups. Young, generally healthy people might make up one classification, healthy middle-aged people another classification, and elderly and disabled people yet another. Each risk (person or group) is categorized as a preferred risk, standard risk, or substandard risk based on the probability of loss, i.e., on the likelihood that the person will contract an illness that generates a claim against the insurer. Thus members of the young group might be considered preferred risks, the middle-aged group standard risks, and the elderly/disabled group substandard risks. People with a very high likelihood of loss—for example human immunodeficiency virus (HIV)-positive individuals—are classified as unacceptable risks and become uninsurable.

Under the insurance principle, each classification is supposed to generate profit; thus the premiums of the young healthy group are not used to help subsidize the greater expense of the elderly or disabled groups. The more likely the loss, the higher the premium. In our classification scheme, the young group would have the lowest premiums, the middle-aged group higher premiums, and the elderly/disabled the highest. Naturally, the only way for the insurer to generate profit from the substandard risk group is to charge its members extremely high premiums (18, pp. 142–149).

Insurance terminology defines a hazard as a condition that increases the likelihood of loss. Coronary heart disease or cancer is clearly a hazard in the field of life insurance. One category of hazard is accusingly termed "moral hazard," referring to a greater likelihood of loss because of deliberate or dishonest acts of the insured. An act of arson by a landlord hoping to collect fire insurance on a deteriorating property certainly deserves the appellation of "moral hazard." But health insurers and health care analysts of conservative persuasion utilize the term "moral hazard" to describe the behavior of people who seek more medical care because they have health insurance (18, p. 18). A prime cause of the high costs of care, according to this mode of thinking, is that most people abuse health insurance by overusing health care, thereby forcing insurers to raise premiums unnecessarily. The assumptions of this line of reasoning are (a) that people love to visit their physicians and do so simply because they are insured, and (b) that patients decide what medical care they will receive. In fact, physicians determine the majority of the demand for medical care, a fact that invalidates the "moral hazard" argument. But whatever the case, taken from the viewpoint of health care as a right, it is desirable that people seek more care by virtue of being insured; improvement in access to care is the very reason health insurance was invented.

Health insurers, nonetheless, attempt to reduce the burden of "moral hazard" by including in their policies deductible and coinsurance provisions, payments meant to discourage people from seeking care. In addition, to prevent people from buying health insurance immediately after contracting a serious illness (behavior considered as highly "morally hazardous") insurers have preexisting illness clauses that exclude coverage for a certain period of time for illnesses that existed before the insurance was obtained.

What does the insurance principle imply for the financing of health care? First, people who need more health care must pay more than people who need less health care. This is the case because people needing more health care are placed in a different classification than people needing less health care and are charged higher premiums. Second, people with lower incomes must pay a greater proportion of their income for health care than people with higher incomes. This is true because within each classification of risks, insurance premiums for people with lower incomes are equal to those of people with higher incomes, with the result that lower-income people pay a higher proportion of their income in insurance premiums. In addition, the deductibles and coinsurance payments consume a greater proportion of the budgets of lower-income people.

The insurance principle thus directly violates the two financing principles of health care as a right: that people who need more care should not pay more than people who need less care, and that lower-income people should not pay a greater proportion of their income than higher-income people. But the difficulty runs even deeper. On the average, people of lower income tend to be people who require more medical care and would therefore be classified as higher risks and charged higher premiums. Thus the most needy people are placed in double jeopardy by the insurance principle. Furthermore, those who have serious illnesses and need health care the most are likely to be unacceptable risks and therefore uninsurable. And individuals with preexisting illnesses can only obtain insurance that initially pays nothing for the very medical care they need. Clearly, these two features of the insurance principle are also in direct violation of the principle of health care as a right.

The Two Principles Coexist

The preceding discussion has emphasized the incompatibility of the insurance principle with the doctrine of health care as a right. But in fact, these two principles have coexisted in U.S. health care for many years. As with any conflicting principles, a unity of opposites underlies the conflict. Both the insurance principle and the principle of health care as a right are based on an agreement that people should pool their risks to prevent a few individuals from suffering catastrophic financial losses at times of major illness. In this regard, health insurance is a progressive social institution. The conflict arises over such questions as who is included in the pool of risk-sharing individuals and—given vast inequality in income, wealth, and need for medical care—how the contributions are distributed among the population. The principle of health care as a right includes every member of society in the risk-sharing pool, while the insurance principle only admits those able to finance the payment of their premiums. Health care as a right redistributes the financial burden from the sick and the poor toward the healthy and the wealthy, while the insurance principle requires people to pay their own way, whether or not they are able to do so.

We now turn to a brief review of the history and structure of the health insurance industry, placed in the context of the interplay between the principle of health care as a right and the insurance principle.

A BRIEF HISTORY OF HEALTH INSURANCE

Thus far we have examined the insurance principle in its pure form. But in practice, the unfettered workings of the insurance principle have been moderated by the success of the U.S. labor movement in achieving employer-sponsored group health insurance. Through the historic strikes of the 1930s and 1940s, labor won the right to bargain with employers for fringe benefits, and forced many employers to provide and pay for health insurance for employees and their families. This labor-led movement determined the dominant structure of U.S. health care financing: by the early 1980s employer-sponsored group private insurance covered 134 million people (19).

The financing principle underlying labor's actions was health care as a right, though the right was reserved for union members rather than for the entire population. Health care as a right was embodied in employer-sponsored group health insurance in two ways: people with higher risk of illness were not necessarily charged more than young healthy people, and—because the employer paid most of the insurance premiums—lower-paid employees did not pay larger proportions of their income for health care than did higher-paid employees.

The advent of Blue Cross combined with the labor movement to strengthen the principle of health care as a right for unionized workers. In the words of Blue Cross analyst Sylvia Law, "Blue Cross is the child of the Depression and the American Hospital Association" (20, p. 6). Because people during the Depression were unable to pay their hospital bills, the hospitals organized Blue Cross plans in which subscribers would pay small premiums to Blue Cross, and Blue Cross would pay the hospital bills for people requiring hospital care. For the hospitals, which controlled Blue Cross, the insurance principle was self-defeating: most people needing hospitals were older, but under the insurance principle older people would be charged premiums they could not afford. Thus Blue Cross utilized the principle of community rating by which all subscriber groups paid the same premium, thereby allowing young healthy groups to subsidize older groups, which enabled those needing most hospital care to afford it (10, Chap. 2; 21, p. 183). It was a case of hospital self-interest coinciding with the principle of health care as a right.

But the for-profit commercial insurance industry, sensing a market opportunity, countered by offering insurance to young healthy groups at rates below those charged by Blue Cross (10, pp. 28-30). The commercial insurers were not concerned with maximizing hospital revenue and had no use for community rating. In 1946 Blue Cross had 19 million subscribers compared with 10 million for the commercials, but by 1951 the commercials exceeded Blue Cross in subscribers (10, pp. 21-24). To protect its market, Blue Cross had no choice but to move from community rating toward the insurance principle, i.e., experience rating—charging each subscriber group a premium that depended on the amount of illness expected (22, p. 330).

Blue Shield was to physicians what Blue Cross was to hospitals. Initially organized by the California Medical Association, and spreading across the nation under physician control, the purpose of Blue Shield was to insure payment to doctors by those less able to afford physician care. As with Blue Cross, Blue Shield's commitment to health care as a right was dependent on the economics of provider reimbursement. Blue Shield payments to doctors covered the entire bill of lower-income patients, while people with higher incomes could be extra-billed by physicians. In that way, physicians could receive payment for their poorer patients but could extract greater fees from people with more money (22, p. 308). Thus Blue Shield approximated the principle of health care as a right, though its reasons were maximization of physician income rather than a strong social conscience. As with Blue Cross, Blue Shield faced the competition of the commercial insurers. In a market economy, the insurance principle will always win out over the principle of health care as a right because the large healthy population can be sold cheaper insurance under experience-rated policies.

During the 1950s, 1960s, and 1970s, as a result of economic expansion and labor pressure, private health insurance grew. Whereas in 1950 private insurance covered only 12.2 percent of consumer health expenditures, in 1983 the figure had reached 56.5 percent (23, p. 317). Between 1951 and 1979, health benefits for all industries went from 1.4 to 5.7 percent of payroll (19). The passage of Medicare and Medicaid in 1965—an affirmation of the public's view that health care should be a right—took the private insurance industry off the hook by providing coverage for millions of unacceptable risks—the elderly—and for millions more unable to afford any insurance premiums at all.

The Erosion of Group Health Insurance

With the 1980s came an entirely new development: the erosion of private health insurance, a product of the persistent late-20th century U.S. economic crisis (19, 24, 25). Corporations facing lowered profits are making concerted attempts to reduce their burden of health insurance benefit payments.

From 1980 to 1984, the percentage of employees covered by employer-sponsored group health plans dropped from 62 to 59.8 percent. The employers' share of the gross medical product, which had risen dramatically from 12.6 percent in 1960 to 28.3 percent in 1983, began to fall in 1985, while the contribution of employees started to rise (19). Coinsurance and deductible payments grew for employer-sponsored group health insurance in the 1980s, as did employee contributions to insurance premiums. [The extent of these changes has been limited by strong labor resistance, as evidenced by such events as the 1989 telephone workers' strike (26, 27).] As employees become responsible for a greater proportion of health care payments, those with lower incomes become less able to afford health care than those with higher incomes, an indication that the financing structure is moving away from the doctrine of health care as a right.

The number of uninsured persons, as measured by the Census Bureau's Current Population Survey, grew from 28.6 million in 1980 to 37 million in 1986 (28, p. 9). This trend has its roots in several interrelated aspects of the changing U.S. economy: the shift from manufacturing to service jobs, from union to nonunion work, from full-time to part-time employment, and from high-wage to low-wage jobs (25).

Another striking development—also related to the corporate drive to reduce health insurance costs—is the bypassing of insurance companies by employers who are themselves underwriting and assuming the risk for the health costs of their own employees. This phenomenon of self-insurance has skyrocketed: in 1975 only 5 percent of employees were covered by self-insured plans, whereas in 1985 the figure was 42 percent (29, 30). Corporations self-insure in order to save money by avoiding the administrative and taxation costs of health insurance companies, to gain more control over the payment of health benefits to hospitals and physicians, and to have health benefits funds available to invest or to use to improve corporate cash flow. By 1985, employers became the leading bearers of risk for health care costs, with a market share exceeding that of commercial insurers or Blue Cross/Blue Shield plans (30). Self-insured plans generally have more premium cost-sharing by employees and higher copayments and deductibles (30), and thus represent an erosion not only of the insurance industry but of the principles of health care as a right.

Another major recent development in the private health insurance sector is the trend toward "managed care," i.e., insurance programs utilizing the cost-control devices of utilization review, preferred provider organizations (PPOs), or health maintenance organizations (HMOs). By 1988, more than 70 percent of Americans with employer-sponsored private health insurance were enrolled in managed care plans, with 18 percent in HMOs (31, 32).

The past ten years have brought particular changes to Blue Cross and Blue Shield ("the Blues"). Until the early 1970s, the Blues were entirely controlled by the health care providers for whom they served as pretreatment collection agencies. But the unrelenting health care inflation of the late 1960s forced Blue Cross to pass on soaring hospital costs to the health consumer in the form of huge premium increases—up to 52 percent in Massachusetts in 1969, 23 percent in Pennsylvania in 1970 followed by another 20 percent in 1971, and 43 percent in New York in 1970 (33). Protests from labor, consumers, and government forced Blue Cross to separate itself from the American Hospital Association (AHA), which owned the Blue Cross insignia and the name "Blue Cross." In 1971, the AHA and Blue Cross Association agreed to eliminate their interlocking directorates and to transfer the Blue Cross name and insignia to the Blue Cross Association (20, p. 19). While these changes were initially only cosmetic, the continuing hospital inflation of the 1970s—plus stiff competition from commercial insurers and HMOs—began to force Blue Cross plans to question the huge hospital bills that they had heretofore been obediently paying. Blue Shield also came into conflict with physicians. By the 1980s, antagonisms were in evidence between the providers and their former servants, the Blues.

Blue Cross and Blue Shield plans tended to merge together into health insurers increasingly indistinguishable from the for-profit commercials. In 1986, Congress recognized this development by removing the Blues' nonprofit tax exemption, thereby ending the Blues' pretense of being charitable community service outfits. Most recently, some Blue Cross plans have discussed converting themselves into commercial businesses. Blue Cross and Blue Shield United of Wisconsin is selling stock and branching into the more lucrative life insurance line (34). Physician relations with the Blues are increasingly strained as the Blues impose cost-control measures on health providers (35). Thus the Blues are well on their way to transforming themselves from hospital and physician collection agencies to "just another insurance company."

Before turning to a critique of the health insurance industry, let us briefly look at the structure and financial prospects of that industry.

INSURANCE INDUSTRY STRUCTURE AND FINANCES

The nation's 77 Blue plans, insuring 77 million people in 1987, generally cover a state or geographic portion of a state. Some states have separate Blue Cross and Blue Shield plans, while in other states they have merged. All the plans belong to the Blue Cross and Blue Shield Association, born of the 1982 national merger of Blue Cross with Blue Shield (36). In addition to their private business, the Blues play a large role as fiscal intermediaries in the Medicare and Medicaid programs, holding 80 percent of Medicare Part A and close to 70 percent of Part B business (35).

In 1970, Blue Cross boards were dominated by health providers, with 42 percent of board members representing hospitals and 14 percent from the medical profession. The 44 percent "public representatives" were generally selected by the incumbent board, and in 21 plans they were chosen by the hospital representatives. Fifty-seven percent of the "public and consumer representatives" to Blue Cross boards were business executives or lawyers (20, pp. 26–29). As a result of the early 1970s' criticisms leveled at hospital domination of Blue Cross, board membership has moved somewhat away from provider domination. By 1978, only 24 percent of Blue Cross directors represented hospitals, 17 percent were physicians, and 59 percent were "public members" (37, p. 210).

Historically, Blue Shield plans have been under the control of local medical societies. In 1976, medical societies actively controlled the selection procedure for physician board members in about two-thirds of Blue Shield plans; in 40 percent of the plans, medical societies approved public as well as physician directors. However, a considerable variation has arisen in Blue Shield board composition and selection; in 1976, 11 plans operated without the approval of their local medical society (38).

The years 1987 and 1988 were disastrous for the Blues. In 1987 the combined plans had losses of $1.9 billion, with another $1 billion deficit in 1988 (39). The Blues' market share of private health insurance dollars dropped from 45 percent in 1965 to 33 percent in 1986 (36). Health insurance generally follows three-year underwriting cycles; during the 1986–88 phase, cost inflation outpaced premium increases, but huge premium hikes in 1988 and 1989 are likely to improve the Blues' financial picture. In addition, greater reliance on managed care, especially the 96 HMOs sponsored by Blues' plans across the country, is expected to reduce benefit payments (40).

Commercial health insurers collected $75 billion in premiums in 1986 (41), well over the Blues' $44 billion. In contrast to the Blues, the largest commercials are not primarily health insurers; health is simply one insurance line, with life insurance generally far more important. In fact, for commercial insurers, health premiums represent only about 18 percent of gross premium income (42). Thus, when commercial health insurers whine about their health insurance losses—$830 million in 1988 for the largest 12 insurers (43)—they generally make up these losses through life insurance profits and income from investments (44, Chap. 2). Jon Gabel, one of the nation's foremost experts on commercial health insurance and a researcher for the commercial insurers' trade association, Health Insurance Association of America, provides a clear explanation of the role of health insurance for commercial companies (42):

> Profits in the health insurance industry are generated almost entirely through investment income. . . . A dollar in health insurance income does not have the same investment income potential as a dollar from other lines of business. In general, the shorter the duration of the policy, the less potential investment profit the premium dollar generates. . . . Policies that incur benefits expenses monthly or weekly, such as health insurance, are less profitable than policies whose benefit expenses may be 30 years in the future, such as life insurance. . . . Given this disparity in income potential, health insurance is likely to serve as a loss leader for other lines of business . . . health insurance may be the vehicle to gain entry into employer group markets.

The commercial insurance industry is made up of over 700 companies (42). The largest insurers are among the world's most massive corporations. Prudential has $116 billion in assets, Metropolitan Life $94 billion, Aetna $49 billion, Connecticut General $31 billion, and Travelers $30 billion (45). The insurance giants hold interlocking directorates with major banks and corporations and have powerful influence over the economy as a result of their billions available for investment. Insurance company directors are among the world's wealthiest people; for example, James Lynn, chief executive officer of Aetna, earned $2.6 million in 1987 (46).

With their enormous financial power, commercial insurers are moving to vertically integrate the health sector by entering the HMO business. Health maintenance organizations have been far more costly to establish than anticipated, and many are in serious financial difficulty. The big commercial insurers, with their huge supply of available capital, are the most likely institutions to ride out the hard times and end up in control of many HMOs. Aetna is moving to acquire partial control of smaller HMOs and could end up running them in the future. Metropolitan Life is positioning itself in the HMO field for the 1990s (47), and Prudential operates a network of HMOs (48). Connecticut General merged with another insurer, INA Corporation, in 1982 to form the holding company CIGNA Corporation, another major player in the HMO movement (48, 49).

The move toward HMOs may create a major restructuring of the private health insurance industry, both the Blues and the commercials. But the dominance of the insurance industry over HMO development is in turn restructuring that movement. Formerly a reform of health care delivery away from office-based fee-for-service practice toward the salaried or capitated group practice of the Kaiser model, HMOs "are becoming increasingly difficult to distinguish from other health plans" (50). Since the organizing of true group practices is expensive and requires medical rather than just financial leadership, insurers anxious to capture the HMO market have simply contracted with existing physicians and hospitals. The only difference from traditional commercial or Blue health insurance is a financial one: the providers—not just the insurers—are at partial or total risk if expenses exceed income. Most HMOs, then, can be considered not as reforms in the organization of health care, but as simply a second generation of health insurance companies.

Some analysts, including those from insurers themselves, are predicting serious financial troubles for the insurance industry. Certain patterns are reminiscent of the savings and loan industry of the early 1980s—lax regulation, low capital requirements, overvalued assets, and sloppy accounting methods. There has been an average of 18 insurance failures in each of the last four years, compared with five per year in the 1970s. The insurance industry holds a large portion of the junk bonds issued by U.S. corporations, as well as potentially risky real estate portfolios. Fraud and mismanagement are also a factor. Particularly for life insurers, AIDS (acquired immune deficiency syndrome) is considered a "ticking time bomb" (51).

The insurance industry has a negative public image, and writers in industry publications are warning that something must be done. When one insurance executive said "We may be the good guys, but the word is not getting out," an insurance columnist responded, "Has it ever occurred to anyone in the insurance industry that it may, in fact, be the bad 'guys,' and that the word is out?" (52). Another analyst predicted that "the domestic life insurance industry is in for the toughest time it has had in 150 years" (53). Such conditions, if true, make it likely that the insurance industry will attempt to improve the profitability of its health business—by increasingly severe cost cutting.

THE CASE AGAINST THE INSURANCE INDUSTRY

High Costs of Health Care

For 40 years, the health insurance industry, in particular the Blues, has contributed to a health care inflation unequalled anywhere in the world. The chief victims of this inflation are the health care consumer, for many of whom health care has been priced out of reach, and the wage earner who pays part of these costs through Social Security deductions, income taxes, and reduced wages resulting from the uncontrolled expenditures of employers on health care benefits. The current backlash against health care inflation threatens to erode the gains made by the doctrine of health care as a right in the group health insurance market and through governmental programs.

How did the insurance industry contribute to the cost crisis? Insurance necessarily increases access to health care; that is its purpose. As a result, both consumers and providers have a tendency to increase the use of medical care—consumers because they feel they need the care, providers because they feel the care is beneficial and because they earn income from providing that care. Because insurance promotes more medical care, the insurer should assume some responsibility to make sure the costs of that care are reasonable. Until recently, Blue Cross and Blue Shield did just the opposite.

Blue Cross paid hospitals under the formula of "reasonable costs" (20, p. 60; 21, pp. 142-143). Hospitals decided the dollar amount of a reasonable cost. If a hospital wished to build a new wing, the loan payments for that capital expenditure were tacked onto the Blue Cross bill. If the hospital wished to set up a cardiac surgery unit (whether or not such a unit was needed) Blue Cross would foot the bill. The result was an enormous overexpansion of the hospital sector, which still plagues the U.S. health system today. With the average hospital only slightly over 60 percent occupied, and with an empty bed costing at least half as much to operate as a full bed, the cost of thousands of empty beds is tacked onto the bill of hospital patients (54).

Blue Shield, the creation of the medical profession, established a payment system in which physicians would be paid a "usual and customary" fee. Physicians could set their own fees and if they were not too far from the fees of other physicians in the area, Blue Shield would pay. Blue Shield also allowed physicians to charge higher fees to patients above a certain income level (55). Nowhere in the world has such a generous physician reimbursement policy existed (56).

The reimbursement principles of "reasonable cost" and "usual and customary fee" were retained in the Medicare program, thereby leading to a worsening of medical inflation. Blue Cross and the AHA supported the Medicare legislation under the condition that Blue Cross become the fiscal intermediary for government payments to hospitals (20, Chap. 3). Similarly, Blue Shield plans became the carriers for Medicare's payment of physicians (22, p. 375). In 23 states, the Blues played a similar role for Medicaid programs (20, p. 46). Naturally, the same generous reimbursement schemes went into effect, with the result that costs of the Medicare and Medicaid programs shot up beyond any expectation. Hospital reimbursement under Medicare was even more generous than under private Blue Cross plans, since the government initially agreed to pay the hospitals their costs plus 2 percent (20, p. 70). In the words of Somers and Somers, who wrote the first definitive book on Medicare, "In no other realm of economic life today are payments guaranteed for costs that are neither controlled by competition nor regulated by public authority, and in which no incentives for economy can be discerned" (57, p. 192).

Commercial insurers have also contributed to health cost inflation, tending to pass along to hospitals and physicians whatever they charge. Many reasons have been given to explain such behavior, which appears to conflict with insurers' primary goal of making profit. Gabel and Monheit (42) argue that insurers are strongly dominated by providers who can successfully argue the medical necessity of their charges and who can refuse to treat patients covered by an overly stingy insurer. Cost-containment policies are expensive to administer. Also, with so many insurers in the market, no single company can truly influence health care costs. These reasons are undoubtedly true, but more significant is that commercial insurers benefit from escalating hospital costs. Let us remember that much of the profit of commercial insurers comes from investment income; the greater the flow of dollars through the company, the more investment income can be generated. Even though insurers will sustain short-term losses by paying out high hospital bills, in the long run these inflating hospital costs justify the raising of premiums which means more money available for investment. In the words of Clark Havighurst, "the industry has always seemed to want someone else to do the cost-containment job, as long as the insurers could continue to handle the money" (quoted in 58, p. 228).

Not only have the Blues and commercials as individual companies fostered an unrelenting health cost inflation, in addition the entire structure of the private insurance system makes control of such inflation impossible. With multiple insurers, no single institution has sufficient financial power to put a lid on medical inflation. For that reason, between 1980 and 1986 medical costs in the United States inflated from 9.2 to 11.1 percent of gross domestic product (59). In contrast, nations having a single payer, or multiple payers coordinated through governmental regulation, have enjoyed lower inflation in the health sector over the same time period: the United Kingdom from 5.8 to 6.2 percent, Japan from 6.6 to 6.7 percent, Australia from 6.6 to 6.8 percent, the Federal Republic of Germany from 7.9 to 8.1 percent, and Canada from 7.4 to 8.5 percent (59).

The 1980s saw the beginning of a backlash from the insurance industry's failure to place any controls on health care costs. But rather than confront the cost-control problem in a logical manner, this backlash seeks to erode the institutions most clearly associated with the doctrine of health care as a right: employer-sponsored group health insurance and governmental programs for the elderly and the poor.

It should be noted that influential conservative economists justify this backlash with an alternative explanation for the rise in health care costs: that health insurance is too comprehensive and thereby suffers from rampant "moral hazard"—people seeking health care not because they need it but because they are insured. This school of thought proposes two remedies: to greatly increase the consumer's share of health costs (e.g., copayments and deductibles) in order to reduce the incidence of "moral hazard," and to eliminate the tax subsidy that employers receive for purchasing health insurance for their employees, thereby taking away the incentive to buy too much insurance (58, 60). These remedies suffer from major flaws. The RAND Health Insurance Experiment showed that high patient cost shares are harmful to the health of lower income people and in particular reduce use of preventive services (61). And projections show that elimination of the tax subsidy for health insurance would reduce the demand for medical care by only 4 to 6 percent and would not substantially contain costs (62).

Justified or not, the current trend (as described earlier in the article) reveals an erosion of private health insurance in an attempt to solve the problem of medical care inflation created in part by the insurance industry.

Administrative Costs

The costs of operating the private health insurance system, including administrative expenses and profits, are high and growing rapidly. In 1986, private health insurers, including the commercials and the Blues, collected $143 billion in premiums and paid out $128 billion in benefits. The difference, $15 billion, constituted 10.4 percent of insurance premiums (41). Between 1980 and 1986, the net cost of private health insurance rose by 185 percent, compared with an 85 percent rise in overall national health expenditures (63). An equally striking statistic is that between 1975 and 1985 the cost of administering health insurance rose 655 percent (64).

In addition to the operating costs of private insurers themselves, the entire structure of multiple private insurers creates large administrative costs for the hospitals and physicians that must bill the insurers. Nations such as Canada, with a single governmental payer of health services, spend far less on administration: about 2.5 percent to administer the government program, and substantially smaller amounts for hospitals and physicians' offices (65; 66, p. 38). Navarro, Himmelstein, and Woolhandler (67) have estimated that the substitution of a Canadian-style single-payer system for the current private health insurance structure would save $69.3 billion in a single year.

Over the years the Blues have had a better ratio of benefit dollars paid to premiums collected: 0.926 in 1979 compared with 0.875 for the commercials. Individual commercial policies have the highest administrative costs with benefit-to-premium ratios running at 0.654 (68, p. 156).

The Blues receive payment from the government for administrative costs in connection with their function as intermediaries and carriers in the Medicare and Medicaid programs. Because these administrative functions have been reimbursed at cost, there is a strong incentive to maximize rather than to minimize them (69). Federal audit agencies have found it difficult to find out exactly what these administrative costs were spent for, and it is likely that administrative functions performed for private beneficiaries have been charged to the government programs (20, pp. 46–49; 69). For Medicare Part A, chiefly administered by Blue Cross plans, the administrative costs charged by Blue Cross went up 200.7 percent from 1967 to 1973, while benefit payments per enrollee rose only 136.6 percent (69). During 1970 and 1971, Congressional hearings found that between 1968 and 1970, shortly after the passage of Medicare, the Richmond, Virginia, Blue Cross paid a highly excessive $1.2 million for furniture bought from a company one of whose officials was a director of Blue Cross (70). In addition, during the 1960s the Washington, D.C., Blue Cross deposited between $10 and $20 million in bank accounts that paid no interest to Blue Cross, yielding an $800,000 profit to the bank; the Blue Cross board chairman was a board member of the bank, and the bank's president was the Blue Cross treasurer who made Blue Cross's investment decisions (71). While such examples may appear petty when contrasted with the $600 billion in U.S. health care expenditures, it is precisely such practices that led health economist Uwe Reinhardt to proclaim that "Our system is the most bureaucratic in the world if measured by the tons of paperwork generated per transaction. For every $100 in health care, we buy $25 worth of pluralism—accountants, advertisers, marketers and financiers" (quoted in 72).

Advertising has been an increasing cost of the health industry. The total bill for health care advertising is projected at $6.5 billion in 1989 (67). How much of this figure can be attributed to the insurance industry and insurance-run HMOs is unknown. In 1987 the Blue Cross and Blue Shield Association alone spent $70.4 million on advertising (73), and during the recent period of greater competition among insurers and insurance-sponsored HMOs, the airwaves and billboards have been increasingly filled with the same language used to sell cars and beer.

The Unfairness of the Insurance Industry

As we have seen above, the insurance principle is by its very nature unfair. As the oft-cited expert on justice, John Rawls (74), has pointed out, the distribution resulting from voluntary market transactions is not fair unless the antecedent distribution of income and wealth is fair. And in the United States, the distribution of income and wealth is not simply unequal, it is becoming increasingly unequal.

Competition makes it inevitable that private insurance markets will evolve toward experience rating, creaming off low-risk groups by offering them lower premiums. As a result, coverage for high-risk groups becomes prohibitively expensive. By its very nature, private insurance cannot insure 100 percent of the population; it must exclude the poorest and least healthy (66, p. 41). Insurance is based on inequality—segmentation of risk (11). Even Mark Pauly (60), champion of the concept of "moral hazard," admits that a major policy issue in health insurance is the inequity of charging more to those who are sick.

Labor-initiated employer-sponsored group health insurance has blunted the intrinsic unfairness of the insurance principle. But the linkage of health insurance to employment also truncates the right to health care. Employers have an incentive not to hire people with chronic health problems because such people enormously raise employer health premiums. Employers understand that a relatively small number of persons with chronic illnesses accounts for a substantial proportion of all medical care spending (75).

For people who are insured through employment, almost a fifth (30 million individuals) lose their insurance within a 32-month period, pointing to the instability of life situations and the fragility of tying health insurance to stable employment (76). In a recession, unemployment becomes a major cause of loss of group health insurance. Other changes in life situation may lead to group health insurance loss; 5 million women aged between 40 and 65 have no insurance as a result of divorce, death of the spouse, or retirement of the spouse (77, pp. 106–107). And employed people who become disabled may lose their health insurance when they need it most. The millions of people who lose eligibility for group health insurance become individual insurance risks.

Individual insurance accounts for 10 percent of total private health insurance premiums (62). Those with individual insurance must subject themselves to an underwriting process involving analysis of previous medical records and laboratory tests to screen for chronic diseases. As Donald Cohodes (78), a high executive in the Blue Cross and Blue Shield Association writes, individual and small group markets are unattractive to insurers. Marketing and administrative costs are high, and insurers frequently lose money because of failure to accurately select out bad risks. Unacceptable risks are rejected, and others are charged premiums far greater than they can afford. In this market, people are victims of the unfettered inequities of the insurance principle.

Harold Luft (79), one of the nation's leading experts on risk selection, predicts that as competition grows in the health sector, insurers—to reduce the possibility of adverse selection (unknowingly insuring higher-risk populations)—will avoid small groups in which one sick person could use up the revenues from the entire group, and will take stricter measures to exclude already sick people.

Inequitable systems tend to discriminate against minorities. Indeed, blacks are less likely to be covered by private insurance than nonblacks and are more likely to be uninsured altogether. In 1985, 22 percent of blacks were uninsured compared with 15 percent of nonblacks. Only 47 percent of blacks had employment-related insurance, compared with 62 percent of nonblacks (80). Clearly, inequities in employment and income are reflected and magnified in the arena of health insurance.

People intensely affected by the insurance principle are HIV-positive individuals. Those with AIDS or suspected AIDS are having more problems obtaining and keeping health and life insurance. One company rejected all applicants from San Francisco. Coverage has been denied to men who are not married or who have jobs commonly held by gays. In every state except California, insurers have won the legal right to require HIV testing for individual policies; those infected are routinely denied coverage. Because it is difficult for companies to exclude AIDS patients from group policies, some companies have placed ceilings on benefits paid for AIDS care (81).

In an article entitled "The Limits of Insurability," Hammond and Shapiro (82) show that from the perspective of insurers, these policies are logical and reasonable. Between 1986 and 1991, AIDS could cost the insurance industry $10 billion in health claims only, with life insurance losses even more serious (83). In 1992, AIDS care is expected to cost $7.5 billion (84). A competitive market requires insurers to classify risks, with each classification paying its own way. If healthy individuals subsidize too many people with AIDS, their premiums will rise and companies with less AIDS cases will corner the market. Those companies with an excess of AIDS patients could face ruin. The example of AIDS also reveals the fragility of employment-based health insurance. Most people with AIDS eventually lose their jobs, and to lose a job is to lose health insurance. And for individual coverage, AIDS falls outside the limits of insurability (82). The treatment of AIDS by health and life insurers, then, is reasonable from the industry's point of view. It is the entire concept of insurance, not the specific policies of the companies, that is at fault. In the words of Benjamin Schatz, director of the AIDS project of the National Gay Rights Advocates, "The AIDS crisis points out the fundamental flaw in our insurance system. Those who most need access to health insurance are least able to get it" (83).

The treatment of the elderly is another sorry chapter in private health insurance history. Because Medicare covers only 45 percent of the health costs of those aged over 65, 66 percent of the elderly have purchased private "Medigap" policies to fill in Medicare's gaps (58, Chap. 4). In 1989, a Congressional committee chaired by Representative John Dingell conducted a probe of the $10 to $15 billion per year Medigap industry. In spite of a law requiring Medigap policies to pay at least 60 cents in benefits for every premium dollar, a federal study revealed that half of Medigap policies paid less than 50 cents on the dollar. In addition, over four million people have two or more Medigap policies even though many policies have a clause stating that they will not pay for benefits covered by another policy. Millions of elderly people are fraudulently duped by aggressive insurance brokers into buying unneeded insurance (77, p. 239; 85).

Another large population group experiencing the unfairness of the private insurance system is low-income Americans, most of whom are priced out of private insurance. The working poor are more likely than higher-income employees to have no employer-sponsored insurance, and most of the nonworking poor are uninsured or Medicaid recipients. The Medicare and Medicaid programs have attempted to salvage the sub-standard risks, unacceptable risks, and those without money to buy insurance. These experiments were initially successful in equalizing access to medical care. But leaving the uninsurables to the government has meant that Social Security and tax financing must bear the costs of the most expensive risk groupings in society. As a result, worsened by the milking of Medicare and Medicaid by providers aided by the Blues, the government has had to cut back on these programs such that Medicare came to cover only 45 percent of health costs for the elderly and Medicaid reimbursement dropped to a level at which many providers ceased accepting recipients. Thus the insurance principle—leaving to the public purse those risks that private insurance prices out of the market—has ultimately eroded equal access to care for those groups covered under the government programs. Insuring low-income people through the public sector and middle- and upper-income groups in the private sector virtually guarantees inequality. Separate but equal has no more validity in health care than it has in education. As Rashi Fein has said, "Programs for the poor tend to become poor programs. The needy are better served by universal programs in which their fate and that of other Americans are inexorably intertwined" (10, p. 123). As a general rule, in nations that establish dual public and private health sectors, the private sector pulls resources away from the public sector such that the latter suffers the pain of rationing while the former enjoys the fruits of plenty (86).

Health Maintenance Organizations: A Second Generation of Health Insurers

The health insurance industry is in transition. Employers are screaming about the rise in health care costs. In one survey of large corporations, health insurance premiums rose by 18.6 percent in 1988 alone (87). Employers have reacted by attempting to force cost-sharing on employees and by moving toward "managed care" including capitated health financing through HMOs. In order to gain greater control over their health expenditures, employers have switched to an unprecedented degree to self-insurance. According to Jensen and Gabel, the growth of self-insurance has been a quiet revolution in health financing: "Within the span of a decade, America's principal bearer for the financial risks of illness passed from Blue Cross and Blue Shield Plans and the commercial insurers to the nation's employers" (30).

Commercial insurers and the Blues, increasingly iced out of the group employee market, must establish a new niche for themselves. They have found it: HMOs and other managed care schemes. Between 1981 and 1987, managed care plans jumped from 4 to 60 percent of employer-sponsored health insurance (29). As noted earlier, the Blues and the large commercials are wading into the HMO business with both feet. At the same time, they are waiting for smaller, regionally based HMOs to drown, ready to rescue them with their billions in capital.

What will insurers do with the HMOs and other managed care plans they control? The HMO was originally conceived to include payment to providers on a capitation basis rather than by the traditional fee-for-service method. Many health reformers supported the HMO idea because it promoted a cost-effective group practice environment exemplified by the Kaiser Health Plan and other organizations with several decades of experience. But the insurance industry entered the HMO arena and tended to turn these enterprises into purely financial structures rather than organized health care practices. Insurer-dominanted HMOs tend to contract with limited panels of physicians and hospitals, and the same physicians and hospitals contract with several other HMOs. In many plans, physicians are paid by discounted fee-for-service. In others, physicians are placed at partial risk for health care costs; for example, every laboratory test, X-ray, or specialty referral ordered by the primary physician might be deducted from the primary physician's capitation payment, thus creating a serious conflict of interest. The positive side of the HMO movement—the development of organized group practice settings—has been subverted; insurers, both commercials and the Blues, have formed HMOs for the sole purpose of preserving their market share. Most HMOs, then, are nothing more than a second generation of private health insurers.

Many HMOs act as little more than insurance intermediaries between the payers and providers of care (50). The insurance industry has turned HMOs, originally seen as a reform in health care delivery, into nothing more than a financial reform in which the HMO, and its country cousin the PPO, is simply a new type of insurance company. Interestingly, in this second-generation insurance enterprise, power has shifted from provider toward insurer while financial risk has shifted from insurer toward provider. What will be the long-term effects of having some of the world's richest and most powerful financial institutions directly run portions of the U.S. health system? It is too early to know. But given the HMOs' capacity, once efficiently organized, to pay out less money for each premium dollar than traditional insurance companies, one might expect reduced access to medical care.

The Undue Financial and Political Power of the Insurance Industry

In 1981, the assets of the U.S. insurance industry, over $700 billion, were greater than the combined worldwide assets of the nation's 50 largest industrial corporations (44, p. 5). Prudential is the nation's largest landlord (44, p. 29). Insurers have dozens of lobbyists hanging around all 50 state capitols, not to speak of Washington, D.C. For example, in Massachusetts in 1981 most interest groups had one or a few lobbyists, while the insurance industry had 60. Insurance lobbyists outnumber all others in virtually every state. State insurance commissioners and their staffs are often former insurance executives or lawyers with insurance company clients, and state legislators on committees handling insurance matters may have significant numbers of members who list their occupation as insurance (44, pp. 29-31).

The health insurance industry has great influence on U.S. health legislation and its implementation. Blue Cross, along with its former twin the AHA, had enormous power in writing the Medicare legislation and its administrative regulations (20, pp. 31-46; 21, pp. 180-181). In another example, recognition that the insurance industry can kill any legislation it considers unacceptable led Senator Edward Kennedy to abandon his original government-run national health insurance proposal in the mid-1970s and substitute a proposal with a major role for the insurance industry (88, pp. 149-151).

ABOLISH THE PRIVATE HEALTH INSURANCE INDUSTRY?

We have discussed five major problems with the private insurance industry's domination of the U.S. health care sector: the industry's responsibility for health care inflation, the industry's waste of billions of dollars in administrative and marketing costs, the unfairness of the insurance principle, the likelihood of increased direct insurance company control over health care delivery through HMOs and PPOs, and the insurance industry's frightening degree of financial and political power. Are these problems sufficiently serious that they justify restructuring the health sector such as to eliminate the private health insurance industry altogether? Is it not possible to reform the industry?

A policy of reform assumes that the goals of the insurance industry could be brought into line with the principles of health care as a right. Such an assumption cannot be justified. In a competitive economy, the job of insurance executives must be to run their companies to the best of their ability. To compete, insurance executives are forced to look for the best risks, to deny insurance to people with no funds, and to cut down the number of subscribers with severe illnesses such as AIDS. That is the logic of private insurance. The difficulty is that the logic of insurance conflicts with the principle that health care is a right, a principle that assures all Americans equal access to care regardless of ability to pay. In a sense, the problems of uninsurance and inequity are not the fault of insurance executives, who are simply attempting to keep their companies afloat and profitable. The problem goes far deeper than the behavior of specific companies—it goes to the very principle underlying private insurance. It is for this reason that reform of the insurance industry cannot succeed in guaranteeing the right to health care to everyone in the United States. Such a guarantee can be made only through the elimination of the insurance principle as the dominant doctrine of U.S. health care financing.

A frequently made argument opposing the elimination of the insurance industry is that most Americans are adequately insured and there is no need to "throw out the baby (private insurance) with the bathwater." This argument has a flaw. A unified public system of health care financing based on the principles of health care as a right will not simply benefit the poor, elderly, and chronically ill—the current victims of the insurance principle. It will benefit almost everyone. Except for those seemingly healthy people who die suddenly before reaching a health facility, most people in society will at some time require highly costly medical care. Small contributions made through the tax structure during the young and healthy years will allow such care to be financed without personal financial hardship at the time of illness. The insurance principle, which charges smaller amounts to the young and healthy, appeals to short-sighted self-interest: pay less now and worry about the future later. Thus the insurance principle causes long-range harm to most people. The logical time to pay for health services is when one is young and healthy, not when one is old and sick.

Another argument against the abolition of the private insurance industry does have some merit: what would happen to the tens of thousands of hard-working, devoted people who make that industry run? This is a real problem, but it can be solved. Consider the situation of military bases closing down. Communities have dealt with such dislocations in one of two ways. Some go into an economic depression and become ghost towns. Others initiate early planning, work to attract new industry, set up retraining programs for workers on the base, and the community thrives. We have all heard of economic conversion from a military to a domestic economy. Similar economic conversion plans can be made for the employees of the private insurance industry. Their expertise in analyzing and processing claims would still be needed. Given the shortage of nurses and other health care workers, insurance company employees might like to be retrained for direct patient care jobs. Opportunities also exist in health planning and public health administration.

A final argument reads: it is impossible to abolish the giant private health insurance industry; the industry is far too powerful. But let us remember, social systems do undergo rapid and profound changes. Who in Poland would have thought a few short years ago that the illegal and repressed Solidarity movement would soon be forming a government? The argument that the insurance industry is too powerful is a strong weapon favoring the industry. A number of health policy analysts might privately state that the United States needs a national health program in which private insurance is no longer part of the landscape. But publicly, such analysts support minor and unworkable reforms because they are afraid to advocate "radical" positions. Yet if every influential person who privately favors a public single-payer health system would publicly state his or her support for such change, the idea would no longer be radical, but would enter the mainstream health policy debate.

Suppose a professor of medical care administration entered the classroom and described a country with the following characteristics. If you are healthy and have a high-paying job, you get health insurance; if you get so sick that you lose your job, you lose your insurance. If you have a low-paying job, and thus can least afford to pay for medical care, you get no health insurance. Private health insurers keep billions of dollars in administrative expenses and profits. With all their money they hire lobbyists and make political campaign contributions in order to keep the system from changing. And in order to spare private health insurers the unprofitable problems of the elderly and the poor, taxpayers and wage-earners—in addition to paying for part of their own health coverage—pay for the care of these unprofitable groups. To which country does the professor refer? The United States of America.

REFERENCES

1. Himmelstein D. U., Woolhandler, S., and the Writing Committee. A national health program for the United States: A physicians' proposal. *N. Engl. J. Med.* 320: 102–108, 1989.
2. Annas, G. J. *The Rights of Hospital Patients.* Avon Books, New York, 1975.
3. Curran, W. J. The constitutional right to health care. Denial in the court. *N. Engl. J. Med.* 320: 788–789, 1989.

4. *Rights and Responsibilities in Modern Medicine*, Vol. 2 in a Series on Ethics, Humanism, and Medicine. *Prog. Clin. Biol. Res.* 50: 9–42, 1981.
5. Veatch, R. M., and Branson, R. *Ethics and Health Policy*. Ballinger, Cambridge, Mass., 1976.
6. Engelhardt, H. T. (ed.). *Rights to Health Care*. Vol. 4 of *J. Med. Philos.*, 1979.
7. Christoffel, T. *Health and the Law*. The Free Press, New York, 1982.
8. Fried, C. Rights and health care–beyond equity and efficiency. *N. Engl. J. Med.* 293: 241–245, 1975.
9. Sidel, V. W. The right to health care: An international perspective. In *Bioethics and Human Rights*, edited by E. L. Bandman and B. Bankman. Little, Brown & Co., Boston, 1978.
10. Fein, R. *Medical Care, Medical Costs*. Harvard University Press, Cambridge, Mass., 1986.
11. Daniels, N. Rights to health care and distributive justice: Programmatic worries. *J. Med. Philos.* 4(2): 174–191, 1979.
12. Shapiro, R. Y., and Young, J. T. The polls: Medical care in the United States. *Public Opinion Q.* 50: 418–428, 1986.
13. HMQ survey: A mandate for high-quality health care. *Health Manage. Q.* 8(4): 3–6, 1986.
14. Public claims right to best care. *Med. World News*, March 14, 1988.
15. Navarro, V. Where is the popular mandate? *N. Engl. J. Med.* 307: 1516–1518, 1982.
16. Berwick, D. M., and Hiatt, H. H. Who pays? *N. Engl. J. Med.* 321: 541–542, 1989.
17. Beauchamp, T. L., and Faden, R. R. The right to health and the right to health care. *J. Med. Philos.* 4(2): 118–131, 1979.
18. Holtom, R. B. *Underwriting Principles and Practices*. The National Underwriter Company, Cincinnati, 1981.
19. Staples, C. L. The politics of employment-based insurance in the United States. *Int. J. Health Serv.* 19(3): 415–431, 1989.
20. Law, S. A. *Blue Cross: What Went Wrong?* Yale University Press, New Haven, 1974.
21. Feldstein, P. J. *Health Associations and the Demand for Legislation: The Political Economy of Health*. Ballinger, Cambridge, Mass., 1977.
22. Starr, P. *The Social Transformation of American Medicine*. Basic Books, New York, 1982.
23. Jonas, S. *Health Care Delivery in the United States*. Springer, New York, 1986.
24. Bodenheimer, T. S. The fruits of empire rot on the vine: United States health policy in the austerity era. *Soc. Sci. Med.* 28: 531–538, 1989.
25. Renner, C., and Navarro, V. Why is our population of uninsured and underinsured persons growing? The consequences of the "deindustrialization" of the United States. *Int. J. Health Serv.* 19(3): 433–442, 1989.
26. Jensen, G. A., Morrisey, M. A., and Marcus, J. W. Cost sharing and the changing pattern of employer-sponsored health benefits. *Milbank Q.* 65(4): 521–549, 1987.
27. *San Francisco Chronicle*, August 21, 1989.
28. Butler, P. A. *Too Poor to be Sick*. American Public Health Association, Washington, D.C., 1988.
29. Gabel, J., et al. The changing world of group health insurance. *Health Aff.* 7(2): 48–65, 1988.
30. Jensen, G. A., and Gabel, J. R. The erosion of purchased health insurance. *Inquiry* 25: 328–343, 1988.
31. Gabel, J., et al. Employer-sponsored health insurance in America. *Health Aff.* 8(2): 116–128, 1989.
32. DiCarlo, S., and Gabel, J. Conventional health insurance: A decade later. *Health Care Financ. Rev.* 10(3): 77–89, 1989.
33. Bodenheimer, T., Cummings, S., and Harding, E. Capitalizing on illness: The health insurance industry. *Int. J. Health Serv.* 4(4): 583–598, 1974.
34. *Am. Med. News*, June 23–30, 1989.
35. *Physician's Financial News*, June 30, 1989.
36. Kenkel, P. J. Losses send Blues scrambling. *Mod. Healthcare* 18(27): 14–19, 1988.
37. Ricardo-Campbell, R. *The Economics and Politics of Health*. University of North Carolina Press, Chapel Hill, 1981.
38. Eisenstadt, D., and Kennedy, T. E. Control and behavior of nonprofit firms: The case of Blue Shield. *South. Econ. J.* 48(1): 26–36, 1981.
39. *New York Times*, April 2, 1989.
40. BC/BS develops new strategies to reverse losses. *Business Insurance*, August 15, 1988.
41. Health Insurance Association of America. *Source Book of Health Insurance Data. 1988 Update*. Washington, D.C., 1988.
42. Gabel, J. R., and Monheit, A. C. Will competition plans change insurer-provider relationships? *Milbank Q.* 61(4): 614–640, 1983.

43. *National Underwriter*, May 1, 1989.
44. Tobias, A. *The Invisible Bankers*. Pocket Books, New York, 1982.
45. The National Underwriter Company. *1989 Argus Chart of Health Insurance*. Cincinnati, 1989.
46. Corporate America's most powerful people. *Forbes*, May 30, 1988.
47. *National Underwriter*, January 23, 1989.
48. A. M. Best Co. *Best's Insurance Reports. Life-Health 1988*. Oldwick, N.J., 1988.
49. Wohl, S. *The Medical Industrial Complex*. Harmony Books, New York, 1984.
50. Feldman, R., Kralewski, J., and Dowd, B. Health maintenance organizations: The beginning or the end? *Health Serv. Res.* 24(2): 191–209, 1989.
51. *New York Times*, April 5, 1989.
52. Kloman, H. F. Finding a cure. Image problem just a symptom, not cause of industry ills. *Business Insurance*, July 10, 1989.
53. *National Underwriter*, April 24, 1989.
54. Califano, J. A. Billions blown on health. *New York Times*, April 12, 1989.
55. Feldstein, P. J. *The Politics of Health Legislation*. Health Administration Press, Ann Arbor, Mich., 1988.
56. Glaser, W. *Paying the Doctor under National Health Insurance: Foreign Lessons for U.S.* Columbia University Bureau of Applied Social Research, New York, 1976.
57. Somers, H., and Somers, A. *Medicare and the Hospitals: Issues and Prospects*. Brookings Institution, Washington, D.C., 1967.
58. Frech, H. E., and Zeckhauser, R. *Health Care in America. The Political Economy of Hospitals and Health Insurance*. Pacific Research Institute for Public Policy, San Francisco, 1988.
59. Schieber, G. J., and Poullier, J. P. International health spending and utilization trends. *Health Aff.* 7: 105–112, 1988.
60. Pauly, M. V. Taxation, health insurance, and market failure in the medical economy. *J. Economic Literature* 24: 629–675, 1986.
61. Brook, R., et al. Does free care improve adults' health? *N. Engl. J. Med.* 309: 1426–1434, 1983.
62. Broyles, R. W., and Rosko, M. D. The demand for health insurance and health care: A review of the empirical literature. *Med. Care Rev.* 45(2): 291–338, 1988.
63. Reinhardt, U. E. The medical B-factor: Bureaucracy in action. *Washington Post*, August 9, 1988.
64. Waldo, D. R., Levit, K. R., and Lazenby, H. National health expenditures, 1985. *Health Care Financ. Rev.* 8(1): 1–21, 1986.
65. Himmelstein, D. U., and Woolhandler, S. Cost without benefit. Administrative waste in U.S. health care. *N. Engl. J. Med.* 314: 441–445, 1986.
66. Evans, R. G. *Strained Mercy. The Economics of Canadian Health Care*. Butterworth, Toronto, 1984.
67. Navarro, V., Himmelstein, D. U., and Woolhandler, S. The Jackson National Health Program. *Int. J. Health Serv.* 19(1): 19–44, 1989.
68. Feldstein, P. J. *Health Care Economics*. John Wiley & Sons, New York, 1983.
69. Vogel, R. J., and Blair, R. D. *Health Insurance Administrative Costs*. Social Security Administration Office of Research and Statistics, DHEW Publication No. (SSA) 76-11856, October 1975.
70. U.S. Senate Subcommittee on Antitrust and Monopoly. *High Cost of Hospitalization*. U.S. Government Printing Office, Washington, D.C., 1971.
71. U.S. House of Representatives Subcommittee on Intergovernmental Relations. *Administration of Federal Health Benefit Programs, Part 2*. U.S. Government Printing Office, Washington, D.C., 1970.
72. Cotton, P. Growing access crisis threatens health system. *Med. World News* 28(14): 30–40, 1987.
73. *Advertising Age*, September 28, 1988.
74. Rawls, J. The basic structure as subject. *Am. Philos. Q.* 14: 159–165, 1977.
75. Etheredge, L. Ethics and the new insurance market. *Inquiry* 23: 308–315, 1986.
76. Monheit, A. C., and Schur, C. L. The dynamics of health insurance loss: A tale of two cohorts. *Inquiry* 25: 315–327, 1988.
77. Hogue, K., Jensen, C., and Urban, K. *The Complete Guide to Health Insurance*. Walker & Co., New York, 1988.
78. Cohodes, D. R. America: The home of the free, the land of the uninsured. *Inquiry* 23: 227–235, 1986.

79. Luft, H. S. Compensating for biased selection in health insurance. *Milbank Q.* 64(4): 566–591, 1986.
80. Long, S. H. Public versus employment-related health insurance: Experience and implications for black and nonblack Americans. *Milbank Q.* 65(Suppl. 1): 200–212, 1987.
81. *New York Times*, August 7, 1989.
82. Hammond, J. D., and Shapiro, A. F. AIDS and the limits of insurability. *Milbank Q.* 64(Suppl. 1): 143–167, 1986.
83. *Wall Street J.,* April 26, 1988.
84. Lifetime cost for an AIDS patient: $60,000. *Physician's Financial News*, April 30, 1989.
85. House panel probes medigap insurance abuses. *Am. Med. News*, May 19, 1989.
86. McCreadie, C. Rawlsian justice and the financing of the national health service. *J. Soc. Pol.* 5(2): 113–131, 1976.
87. *Am. Med. News*, February 24, 1989.
88. Navarro, V. *Medicine Under Capitalism.* Prodist, New York, 1976.

CHAPTER 6

Premiums without Benefits: Waste and Inefficiency in the Commercial Health Insurance Industry

Robert M. Brandon, Michael Podhorzer, and Thomas H. Pollak

OVERVIEW

The U.S. system of health insurance is wasteful and inefficient. For every dollar the commercial insurance industry paid in claims in 1988, the industry spent 33.5 cents for administration, marketing, and other overhead expenses. Thus, not including profits, the commercial insurance industry spent 14 times as much on administration, overhead, and marketing per dollar of claims paid as did the Medicare system, and 11 times as much per dollar of claims paid as the Canadian national health system. Had an efficient public program such as Medicare or the Canadian system provided the same amount of benefits, consumers and businesses served by commercial insurers would have saved $13 billion.

The roughly 30 cents-per-dollar-of-claims-paid difference in administrative, overhead, and marketing expenses between commercial insurers and public programs did not buy better health care. It paid for functions that are not necessary when coverage is provided by a comprehensive and unified public program. In order to lower its risks of paying claims and increase its chances of earning profits, each insurance company spends vast amounts of money on underwriting, marketing, and denying claims. Underwriting divides people into narrow segments based on their probable need for medical care. The irresistible motive for segmenting is that each time an insurance company can find a segment likely to need medical care, it can charge higher rates or deny coverage altogether, lowering its risks of paying claims. The commercial insurance companies spend a great deal of money on marketing, aggressively competing with each other to insure those segments that underwriting has determined to be most lucrative. Since the companies have so little control over medical expenditures and fees, they rely on expensive internal bureaucracies to reject claims submissions from groups or individuals once they are insured. The system is rational and indispensable for each company, but

Originally published in the International Journal of Health Services, 21(2): 265–283, 1991.

irrational and dispensable for the nation. Incredibly, the commercial insurance way of paying for health care leaves Americans spending more to deny people coverage than it would cost to provide everyone with coverage.

This report is based on documents filed by commercial insurance companies with regulatory bodies. These filings have been tabulated on a national, state-by-state, and company-by-company basis. The administrative, overhead, and marketing costs documented in this report represent only a fraction of the total waste attributable to the insurance industry. Not included in this estimate are the profits of commercial health insurers, and the administrative, overhead, and marketing expenses of insurance firms for whom comparable state-by-state data are not available (most notably Blue Cross/Blue Shield). Nor are the administrative and paperwork costs that the insurance companies impose on doctors, hospitals, businesses, and consumers counted. Finally, the kind of savings that nations with comprehensive public programs have been able to achieve by bargaining with doctors and hospitals for reasonable prices have not been estimated. A full accounting of the social costs of the insurance industry would be many times the total represented in this report.

The major findings of this report are:[1]

- Commercial insurance companies spent 33.5 cents to provide a dollar of benefits, 14 times more than it cost Medicare (2.3 cents) and 11 times more than it cost the Canadian national health system (3 cents).
- Not including profits, commercial insurance companies spent $14.9 billion to provide $44.5 billion in health benefits, at least $13 billion more than it would have cost had the same amount of benefits been provided by a system as efficient as Medicare or the Canadian national health system.
- Administrative, overhead, and marketing costs amounted to $316 for typical individual coverage under employer-provided plans, and $675 for typical family coverage under employer-provided plans. Had benefits been provided as efficiently as they are by Medicare or the Canadian national health system, the cost for an individual could have been reduced by $281 and the cost for a family policy could have been reduced by $599.
- Administrative, overhead, and marketing costs were even greater for those who could not obtain group coverage. It cost commercial insurers 73 cents to provide one dollar of benefits to those who were not part of regular group plans. Workers for companies that do not provide health insurance, the self-employed, farmers, and those with preexisting conditions are some of the most common examples of people who cannot obtain standard group coverage.
- The $13 billion difference between what it cost commercial insurers and what it would have cost a public program to provide the same benefits in 1988 would have been sufficient to provide insurance coverage to 11 million Americans then without insurance.
- Between 1981 and 1988, the administrative, overhead, and marketing costs of the commercial insurance companies increased by 93 percent, far more than the increase in premiums sold (73 percent) or benefits paid (77 percent). In other words,

[1] Unless otherwise indicated, all figures are for 1988 in 1988 dollars. See the Appendix for a definition of terms.

administrative, overhead, and marketing costs of the companies have increased even faster than health costs themselves and now consume an even greater share of the premium dollar than they did in 1981.
• The top ten commercial insurance companies in the United States in 1988 were, in order of direct premiums earned, Prudential, Aetna, Metropolitan Life, Travelers Insurance, Principal Mutual, Connecticut General, Continental Assurance, Guardian Life, Mutual of Omaha, and Provident Life and Accident.[2]

Figure 1 compares the efficiency of the commercial health insurance industry with the efficiency of Medicare and the Canadian national health system. Table 1 provides a summary of the key findings of this report.

INTRODUCTION

The health care system is in crisis. Health care in the United States is unaffordable, inefficient, and inequitable. Costs have been escalating at an annual rate far exceeding inflation. Americans spend far more for health care than their international competitors yet lag behind them on all measures of health. The United States spent over $600 billion on health care in 1989. Per capita health care spending was $2,051 compared with an average of only $1,069 for our major international competitors (Japan, West Germany, France, the United Kingdom, and Canada) (1). Yet on three commonly used indicators of public health, the United States lags behind. The United States ranks poorest among those countries on measures of infant mortality and child mortality and leads only the United Kingdom on life expectancy (2).

Many people can no longer afford health care. Twenty-eight percent of all Americans—63 million people—were without insurance for a substantial amount of time during a recent 28-month period, according to the Census Bureau (3). A recent study reports "57 percent of Americans who had someone in their family needing medical care reported some problems paying for it; for 25 percent, these payments caused financial difficulties" (4).

Private health insurance accounted for $174.9 billion, or 32.4 percent, of the $539.9 billion spent on health care in 1988, the most recent year for which information is available. Commercial life and health insurance companies—the focus of this study—accounted for over $55.4 billion of this amount (5, 6). Based on the most recently available data, Blue Cross/Blue Shield accounted for 29.3 percent of the private health insurance market and HMOs (health maintenance organizations) and self-insured plans accounted for an additional 31.2 percent (7). (Of the $157 billion spent on private insurance in 1987, Blue Cross/Blue Shield collected over $46 billion and self-insurance and HMO plans collected the remaining $49 billion.) In addition, consumers paid $113.2 billion in out-of-pocket expenses—for deductibles, co-insurance payments, and care that private health insurance policies do not cover (8).

---

[2] The list is somewhat different in terms of net premiums written: Prudential, Metropolitan Life, American Family Life Insurance Co. of Columbus, Mutual of Omaha, Connecticut General, Health Care Service Corp., Aetna, Principal Mutual Life Insurance Co., Travelers Insurance Co., and Continental Assurance Co. Together, these companies accounted for 16.7 percent of the commercial health insurance market. See the Appendix for the difference in definitions.

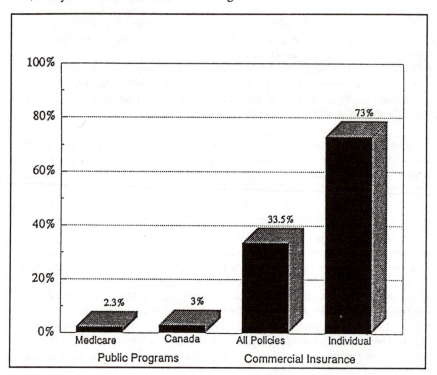

Figure 1. Overhead expenses as a percentage of claims: Medicare, Canada, and commercial insurers, 1988.

The remainder of this report is divided into three sections. The first explores the ways in which the insurance industry adds social costs to the health care system. The second details the national performance of commercial insurance companies in 1988. The third section compares the performance of the commercial insurance industry with two public programs: Medicare and the Canadian national health system.

THE NATURE OF INSURANCE INDUSTRY INEFFICIENCY

Paying for health care through private insurance imposes three types of cost on the nation. This section illustrates each kind of cost, although only one—administrative, overhead, marketing, and claims—is the focus of this report.

Health Care Cost Containment

The fact that many people are either denied coverage or are priced out of the health insurance market is a symptom of the larger systemic problem of controlling costs in a health care system with over 1,500 private health insurers. Insurance companies resort

Table 1

Summary of commercial health insurance statistics, United States, 1988[a]

Premiums	$55.2 billion
Claims	$44.5 billion
Difference	$10.7 billion
Administration, commissions, marketing, and other overhead expenses	$14.9 billion
Expenses per dollar of claims	33.5 cents
Expenses per dollar of premiums collected	26.9 cents
Waste, as compared with Canada (3 cents per dollar of claims paid)	$13.2 billion
Waste, as compared with Medicare (2.3 cents per dollar of claims paid)	$13.6 billion

[a]Sources: A. M. Best Co. *Best's Insurance Reports 1989* and *Best's Life-Health Industry Marketing Results 1989*. Oldwick, N.J., 1989. Citizens Fund calculations.

to huge premium increases and denial of coverage because they see this strategy as the best way to stay profitable in a world of rapidly escalating prices. The best way to bring those costs under control is to create a single-payer system similar to the Canadian health care system, in which one payer determines the fee structure and budgets for providers and prevents redundant acquisitions of expensive new technologies.

In the current system, the hundreds of insurance companies and millions of individual and business consumers are without significant leverage to control the costs of doctors, hospitals, and drug companies. A free-market approach only works well when both buyers and sellers have information. Where the buyers are hostage to the expertise of sellers, a free market is not the best system of providing a product. If a person needs an appendectomy, for example, he or she is not in a position to shop around for the best-priced hospital, surgeon, and anesthesiologist. The patient is likely to have an established relationship with a particular family practitioner who, in turn, has established relationships with particular hospitals and specialists.

A single-payer system, on the other hand, allows the government to bargain with these groups to set reasonable rates that allow doctors and hospitals to make reasonable profits while still providing care to all. In Canada, for example, doctors work for themselves and are paid a fixed amount for each procedure just as they are in the United States. The difference is that the fee they are paid is set by a provincial commission based on a rational assessment of the time, training, and equipment required by the physician for the particular procedure and negotiations between doctors, hospitals, and the government. And in Canada, annual budgets are set for each hospital. In the United States, by contrast, businesses and individual consumers buying private insurance are at the mercy of hospitals, doctors, and drug companies who can set whatever rate they want. For example, the average cost of an adult checkup is only $32 in Canada compared with $53 in the United States. For surgical procedures, the gap is even wider. An appendectomy costs only $180 in Canada compared with $797 in the United States (data are for 1987) (9). The result is that Canadians can spend far less per capita on health care and receive better care overall.

The Burdens Imposed on Medical Care Providers, Consumers, and Businesses

The commercial insurance industry's practices, as well as the barriers erected to paying claims, impose significant costs on the medical care providers, consumers, and businesses that must live by their rules, including the following:

Paperwork for Providers. Each insurance company has its own unique forms that must be filled out by doctors and hospitals. Administrative expenses consume 18 percent of an average U.S. hospital's budget compared with only 8 percent in Canada (10).

Paperwork for Individuals. Individuals face a daunting task shopping for health insurance. The structure of benefits is far from uniform. Some policies promise no premium increases for a number of years whereas others may be initially less costly but allow for rapid escalation of premiums and cost-sharing upon renewal. Others may provide high deductibles and lower prices. Many people report experiencing difficulty in getting claims paid and bills corrected.

Paperwork for Business. Businesses face costs similar to those faced by individuals. Many businesses have been forced to hire full-time health care administrators to manage coverage and expensive health benefits consultants to help find the best policies.

Churning Business. The General Accounting Office estimates that roughly one-third of small businesses leave their insurance companies or are not renewed each year. Unfortunately, the effect on employees of a business changing insurance companies can be devastating. Pregnancies or serious illnesses that occurred under the previous policy are usually excluded from coverage under preexisting condition exclusion clauses. In the second and subsequent years of a policy, some preexisting condition exclusions expire or employees may develop new medical problems; either event leads to higher insurance premiums. The higher insurance premiums, once again, force the employer to find a new insurance company offering lower rates, and the cycle begins again (11).

Blocking Employment Mobility. Many people with conditions as common as pregnancy and asthma are effectively deterred from finding new jobs because insurance will rarely cover preexisting conditions of new employees.

Insurance Industry Administrative, Overhead, and Marketing Costs

The focus of this study is the commercial insurance industry's excessive administrative and marketing expenses. The industry wastes billions of dollars each year on practices that other countries and financing systems avoid. The following are among the reasons for the excessive health insurance costs:

Denying Coverage. Resources are wasted weeding out unprofitable groups and individuals. The insurance companies usually evaluate each group before deciding to offer initial coverage, and then repeat the process every year before deciding to renew. In small groups, if one person has a serious illness, coverage is sometimes denied (or effectively denied through dramatic premium increases) to the group the next year. Making those distinctions is expensive. In addition, the industry is going to great lengths to deny coverage to new applicants who do not fall into "safe" occupational or industrial categories. Applicants are often investigated and their backgrounds verified to determine whether they fall into a wide range of categories. Those groups include people with preexisting conditions, people who work in low-paying or seasonal jobs, small businesses, government-financed nonprofit organizations, health care and hazardous occupations, and those in professions that have been redlined by the insurance industry (12). Businesses and persons denied coverage by one insurance company are likely to apply to another company, and the cycle of applications, investigations, and verification begins again.

Setting Rates. In order to maximize profits, the insurance industry determines an "experience rating" for each group and individual. This experience rating is based on the insurance company's actual cost experience with the policy holder or policy holders with similar characteristics. In contrast to single-payer systems where the government relies on general revenues to spread the risk across the entire population or employs a very simple system for calculating premiums, the current system requires enormous resources to administer since the insurance industry tries to assess the specific risk for virtually every group or individual policy it writes.

Advertising, Marketing, and Commissions. In 1988, the commercial health insurance industry spent over $292 million in advertising and paid out $6.9 billion in commissions. Commissions alone are equal to 12.6 percent of total premium income. Commercial health insurers have been especially aggressive in marketing to large groups, which they consider more profitable than either small groups or individuals.

Denying and Processing Claims. Insurance companies administer many different types of policies with varying degrees and types of coverage. In addition to managing a multiplicity of forms, insurance companies devote a great deal of time and resources reviewing, challenging, and denying claims submissions. A single plan available to all people would dramatically simplify the processing of claims—as is the case in the Canadian and Medicare systems.

Monitoring Providers. Insurance companies duplicate each other's monitoring of providers to prevent overbilling.

Profits. From 1979 to 1988, the insurance industry made over $7.3 billion in profits from health and accident insurance. *Valueline Investment Survey* reports (13):

> We look for strong earnings gain from most of the group health participants over the next three to five years. That's because annual rate increases (estimated at 15 percent–25 percent for large cases and 35 percent–45 percent for small cases) are still running well in excess of the trend factor—the annual growth rate of medical claims costs per risk. . . . [M]any of the group health carriers have modified their policies, and increased out-of-pocket provisions. And these claim reductions are likely to show up on the bottom line, too.

Excessive Compensation for Industry Executives. A study by the accounting firm Ernst & Young (14) reveals that insurance company compensation to executives in three of four positions studied was significantly higher than in other industries. (Compensation for chief executive officers, chief operating officers, and chief financial officers was 20, 37, and 9.7 percent higher, respectively, than for companies of similar size in other industries.)

HEALTH INSURANCE INDUSTRY PERFORMANCE IN THE UNITED STATES

This section quantifies the administrative expenses of the commercial health insurance industry. (See the Appendix for a full description of technical measures used.)

An Overview of Health Insurance Industry Expenses

In 1988, commercial insurance companies paid $44.5 billion to policy holders in claims. These companies also reported $14.9 billion in administrative, marketing, and other overhead costs.[3] These expenses are itemized in Table 2.

Administrative, Overhead, and Marketing Expenses and Claims

For the health insurance consumer, the test of the insurance industry's efficiency is how much insurance companies spend to provide a dollar of benefits. In this report, this ratio is called the expense-to-claims ratio; it is administrative, marketing, and other overhead expenses divided by claims. Since administrative, overhead, and marketing expenses totaled $14.9 billion, and claims paid amounted to $44.3 billion, the expense-to-claims ratio was 33.5 percent in 1988. In other words, for every dollar that the commercial health insurance industry paid out in claims, the insurance industry spent 33.5 cents for administration, marketing, and other overhead expenses (5).

The typical employer-provided group policy cost $1,176 for individual coverage, of which the commercial insurance industry spent $316 for administration, overhead, and marketing. An employer-provided family policy cost $2,508, of which $675 was spent on administration, overhead, and marketing. Individual policy holders have traditionally paid much higher premiums than people who are able to obtain insurance as part of a group. As Table 3 makes clear, overhead expenses were far higher in relation to claims for nongroup policies—mostly individual policies—than for the standard group policies. The expense-to-claims ratio for these policies was an enormous 73.1 percent. In other words, for each dollar in benefits to those unable to participate in a group, the commercial insurance industry spent 73 cents on administration, marketing, commissions, and other overhead expenses.

Table 3 also documents the steep rise in administrative, overhead, and marketing expenses since 1981. These data dispel the popular misconception that premium increases merely reflect medical price inflation. The reality is that industry inefficiency contributed to the premium increases. While the annual amount of claims paid increased by 76.6 percent from 1981 to 1988, insurance industry expenses increased by 92.8 percent. As a share of claims, they rose from 30.7 to 33.5 percent.

Other Measures of Health Insurance Performance

In addition to the expense-to-claims ratio, there are two other commonly used measures of health insurance efficiency: the expense-to-premiums ratio[4] and the loss

---

[3] One misconception is that federal income taxes account for the large differences between the expenses of the commercial insurance industry and nonprofit or governmental insurers. However, income taxes are not included in the measures of expense used in this study. If they were, one would see that the health insurance industry reported a net *gain* from federal income taxes in 1988 since companies were able to deduct health insurance underwriting losses from the profits made in other profitable lines of insurance and investments.

[4] The insurance industry calls this ratio simply the "expense ratio." This report refers to it as the expense-to-premiums ratio for clarity and to remind readers of the difference between it and the expense-to-claims ratio.

Table 2

Health insurance industry expenses, 1988[a]

	Expenses, millions of dollars	Percent of claims	Percent of premiums
Commissions	6,957.3	15.7%	12.5%
Advertising	292.1	0.7%	0.5%
Salaries and wages	4,014.6	9.1%	7.2%
Insurance industry employee and agent benefits	488.4	1.1%	0.9%
Printing, postage, and phone	923.7	2.1%	1.7%
Rent and other expenses	2,238.3	5.0%	4.0%
Total expenses	14,914.4	33.5%	26.9%

[a]Source: Estimates from reference 5.

Table 3

National health insurance statistics, 1981 and 1988[a,b]

	Billions of dollars			Expense-to-claims ratio	Expense-to-premiums ratio
	Claims	Premiums	Expenses		
1988					
Group	35.8	41.3	8.5	23.8%	20.7%
Individual and other	8.8	13.9	6.4	73.1%	44.7%
All policies	44.5	55.2	14.9	33.5%	26.9%
1981					
Group	20.8	24.5	4.3	20.9%	17.7%
Individual and other	4.4	7.3	3.4	76.8%	45.7%
All policies	25.2	31.9	7.7	30.7%	24.2%
Change from 1981 to 1988					
Group	72.0%	68.6%	95.9%	13.9%	16.9%
Individual and other	98.1%	88.8%	88.6%	-4.8%	-2.2%
All policies	76.6%	73.3%	92.7%	9.1%	11.2%

[a]Source: reference 5; Citizens Fund calculations.
[b]Claims are claims incurred; premiums are net premiums earned. See text for definition of ratios; Appendix for definition of terms.

ratio. Both of these measures are inferior to the expense-to-claims ratio for the purpose of measuring insurance industry inefficiency.

The expense-to-premiums ratio is simply expenses divided by premiums. As stated above, administrative, overhead, and marketing expenses were $14.9 billion in 1988. Since premiums were $55.2 billion, the expense-to-premiums ratio was 26.9 percent. In other words, for every dollar commercial health insurers collected in premiums, they spent 26.9 cents on administrative, marketing, and other overhead expenses. The expense-to-premiums ratio and the expense-to-claims ratio measures differ only in that they compare expenses with different indicators. The expense-to-claims ratio measures efficiency from the perspective of the health insurance consumer or the policy maker. The consumer wants to know, "How much do I have to spend on insurance administration for each dollar of benefits I actually get back?" On the other hand, the insurance company executive wants to know, "How much of each dollar I collect in premiums must be spent for overhead expenses and taken out of profits?" Estimating the amount that could be saved in administrative waste—$13 billion—is unaffected by whether expense-to-premiums or expense-to-claims ratio is used since both measures are based on identical definitions of administrative expense.

Another measure used by the insurance industry is the loss ratio. The loss ratio is simply the total claims divided by total premiums. This measure does not address administrative, overhead, and marketing expenses directly. Rather it indicates the percentage of premiums sold that were spent paying claims. The remainder (mathematically 100 percent minus the loss ratio) is the amount left over after claims have been paid. These funds are used to pay administrative, marketing, and other overhead expenses as well as to provide profit. The loss ratio will tend to understate expenses since it makes no allowance for additional income that insurance companies receive from investments. Investment and other income derived from health insurance funds in 1988 totaled $5.5 billion in addition to the $55.2 billion received in premium income. In addition, since the industry lost money in 1988, the loss ratio implies a greater efficiency than the industry actually achieved. Policy holders are likely to pay for these losses in higher prices in subsequent years.

The loss ratio varies from year to year depending upon how well the insurance industry has anticipated claims for the year. In the past several years, many companies have underestimated the amount of claims they would have to pay out, so their loss ratios have been high and they have lost money as a result. Since this ratio is heavily influenced by the industry's calculation or miscalculation of expected claims, it is a less reliable indicator than either of the other two ratios. There are, however, three reasons for paying attention to the loss ratio. The first is that it does provide an annual snapshot of how much more the public actually pays in premiums than it receives in benefits. Second, when profits are earned, the measure adds that profit to the administrative costs so that a more complete picture of the public costs of the insurance industry is visible. And third, because of inconsistencies between what the insurance companies report nationally and in each state, it is impossible to compute the expense-to-claims ratio for each company in each state. On the other hand, the companies do report their loss ratios on a state-by-state basis.

In order to make the loss ratio conceptually consistent with the expense-to-claims and expense-to-premiums ratios, this report recomputes the loss ratio as an "excess-premiums-to-premiums-ratio," and as an "excess-premiums-to-claims ratio." Excess premiums are simply the difference between premiums collected and claims paid. The ratios are this number divided by either premiums or claims. Thus, the excess-premiums-to-premiums ratio is simply 100 percent minus the loss ratio. If a company collected $100 in premiums and paid $80 in claims, its excess-premiums-to-premiums ratio would be 20 percent [(100 − 80)/100]. The expense-to-claims ratio for the same company would be 25 percent [(100 − 80)/80]. These two measures are conceptually consistent with the other indicators used in that they measure what the company retains for expenses and profits rather than what they pay in claims.

Figure 2 and Table 3 confirm that the overall conclusions of this report are unaffected by the choice of industry performance measure. The measures were fairly stable in the 1980s and basically followed the same trends.

The Top Ten Health Insurers

Unfortunately, the information each company provides is inadequate to compute an expense-to-claims ratio. For that reason, we will summarize the performance of the top ten companies by detailing their expense-to-premiums ratios and their excess-premiums-to-claims ratio, as just described. Table 4 shows, for example, that in 1988 Prudential, the leading company, earned $4.4 billion of premiums. Its expense-to-premiums ratio nationally was 17.9 percent, meaning that for every dollar it collected in premiums, 17.9 cents were spent on administration, overhead, and marketing. Prudential had an excess-premiums-to-claims ratio of 9 percent meaning that for every dollar it paid in claims, it had 9 cents available for administration, overhead, marketing, and profits. As a comparison between the expense-to-premiums ratio and the excess-premiums-to-claims ratio suggests, Prudential lost money on its health underwriting in 1988. (However, the company's $7.4 billion in investment income more than offset its $192 million health insurance underwriting loss.) Although no company can be as efficient as a comprehensive and uniform public program and these ratios are subject to some change from year to year, the wide variation among these companies suggests that policy holders and regulators might profitably subject the operations of these companies to greater scrutiny, particularly when rate increases are requested.

Table 5 (on pages 86–87) shows data for each state.

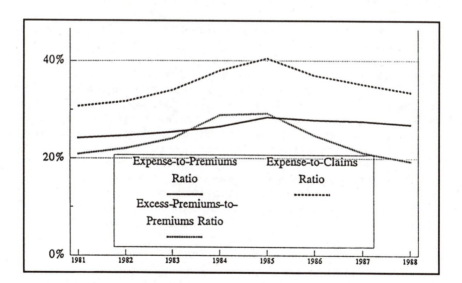

Figure 2. Expense-to-premiums, expense-to-claims, and excess-premiums-to-premiums ratios, 1981–88.

Table 4

Top ten health insurers in the United States, 1988[a]

	Premiums, millions of dollars	Expense-to-premiums ratio	Excess-premiums-to-claims ratio
Prudential Insurance America	4,398	17.9%	9%
Aetna Life Insurance	2,344	19.3%	8%
Metropolitan Life	1,993	33.6%	31%
Travelers Insurance	1,862	10.8%	39%
Principal Mutual	1,599	28.0%	14%
Connecticut General Life Co.	1,527	15.4%	2%
Continental Assurance	1,368	18.7%	14%
Guardian Life Insurance	1,157	20.2%	11%
Mutual of Omaha	1,125	18.2%	32%
Provident Life and Accident	1,074	12.8%	19%

[a]Sources: A. M. Best Co. *Best's Insurance Reports 1989* and *Best's Life-Health Industry Marketing Results, 1989*. Oldwick, N.J., 1989. Citizens Fund calculations.

COMPARISON OF EXPENSES WITH MEDICARE AND CANADA

The U.S. government, much maligned for its inefficiency, does a far better job than commercial insurance companies when it comes to efficiently administering health care programs. For example, administrative expenses are only 2.3 percent of Medicare claims (a 2.3 percent expense-to-claims ratio) including payments to carriers and intermediaries (Table 6) (15, 16). If the private health insurance industry were as efficient as the U.S. Medicare system, consumers would save over $13 billion each year.

Other nations have far more efficient systems of health care financing than the U.S. commercial health insurance industry. For example, the Canadian government pays all major health care expenses for all Canadians. Their overhead expenses—primarily administrative since they have no marketing or commission expenses—are only 2.5 percent of claims (10). This study uses a more conservative estimate of 3 percent of claims (Table 6). If the United States were to adopt an approach along the lines of Canada's single-payer system, the American consumer would save an estimated $13 billion on administration, marketing, and other overhead costs incurred by the commercial insurance companies alone. Other studies estimate total health care administrative savings from a single-payer approach to be $45 billion or more (17). Table 7 (on pages 88–89) shows the estimated savings for each state. According to a 1988 survey on health insurance premiums, the cost per person for employer-provided individual insurance coverage averaged $1,176 per year (18). Using this average, the $13 billion of waste identified in this report is sufficient to provide insurance to 11 million uninsured people.

APPENDIX

The "commercial health insurance industry" in this study includes only life and health insurance companies. Excluded are property and casualty insurance companies that write health insurance. The property/casualty companies account for approximately $3.4 billion, or 6.3 percent, of the $54.9 billion in direct premiums written by commercial health insurers. However, complete data for these companies were not available at the time of publication.

Insurance companies use different definitions of the terms premiums and claims, depending on the purpose for which reporting is required. This appendix explains the different meanings of these definitions, and when they are used in the report.

Premiums and Claims (Losses). The work "premiums" is used in the text and tables to refer to four possible measures, all of which on a national basis equal roughly the same amount for analytical purposes. Likewise, the word "claims" is used to refer to several different measures, which on a national basis are roughly equal. This report uses the word "claims" to refer to what the industry calls "losses": the amount companies pay out in benefits or claims plus the amounts they set aside as reserves for claims that will be paid in future years. In 1988, the commercial insurance industry reported paying out over $41.0 billion in health insurance benefits and set aside $3.3 billion for future reserves.

Direct versus Net Measures. If the word "direct" is used, the measure refers only to premiums, or corresponding claims, based on policies actually written by the company. What these categories exclude are the premiums and claims related to policies that one company may have bought from another company. For example, if ABC Insurance Co. wrote $100 worth of policies itself, sold $20 worth to EFG Insurance Co., and bought $60 worth of policies from XYZ Insurance Co., its direct premiums written would still be $100. On the other hand, its net premiums written would be $140 ($100 + $60 – $20). The totals for "direct" measures are consistently lower than "net" measures for several reasons. First, some of the data for the "direct" calculations that were collected by A.M. Best Co. required voluntary submissions by companies of state-specific business. A.M. Best Co. officials acknowledge that these data are likely to be less accurate than the "net" measures. In addition, the "direct" measures do *not* include international business, which for at least a few companies may be a significant portion of their business. All national numbers, unless otherwise cited, refer to "net" measures.

Written versus Earned Premiums. The difference between premiums "written" and premiums "earned" is the difference between actual premiums and accrued premiums in a particular year. For example, if a premium is received on December 30, 1989, to pay for insurance coverage beginning in January 1990, that premium is included among premiums "written" in 1989 but would be considered a premium "earned" in 1990.

Losses Paid versus Losses Incurred. The distinction between losses "paid" and losses "incurred" parallels the distinction between premiums. If, for example, a claim was paid on January 2, 1990, for a bill submitted in December 1989, that claim or loss was "incurred" in 1989 yet was "paid" in 1990.

As Table 8 makes clear, on a national level, the differences in definitions are analytically insignificant. The distinctions drawn by the definitions are occasionally significant, however, on a company-by-company basis. For example, a company that either buys or sells a large number of policies from other insurance companies will have significantly different direct premiums earned and net premiums earned. Because companies do not disclose all four definitions nationally and in each state, this report merely reproduces those measures the companies did disclose.

Table 5

Premiums, claims, and expenses, 1988[a,b]

	Thousands of dollars				
	Premiums	Claims	Excess premiums	Overhead expenses	Expense-to-claims ratio
Alabama	$790,622	$626,077	$164,545	$212,677	34.0%
Alaska	164,447	154,400	10,047	44,236	28.7%
Arizona	733,004	618,405	114,599	197,178	31.9%
Arkansas	367,823	443,050	−75,227	98,944	22.3%
California	6,160,011	5,115,242	1,044,769	1,657,043	32.4%
Colorado	715,414	620,014	95,400	192,446	31.0%
Connecticut	911,355	644,960	266,395	245,154	38.0%
Delaware	117,840	78,028	39,812	31,699	40.6%
Florida	3,074,388	2,609,809	464,579	827,010	31.7%
Georgia	1,529,444	1,191,546	337,898	411,420	34.5%
Hawaii	105,027	102,706	2,321	28,252	27.5%
Idaho	129,032	134,895	−5,863	34,710	25.7%
Illinois	3,867,265	3,080,439	786,826	1,040,294	33.8%
Indiana	1,099,982	786,782	313,200	295,895	37.6%
Iowa	552,414	404,386	148,028	148,599	36.7%
Kansas	437,769	365,449	72,320	117,760	32.2%
Kentucky	559,498	400,911	158,587	150,505	37.5%
Louisiana	828,049	702,171	125,878	222,745	31.7%
Maine	222,912	206,647	16,265	59,963	29.0%
Maryland	839,119	634,506	204,613	225,723	35.6%
Massachusetts	1,076,172	735,929	340,243	289,490	39.3%
Michigan	1,401,957	1,106,517	295,440	377,126	34.1%
Minnesota	770,758	554,486	216,272	207,334	37.4%
Mississippi	522,871	385,102	137,769	140,652	36.5%
Missouri	1,329,191	1,020,227	308,964	357,552	35.0%
Montana	148,507	102,011	46,496	39,948	39.2%
Nebraska	406,373	274,897	131,476	109,314	39.8%
Nevada	234,040	242,662	−8,622	62,957	25.9%
New Hamsphire	202,534	158,176	44,358	54,482	34.4%
New Jersey	1,784,385	1,516,755	267,630	480,000	31.6%
New Mexico	257,386	216,309	41,077	69,237	32.0%
New York	4,756,523	3,566,077	1,190,446	1,279,505	35.9%
North Carolina	1,167,591	864,867	302,724	314,082	36.3%
North Dakota	105,729	114,840	−9,111	28,441	24.8%
Ohio	1,983,005	1,466,261	516,744	533,428	36.4%
Oklahoma	637,854	542,585	95,269	171,583	31.6%
Oregon	413,566	291,568	121,998	111,249	38.2%
Pennsylvania	1,636,156	1,211,806	424,350	440,126	36.3%
Rhode Island	128,633	104,258	24,375	34,602	33.2%
South Carolina	615,893	474,587	141,306	165,675	34.9%

Table 5

(Continued)

| | Thousands of dollars | | | | |
	Premiums	Claims	Excess premiums	Overhead expenses	Expense-to-claims ratio
South Dakota	$171,515	$219,322	$–47,807	$46,138	21.0%
Tennessee	1,104,616	885,482	219,134	297,142	33.6%
Texas	3,818,214	3,207,894	610,320	1,027,100	32.0%
Utah	256,397	246,305	10,092	68,971	28.0%
Vermont	95,148	70,159	24,989	25,595	36.5%
Virginia	1,020,085	712,800	307,285	274,403	38.5%
Washington	600,603	422,669	177,934	161,562	38.2%
West Virginia	317,857	246,948	70,909	85,504	34.6%
Wisconsin	1,032,670	808,037	224,633	277,788	34.4%
Wyoming	87,787	65,069	22,178	23,615	36.3%

[a]Sources: reference 5 and A. M. Best Co. *Best's Life-Health Marketing Results*. Oldwick, N.J., 1989. Citizens Fund calculations.

[b]Premiums: direct premiums earned; claims: "losses incurred" includes reserves and claims incurred; excess premiums: premiums minus claims; overhead expenses: estimated administrative, marketing, and other overhead expenses using national average expense-to-premiums ratio; expense-to-claims ratio: expenses divided by claims.

Table 6

Estimated insurance expenses for the United States under different health care financing systems[a]

	Expense-to-premiums ratio	United States, thousands of dollars	Individual coverage, dollars	Family policy, dollars
Premiums collected by commercial insurers		55,245,526	1,176	2,508
Estimated expenses under different systems				
Commercial insurers	26.9%	14,914,400	316	675
Medicare[b]	2.3%	1,024,142	27	58
Canada[b]	3.0%	1,335,837	35	75
Difference between Canada and commercial insurers	23.9%	13,578,563	281	599

[a]Source: National data on expenses and premiums from reference 5.

[b]National premiums are estimates of what administrative expenses would have been if the expense-to-claims ratio had been the same as Medicare and Canada, respectively.

Table 7

Estimated savings from a single-payer system, 1988, thousands of dollars[a,b]

	Excess premiums	Expenses	Estimated single-payer expenses	Savings: expenses vs. sing. pay.	Savings: excess prem. vs. sing. pay.
Alabama	164,545	212,677	18,782	193,895	145,763
Alaska	10,047	44,236	4,632	39,604	5,415
Arizona	114,599	197,178	18,552	178,626	96,047
Arkansas	−75,227	98,944	13,292	85,653	−88,519
California	1,044,769	1,657,043	153,457	1,503,586	891,312
Colorado	95,400	192,446	18,600	173,846	76,800
Connecticut	266,395	245,154	19,349	225,806	247,046
Delaware	39,812	31,699	2,341	29,358	37,471
Florida	464,579	827,010	78,294	748,716	386,285
Georgia	337,898	411,420	35,746	375,674	302,152
Hawaii	2,321	28,252	3,081	25,171	−760
Idaho	−5,863	34,710	4,047	30,663	−9,910
Illinois	786,826	1,040,294	92,413	947,881	694,413
Indiana	313,200	295,895	23,603	272,292	289,597
Iowa	148,028	148,599	12,132	136,468	135,896
Kansas	72,320	117,760	10,963	106,796	61,357
Kentucky	158,587	150,505	12,027	138,478	146,560
Louisiana	125,878	222,745	21,065	201,680	104,813
Maine	16,265	59,963	6,199	53,764	10,066
Maryland	204,613	225,723	19,035	206,688	185,578
Massachusetts	340,243	289,490	22,078	267,412	318,165
Michigan	295,440	377,126	33,196	343,931	262,244
Minnesota	216,272	207,334	16,635	190,699	199,637
Mississippi	137,769	140,652	11,553	129,099	126,216
Missouri	308,964	357,552	30,607	326,946	278,357
Montana	46,496	39,948	3,060	36,888	43,436
Nebraska	131,476	109,314	8,247	101,067	123,229
Nevada	−8,622	62,957	7,280	55,677	−15,902
New Hampshire	44,358	54,482	4,745	49,736	39,613
New Jersey	267,630	480,000	45,503	434,497	222,127
New Mexico	41,077	69,237	6,489	62,748	34,588
New York	1,190,446	1,279,505	106,982	1,172,522	1,083,464
North Carolina	302,724	314,082	25,946	288,136	276,778
North Dakota	−9,111	28,441	3,445	24,996	−12,556
Ohio	516,744	533,428	43,988	489,441	472,756
Oklahoma	95,269	171,583	16,278	155,305	78,991
Oregon	121,998	111,249	8,747	102,502	113,251
Pennsylvania	424,350	440,126	36,354	403,772	387,996
Rhode Island	24,375	34,602	3,128	31,475	21,247
South Carolina	141,306	165,675	14,238	151,438	127,068

Table 7

(Continued)

	Excess premiums	Expenses	Estimated single-payer expenses	Savings: expenses vs. sing. pay.	Savings: excess prem. vs. sing. pay.
South Dakota	−47,807	46,138	6,580	39,558	−54,387
Tennessee	219,134	297,142	26,564	270,577	192,570
Texas	610,320	1,027,100	96,237	930,863	514,083
Utah	10,092	68,971	7,389	61,582	2,703
Vermont	24,989	25,595	2,105	23,490	22,884
Virginia	307,285	274,403	21,384	253,019	285,901
Washington	177,934	161,562	12,680	148,882	165,254
West Virginia	70,909	85,504	7,408	78,095	63,501
Wisconsin	224,633	277,788	24,241	253,547	200,392
Wyoming	22,718	23,615	1,952	21,663	20,766

[a]Sources: reference 5 and A. M. Best Co. *Best's Life-Health Marketing Results*. Oldwick, N.J., 1989. Citizens Fund calculations.

[b]Current excess premiums: direct premiums earned minus direct claims; current expenses: expenses estimated by multiplying the national average expense-to-premiums ratio by the state direct premiums; estimated expense, single-payer system: direct premium earned times 3%; savings, expenses vs. single-payer: column 2 minus column 3; savings, excess premium vs. single-payer: column 1 minus column 3.

Table 8

Definitions of premiums and claims used by the insurance industry

Premiums	Amount, 1988	Claims	Amount, 1988
Direct premiums written	$51.5 billion	Direct losses paid	$38.5 billion
Direct premiums earned	$51.7 billion	Direct losses incurred	$41.1 billion
Net premiums written	$55.5 billion	Net losses paid	NA
Net premiums earned	$55.2 billion	Net losses incurred	$44.5 billion

In keeping with the reporting practices of the A.M. Best Co., the national expense-to-premiums ratios use the net premiums written statistic as the measure of premiums. The expense-to-claims measure compares expenses to net losses incurred. State-specific measures of premiums and losses are limited to the "direct" series of measures; no "net" numbers are available. Thus, expense-to-premiums and expense-to-claims measures use the national expense ratios for particular companies or lines of insurance and compare those with direct premiums written and direct losses incurred statistics.

Types of Policies. The term "group policies" includes only those policies that are classified as group plans by the National Association of Insurance Commissioners. "Individual and other policies" includes credit, collectively renewable, non-cancelable, guaranteed renewable, non-renewable for stated reasons only, and "all others." Although collectively renewable policies are a special type of group policy, for analytic purposes this was kept separate from the standard group policies. As a percentage of "individual and other policies," collectively renewable policies account for between 5 and 6 percent of the total on all measures. All the other types of policies lumped under "individual and other policies" are primarily or exclusively individual policies.

REFERENCES

1. OECD Secretariat. Health care expenditure and other data: An international compendium from the Organization for Economic Cooperation and Development. *Health Care Financing Review 1989 Annual Supplement*, pp. 111–194. Baltimore, Md., December 1989.
2. Citizens Fund. *Spending More, Getting Less*. Washington, D.C., 1990. Data from U.S. Department of Health and Human Services, Health Care Financing Administration. *Health Care Financing Review 1989 Annual Supplement*. Baltimore, Md., December 1989.
3. Rich, S. 28% in U.S. seen lacking steady health insurance: Census study finds long gaps in coverage. *Washington Post*, April 12, 1990, p. A-19.
4. Aday, L., Flemming, G., and Anderson, R. *Access to Medical Care in the U.S.? Who Has It, Who Doesn't*, pp. 56–57. Pluribus Press, Chicago, 1984. Cited in Blendon R., et al. Satisfaction with health systems in ten nations. *Health Aff.*, Summer 1990, p. 192.
5. A. M. Best Co. *Best's Aggregates & Averages: Life-Health, 1989*, p. 48. Oldwick, N.J., 1989.
6. A. M. Best Co. *Best's Aggregates & Averages: Property-Casualty, 1989*, pp. 214–216. Oldwick, N.J., 1989.
7. Health Insurance Association of America. *Source Book of Health Insurance Data*, p. 24. Washington, D.C., 1989.
8. Levit, K., Freeland, M. S., and Waldo, D. R. National health care spending trends: 1988. *Health Aff.*, Summer 1990, pp. 171–174.
9. Total medical care without bills. *St. Petersburg Times*, April 2, 1989.
10. Himmelstein, D. U., and Woolhandler, S. Cost without benefit: Administrative waste in U.S. health care. *N. Engl. J. Med.* 314: 443, 1986.
11. U.S. General Accounting Office. Health Insurance: Availability and Adequacy for Small Businesses, p. 6. Testimony of Mark V. Nadel before the Subcommittee on Health and the Environment, Committee on Energy and Commerce, U.S. House of Representatives, October 16, 1989.
12. Freudenheim, M. Health insurers, to reduce losses, blacklist dozens of occupations. *New York Times*, February 5, 1990.
13. *Valueline Investment Survey*, December 15, 1989.
14. Ernst & Young. *Health Care Versus Other Industries: Executive Compensation Study 1990*. Atlanta, 1990.
15. Committee on Ways and Means, U.S. House of Representatives. *Overview of Entitlement Programs: 1990 Greenbook, Background Material and Data on Programs Within the Jurisdiction of the Committee on Ways and Means*, p. 158. June 5, 1990.
16. Lazenby, H., Health Care Financing Administration. Personal communication.
17. Himmelstein, D., and Woolhandler, S. Free care: A quantitative analysis of health and cost effects of a national health program for the United States. *Int. J. Health Serv.* 18: 393–399, 1988.
18. Health Insurance Association of America. *Source Book of Health Insurance Data, 1989*, p. 21. Washington, D.C., 1989.

CHAPTER 7

Private Insurance Reform
in the 1990s:
Can It Solve the Health Care Crisis?

Thomas Bodenheimer

THE ACCESS/COST CRISIS

• Timmy Dawkins, son of a small-town school teacher, developed cancer; the following year the insurance company hiked premiums to all the school's employees by 200 percent, and 20 other companies refused to insure the school at all (1).

• Buzz Gammel, owner of a small business, developed a brain tumor; a few months later his insurance announced a rate increase from $1,352 to $10,068 per month, which Mr. Gammel was unable to afford (2).

• Dean Meyer, former director of the California Insurance Brokers Association, developed coronary artery disease; the only insurance he could obtain has a preexisting illness clause, denying benefits for any costs associated with heart disease (1).

• In 1989, New York Life Insurance canceled five group plans, leaving 120,000 individuals without coverage. One of those was James Snyder, a lawyer who had just contracted leukemia. He was unable to obtain new coverage.

• Ronald Katz, an architect, had two insurance policies canceled—United of Omaha and Blue Cross—after he contracted AIDS (2).

• An uninsured janitor in his thirties with rheumatic heart disease was admitted to a coronary care unit, where his bill came to $26,000. To pay the bill he was forced to sell his car, which he used to travel to work. As a result he lost his job and was forced onto welfare.

• When a 59-year-old woman retired from her job as a bookkeeper, she converted her group insurance to an individual policy. After three years she missed one monthly insurance payment, at which time her insurance was canceled. When she reapplied for coverage, she was rejected due to her high blood pressure.

• A 35-year-old employed black man arrived at a private hospital emergency room with fever and cough—he had delayed treatment because of lack of health insurance. He was found to have acute leukemia, potentially curable with chemotherapy. Due to

Originally published in the International Journal of Health Services, 22(2): 197–215, 1992.

treatment delay, the illness was too far advanced and after several months of heroic measures, he died.

• A 58-year-old Hispanic clerical worker had restrictive lung disease from a spine deformity. She depended on a home IPPB (intermittent positive pressure breathing) machine to assist her breathing. She was finally forced to resign from her job, lost her insurance, and could not afford to rent the IPPB machine. The medical supply company came and took the machine away.

• A man whose Medicaid benefits were terminated died of a treatable perforated ulcer because he delayed seeking care for 10 days. An uninsured cardiac patient died of a presumed myocardial infarction after running out of cardiac medications that he could not afford to buy. A hypertensive patient without health insurance died of a stroke after becoming unable to afford her blood pressure medications (3).

• Two neurosurgeons at a private hospital refused to see a young uninsured man who was going into a coma after a severe beating in the head. The patient died shortly after being transferred to a county hospital (4).

As these examples show, the United States is facing a two-part health crisis: a crisis of access and a crisis of costs. In 1987, 37 million Americans were uninsured, 18 percent of the nonelderly population. Health care costs are rising at twice the general rate of inflation.

Health care financing is dominated by the private health insurance industry, which insured about 180 million Americans and received $175 billion in premium income in 1988 (5). Private health insurance policies can be divided into two major categories: large employer group plans and small group/individual plans. The costs of large group plans are inflating rapidly: between 1973 and 1983, employer-paid health insurance costs rose by 16.4 percent annually (6), followed by increases of 18.6 percent in 1988, 20.4 percent in 1989, and 17.1 percent in 1990 (7–9). While large employers pay the majority of premium costs, the employee share is rising, creating hardship for working families (5). In one survey of 178 plans, employee premium contributions jumped 70 percent between 1987 and 1989 (10).

Difficulties with small group/individual plans are far worse, since prospective entrants into many of these plans must undergo medical underwriting, that is, medical reviews to determine their insurability and their premium rate. Companies with under 25 employees employ about 30 percent of the work force, including 48 percent of the uninsured. Such small businesses are charged about 20 percent more than large businesses for identical health insurance coverage. Small employers can seldom buy coverage without preexisting condition exclusions, and firms with employees having chronic health problems are often unable to obtain coverage at all (11). If an employee develops a costly illness, the group may face a premium increase of 200 to 300 percent in a single year, or may have coverage canceled (12, 13). Many health insurers have blacklisted about 40 occupations with increased risks of accidents, alcoholism, or AIDS (14). The same difficulties beset people seeking individual health insurance.

THE REFORM PROPOSALS

Attempting to solve these problems, a number of reform proposals have surfaced at the state governmental level. These include Medicaid expansion for the below-poverty or near-poverty uninsured, state subsidy to individuals and/or businesses for the purchase of health insurance, risk pools for the medically uninsurable, insurance industry–initiated reforms within the small group market, the promotion of "stripped down" insurance plans that reduce premium cost, and state mandating of employer-sponsored health insurance for the employed uninsured. While a potpourri of other proposals can be found in various state capitols, this listing is sufficient to capture the general thrust of health insurance reform.

Medicaid Expansion

The proportion of persons below the poverty line covered by Medicaid fell from 70 percent in the mid-1970s to 46 percent in 1985 (15). One simple way to insure a portion of the uninsured is to extend Medicaid to everyone below the poverty line, which a few states have done. Delaware, for example, is financing Medicaid expansion through a cigarette tax, and Maine through cigarette and alcohol taxes (16).

On a national level, expansion of Medicaid to the below-poverty population is estimated to cost $14 billion in its first year (17). This approach is supported by the American Medical Association and the private insurance industry. For insurers, removing the poor (who cannot afford insurance) from the private market removes industry responsibility for a portion of the uninsurance problem without encroaching into an area of possible insurance expansion (18). An important weakness of Medicaid expansion tied to the federal definition of poverty is that the poverty line, in relation to the cost of living, is far lower than it was initially set in 1963 (19).

Medicaid expansion can extend above the poverty line through the mechanism of "Medicaid buy-in." Under one version of such a plan, people below the poverty line would receive Medicaid with no premium, people between 100 and 200 percent of poverty would pay a premium equivalent to 3 percent of adjusted gross income, while those over 200 percent of poverty would pay a full community-rated premium that would reflect the collective experience of all persons covered in the Medicaid buy-in program. Versions of the Medicaid buy-in are included in the federal Mitchell–Kennedy bill as well as the universal health insurance plan of Massachusetts. A number of states have proposed but not passed buy-ins (20).

Oregon's now-famous rationing experiment is in fact a novel approach to Medicaid expansion. In order to expand Medicaid to all people below the poverty line without incurring unacceptable expenditure increases, Oregon proposed to limit benefits offered under Medicaid to those medical interventions found by a commission and the legislature to be the most cost-effective. The trade-off was increasing the population covered in exchange for reducing the comprehensiveness of the coverage. Thus far the program has not been implemented because it requires a federal waiver (21, 22).

State Subsidy to Buy Insurance for the Poor

An alternative approach to the uninsured poverty and near-poverty populations is state subsidy of individuals or employers for the purchase of health insurance. Hawaii funds subsidized health insurance for 50,000 low-income people who are uncovered by the state's employer mandate law. Washington State's Basic Health Plan of 1987 has a somewhat new twist on a state subsidy; rather than using tax funds to help low-income people purchase private insurance, Washington requires that the insurance be purchased from a public entity that is separate from Medicaid—an insurance company within state government. Under this program, families with incomes below 200 percent of poverty (57 percent of the state's uninsured) can purchase health insurance on a sliding scale based on income, with the state paying up to 90 percent of the health plan's cost. The program requires providers to be paid by capitation for cost-control purposes. Copayments are charged except for preventive care, and a waiting period of 12 months is required for the coverage of preexisting illnesses. The monthly cost in 1989 was about $90 per member, split between state funds and enrollee premiums (23).

Oregon has a subsidy to employers rather than to individuals; businesses with under 25 employees receive tax credits if they buy health insurance for their employees. In 1990, Oklahoma awarded a $15 per month tax credit for businesses that choose to obtain low-cost private health insurance for employees. California has a similar tax credit program, which does not start until 1992 (12, 24, 25). Such partial subsidies to employers are problematic since there is little reason for employers who pay nothing for health insurance to participate.

High-risk Pools

A particular grouping among the uninsured are the medically uninsurable, whom private companies refuse to insure because of preexisting health conditions. Nineteen states have established high-risk pools for the medically uninsurable (24). Under such pools, the state requires all health insurers to join an association, which selects a carrier to administer the program. Eligibility is limited to people who have been rejected by at least one insurer for medical reasons and/or who cannot find insurance at rates lower than the price of risk-pool premiums. Premiums are generally set at 125 to 400 percent of the average cost of an individual policy for a healthy person in that state. With deductibles ranging from $150 to $2,000 per year and annual premiums as high as $2,500, risk pools are geared to help middle-class uninsurable persons; low-income people cannot afford the policies. Maine and Wisconsin partially subsidize these policies for the poor, but even with the subsidy, pool coverage is more expensive than any similar private insurance policy. All of the pools lose money, which in some cases is partially made up by a state subsidy (26).

The problem with risk pools is that the risk is spread only over the sickest portion of the population, thereby necessitating very high premiums, state subsidy, and/or chronic loss of money by the pools. Due to high premiums, the pools are extremely limited in scope. Of the 37 million uninsured, 1 to 2 million are medically uninsurable; as of 1988, only 27,000 had actually enrolled in high-risk pools (26, 27).

Insurance Industry Reforms

Over the past few years, the insurance industry has come under heated public pressure to change its practices; the industry itself admits its public image is tarnished (28, 29). In the health insurance arena, consumer criticism has concentrated on the issues of policy cancellations and massive premium increases for seriously ill individuals, both those with AIDS and those with other chronic or mortal conditions (1). In 1990 Congressional testimony, the National Association of Insurance Commissioners admitted: "In addition to the thousands of complaints we, as regulators, receive relating to massive [premium] increases in a particular year because of health status, we receive thousands of complaints that, the company just dropped me" (12). The Association regards these insurance company actions as "abusive practices." Adding to consumer complaints, the industry is concerned about growing interest in publicly financed national health insurance that would eliminate or substantially reduce the private health insurance market. Asked about the Canadian approach to health insurance, Carl Schramm, president of the Health Insurance Association of America (HIAA), said "We'd be out of business. It's a life-and-death struggle" (18).

In response to the criticisms and the threat of government-run health insurance, commercial health insurers have proposed a set of minor reforms that could eliminate some of the industry's "abusive practices." HIAA testimony before the U.S. House Committee on Small Business outlines the industry's proposal. HIAA suggests that no individuals in small-group plans should be excluded because of high medical risk, nor should small-group policies be canceled due to the deteriorating health of a member of the group. Individuals with health insurance who have met preexisting illness restrictions should not be faced with new restrictions if they change jobs or if the employer changes insurance carrier. The HIAA proposes limits on how much premiums should vary for employer groups of similar composition and how much carriers can raise rates for a specific group. To allow these reforms, the HIAA would require the government to set up a private nonprofit reinsurance organization (reinsurance means insuring the insurance company for individuals with large claims). Carriers and employers would pay a premium for the reinsurer, who in turn would reimburse the carrier for claims associated with high-cost persons. Such a program would spread high-risk people broadly throughout the private small-group market. The reinsurance mechanism would of necessity sustain financial losses since carriers would only reinsure in cases whose claims are expected to exceed the price of reinsurance. If the losses exceed 4 percent of premiums, a second tier of losses would be spread across health benefit plans of both small and large employers to provide a larger private financing cushion. If the second tier is inadequate to absorb reinsurer losses, a safety valve (read: bailout) of government funds would become available. According to the HIAA spokesperson, "A major objective of these reforms should be to ensure a viable private marketplace over the long term" (12). The reinsurance pool concept will have its first test in Connecticut, where it began on May 1, 1991 (30).

This program to insure the insurance industry does have the capacity to reduce the cancellations and to moderate the premium increases associated with small-group members who become sick. To finance these improvements, premiums generally would go up, and a government bailout mechanism would be established. But the reforms do not assist those employers and individuals who simply cannot afford to purchase private health insurance. According to the HIAA's own testimony, three-fourths of the employed uninsured have annual incomes less than $10,000, making them unable to buy health insurance. And many of the small businesses that do not insure their employees have low profit margins and high failure rates. For these reasons, such reformed insurance plans would probably achieve less than a 20 percent market penetration rate among uninsured small businesses (31). Even the HIAA admits that solutions are not possible without government funding: all people below the poverty line should be insured through an expansion of Medicaid, and the employee share of employer-sponsored insurance for workers under the poverty line should be picked up by Medicaid (12). Aside from their limited capacity to solve the problem of health access, the HIAA reforms provide no answer to unabated health cost inflation.

The HIAA proposal is not a surprising one: eliminate the worst abuses to ward off the potential of public universal health insurance, stabilize the small-group health insurance market through a government-guaranteed reinsurance mechanism, and take the insurance industry off the hook for the lowest-income people.

Stripped-down Insurance Benefits

HIAA and Blue Cross/Blue Shield support another proposal to extend health insurance to the uninsured: the marketing of "stripped-down" insurance policies with high deductibles, high copayments, and reduced benefit packages. Currently, many states mandate that policies include a broad array of benefits, thereby denying insurers the option of selling lower-cost policies. The trend toward broad benefits is now reversing, and more and more states (including Oregon, Virginia, Oklahoma, Colorado, Florida, Illinois, Kansas, Kentucky, Missouri, Rhode Island, and Washington) are allowing low-cost, limited benefit policies (32). Such pared-down policies may cost $60 per month, which, according to one Blue Cross executive, is an insufficient cost reduction to make coverage affordable to small employers. With their large increases in out-of-pocket costs, these plans discriminate against low-income families. One pared-down insurance policy has a $1,000 per person deductible, 30 percent copayment for hospital and ambulatory services, and no mental health, or alcohol/drug treatment (33).

Employer-mandated Health Insurance

The extension of private insurance to the uninsured can be attempted by subsidizing or reducing the premium cost for the individual, or alternatively, by inducing the employer to buy insurance for employees. Purchasing insurance through the employer can be approached in one of two ways: by an incentive-based strategy (tax credits, subsidized insurance, or stripped-down low-cost insurance) or by a mandatory strategy (34). Over the past two years, the mandatory strategy has become an increasingly popular approach for politicians seeking to reduce the number of uninsured without creating increased government spending.

Under employer-mandated health insurance (EMHI), the government mandates (which means forces) all employers to provide health insurance for their employees. Because most large employers already provide such insurance, EMHI specifically targets small businesses to come up with much of the financing for the employed uninsured population. At the federal level, the Mitchell–Kennedy bill calls for EMHI, as does the blue-ribbon National Leadership Commission on Health Care and the bluer-ribbon Pepper Commission. Several states have versions of EMHI on their legislative agendas.

Hawaii is the only state with a true employer mandate. Passed in 1974, Hawaii's Prepaid Health Care Act (PHCA) requires employers to provide health insurance to most employees who work 20 or more hours per week. In order to comply with the federal Employee Retirement Income Security Act (ERISA), which prohibits states from mandating employers to provide health insurance, Hawaii received a federal exemption from ERISA in 1983. Hawaii has a fund to subsidize very small businesses to comply with the law. PHCA leaves out part-time employees and farm workers, and does not require coverage for dependents, thereby failing to cover about 5 percent of the nonelderly population (24).

Since employer mandate programs only reach the employed uninsured, they are often accompanied by proposals to extend Medicaid and/or to subsidize private insurance for the poor and near-poor. In 1989 Hawaii initiated a state-funded subsidy to assist the 50,000 people not covered by Medicare, Medicaid, or PHCA to buy private health insurance. Those below the poverty line will be charged no premiums but a copayment for services; the near-poor will contribute premiums and copayments on a sliding scale. The state will pay private insurers an average of $500 per enrollee (35).

While Hawaii's PHCA appears to be working, that state has unique features that make the program an unlikely model for the rest of the United States. The state has had a plantation-type economy with a tradition of employers providing direct health care through company hospitals and physicians. Hawaii also has a strong union movement, which has forced employers to provide health benefits voluntarily, and a strong Democratic Party, which enacted a liberal Medicaid program (25). Accordingly, at the time the PHCA was passed, 90 percent of the population was already insured; thus the EMHI program insured less than 50,000 additional people (36). Hawaii is the state closest to a single payer system, with 65 percent of the population insured under the Blue Shield plan; this concentration of insurance coverage might have the effect of reducing administrative waste and thereby helping to control costs. Hawaii's geographic isolation prevents businesses faced with employer-mandated health insurance from moving to nonmandate states (25). Health insurance rates in Hawaii are unusually low because the state has low rates of cancer, heart disease, and emphysema (37). At the time of implementation of PHCA, health insurance premiums were about 20 percent less than for the nation as a whole (36). Rates of hospitalization in Hawaii are low, and the percentage of total personal health care spending going to hospitals is one of the lowest in the nation (38). Yet one aspect of the Hawaii story is typical of mainland United States: its health costs are expected to inflate 17.4 percent per year in the 1990s (39).

In order to get around the ERISA prohibition on mandating employers to provide health insurance, a sleight of hand has been invented with the enigmatic name "pay or play." The pay or play version of EMHI gives employers two options: purchase health insurance for all employees (play) or pay a tax to finance health insurance for the uninsured. It is unlikely that employers consider the former option as "playing"; they clearly see both choices as "paying." Pay or play lies at the heart of the 1988 Massachusetts universal health insurance legislation, scheduled to be implemented by 1992. As a companion to its pay or play program, Massachusetts enacted a variety of programs to cover the unemployed uninsured.

The Massachusetts EMHI program is in trouble even before it has been fully implemented. The program passed in part because Governor Dukakis offered the state's hospitals substantial increases in their rates in order to gain support for the program, and in part because the state's economy was in a boom period, which appeared to make funding for the program—both by business and the government—less of an obstacle (20). But with the economy headed rapidly downward, and with the hospital payoff overly expensive, the state's new governor campaigned on a promise to repeal the program. At the very least, implementation of the EMHI provision of the Massachusetts law will be delayed and the benefit package watered down to reduce the costs of the program to employers (40).

Only Oregon has followed Massachusetts' example, with its mandatory pay or play program to begin in 1994 only if the voluntary tax credit plan for employers to purchase employee health insurance fails. Oregon would also apply the rationing scheme proposed for its Medicaid expansion to the pay or play program (24).

New York State has come up with an imaginative and controversial species of EMHI: UNYcare. In essence a pay or play proposal with tax subsidies for the unemployed uninsured to purchase insurance, UNYcare adds a cost-control mechanism that would reimburse health providers through a state-run "single payer," which would then turn around and collect from the insurers (41). Organized medicine, which generally favors EMHI plans, is not surprisingly antagonistic to UNYcare, which would exert strong control over physician reimbursement (42).

While other states may pass EMHI programs, their enactment will not be easy. Vehement business opposition, especially from small employers, is widespread. The HIAA opposes EMHI, perhaps because such a program might force private insurers into a perilous small-group market they have been increasingly trying to forsake. However, the insurance industry is not uniformly against EMHI; in California, for example, the large commercial insurers Aetna and Travelers oppose EMHI, while Blue Cross, Blue Shield, Kaiser, and Pacific Mutual Life favor such a program (43). The hospital industry and organized medicine support EMHI. If EMHI passes in more states, it will likely be accompanied by stripped-down insurance benefits to make the program less costly (44).

A CRITIQUE OF INSURANCE REFORM

Listed above are some of the multitudinous ways in which states are attacking the problem of uninsurance. But the totality of this listing makes up more than the sum of its parts. Taken together, these reforms represent a particular, and a unified, philosophy of health care financing. The approach combines (*a*) private group health insurance for people who are employed, including tax subsidies to assist small employers/lower-income workers to purchase such private insurance, and reductions in coverage to make premiums more affordable, while increasing out-of-pocket costs; with (*b*) tax-financed care for the poor/elderly and partial tax subsidies for the purchase of individual private health insurance for the unemployed near-poor.

This philosophy of health insurance reform is sometimes labeled a public-private partnership. But in truth, such a description misses the mark, for under this system the private insurers are allowed to benefit from the premiums of the healthier portions of the population while being spared the high costs of the sicker portions (who tend to be concentrated among the elderly and the poor), which costs are passed to the public sector (i.e., the taxpayer) to finance. For people who are generally healthy but too poor to buy the products of the private insurance industry, the taxpayer is again called upon to assist by subsidizing the purchase of premiums. Rather than a partnership, the public-private relation more closely resembles the dynamic between imperial nations and their colonies: the mother country is subsidized by the colony through the extraction of the colony's mineral or agricultural wealth, while leaving to the colony the most difficult and expensive social problems with a diminished financial base for confronting those problems. Analogously, the government (the colony) subsidizes the private insurance industry (the imperial nation) by making insurance premiums more affordable to employers and employees through the federal income tax deduction for employer-sponsored health insurance, which in 1987 deprived the federal government of $36 billion in tax revenues (45), and through other public subsidies such as those discussed above. In this way, the most costly patients are left to the public sector, which has less resources to pay for them on two accounts: (*a*) because the subsidies have reduced its revenues and (*b*) because businesses and individuals, already paying for their own health care through premiums, understandably resist paying more for other people's health care through taxes.

Having thus characterized the general philosophy of U.S. health insurance and insurance reform, let us consider the difficulties created by such an approach. We will examine three major areas: (*a*) the underwriting principle, (*b*) the linking of health insurance to employment, and (*c*) the search for funds in a deficit-laden society; the need to combine universal access with cost control.

The Underwriting Principle

Insurance is a social mechanism by which people reduce the adverse financial consequences of an unpredictable event by paying small amounts in advance to an institution, which in turn pays all or part of the costs incurred by the event. Insurance allows people to pool their risks in order to prevent catastrophic financial losses. The kinds of institutions that can provide insurance include employers, unions, member-run cooperatives, governments, or private companies that sell insurance as a commercial venture.

Many nations provide health insurance through governments (e.g., Canada) or through employee-oriented private funds set up for particular occupational groups or workplaces (e.g., Germany). In contrast, the United States relies most heavily on companies that sell insurance as a business venture. Historically, U.S. health insurance was developed by health providers through Blue Cross and Blue Shield to increase the purchasing power of potential patients, but due to fierce competition from commercial insurers, almost the entire health insurance apparatus, including the Blues, has now become commercial in essence (46).

The dominance of a business-oriented health insurance industry calls attention to the distinction between "insurance" and "underwriting." While insurance has a social purpose, underwriting is a business technique whose purpose is to maximize market competitiveness and minimize financial loss in the conduct of the insurance business. According to the underwriting principle, people are separated into homogeneous groups and classified according to their risk of creating a claim against the insurer. Underwriters evaluate, select (or reject), and classify risks, and establish the amount of coverage to be offered to each acceptable risk and the amount of premium to be charged (47). In the health field, young healthy people might make up one risk classification, healthy middle-aged people another classification, and elderly and disabled people yet another. Each risk (person or group) is categorized as a preferred risk, standard risk, or substandard risk based on the probability of loss, that is, on the likelihood that the person will contract an illness that generates a claim against the insurer. Members of the young group might be considered preferred risks, the middle-age groups standard risks, and the elderly/disabled group substandard risks. People with a high likelihood of loss—for example HIV-positive individuals, disabled people, or the elderly—may be classified as unacceptable risks and become uninsurable. One central feature of the underwriting principle is "experience rating"—the setting of premium rates based on the past experience of different groups in generating losses. Experience rating is generally practiced by both the commercial health insurers and the Blues.

The purpose of underwriting is to maximize profits or net income for insurance companies. In his book published by the National Underwriter Company, an organization representing the insurance industry, Robert Holtom emphasizes the aspect of profit: "The principal responsibility of an underwriter is to make a profit for his company" (47). Under the underwriting principle, each classification is supposed to generate profit; thus the premiums of the young healthy group are not used to help subsidize the greater expense of the elderly or disabled groups. The underwriting principle enables the company to attract a large number of customers because the bulk of the customers, who are at low risk, are not charged to cover those customers at higher risk. The underwriting principle implies that people who need more health care must pay more than people who need less health care. Moreover, people requiring more health care tend to have lower incomes than healthy people; they are less capable of paying insurance premiums. Thus the very people who need health care the most are placed in serious jeopardy by the underwriting principle: if they can obtain insurance at all, they must pay more than other people even though their income is likely to be less (46). According to health policy consultant Lynn Etheredge: "fragmenting and skimming the risk pool—that is, by not insuring people with high health expenses . . . is a relatively easy, widely practiced, and profitable strategy" (6).

Private insurance for the middle and upper classes coexisting with public insurance for the poor guarantees inequality; where dual private and public sector programs exist "the private sector pulls resources away from the public sector such that the latter suffers the pain of rationing while the former enjoys the fruits of plenty" (46). Meanwhile, the insurance industry is off the hook for its high risks while the industry benefits from insuring those less likely to need benefits.

All of the reforms that endeavor to increase private insurance coverage of poor or uninsurable people leave in place the underwriting principle. Tax subsidies to assist in the purchase of private insurance do not change the insurance industry practice of charging higher premiums to individuals and groups with higher use of health services. High-risk pools do allow uninsurable people to become insurable, but at very high premiums—so high that less than 3 percent of uninsurables can afford the policies (26). HIAA proposals to reduce the spread of premiums among different groups and to limit rate increases only serve to cushion the underwriting principle in order to prevent this sacred principle from being eliminated. And while some EMHI plans (Hawaii's, for example) place small businesses in one community-rated pool, this is by no means a necessary component of such plans, which can generally be expected to charge groups with more health care usage more than groups with less.

The Linking of Health Insurance to Employment

There is no logical reason why health insurance should be tied to employment. Historically, 1940s' wartime restrictions on wage increases led unions to pressure for fringe benefits including health insurance, and postwar bargaining produced an explosion of employer-sponsored health coverage (48). But there is no reason why this historical accident linking employment and health insurance should continue, and there are many arguments why it should not.

1. The U.S. economy faces growing foreign competition, with steady declines in the world market share of numerous products (49). While health costs are by no means the major reason for this trend, they do contribute. Because employers in other nations tend to pay less for the health care of their employees, they have an advantage over U.S. employers. This U.S. disadvantage grows each year as the costs of employer-sponsored health insurance inflate at rapid rates. The separation of health insurance from employment has the potential to relieve this situation.

2. Employer-based health insurance prolongs the current fragmentation of the insurance market whereby healthy groups have lower premiums than less healthy groups, and small groups are vulnerable to the illness of one employee. This fracturing of the insurance market fails to spread the risk of large medical expenditures, thereby diluting the positive social contribution of health insurance (50).

3. Millions of workers change jobs each year; many move to jobs that do not offer health insurance immediately upon employment, others switch to jobs that do not offer health insurance at all. Those with preexisting illnesses may face major restrictions in new health insurance policies. Although employees can continue their previous health insurance under the COBRA law, they must pay for the insurance themselves, which may cost between $1,500 and $8,000 per year for a single individual (51). Thus an employer-based system fails to provide an essential feature of health insurance: portability (50).

4. Workers who are laid off or who must leave jobs for health reasons lose their employer-sponsored insurance at critical times in their lives; often they are unable to afford continuing insurance through the COBRA program.

5. Employment-related health insurance has major impacts on families. Dependents of workers may lose their insurance if the insured person dies or becomes disabled or unemployed. Divorces and other changes in family patterns may leave children and spouses uninsured if coverage is based on one family member's job (52).

6. Since many families have two working members, and since many group insurance policies cover dependents, the requirement that the employers of both working members insure their employees could mean that many people have two health insurance policies, a wasteful and confusing arrangement.

7. Many workers are part-time or seasonal; these workers are generally ineligible for job-related health insurance, even under EMHI plans.

8. The linkage of health insurance and employment may have a major effect on employability or conditions of employment. Employers, especially small businesses, tend to look for good health as a condition of employment, knowing that poor health will lead to higher health insurance costs. Chronically ill persons can be identified by health claims data prior to hiring (6). In addition, EMHI programs, which generally require insurance for employees who work more than half-time, may lead employers to hire more part-time workers in order to evade the requirement to purchase health insurance.

9. An employee whose child had asthma or an executive with ulcers must think twice about changing jobs; for small businesses, insurers may reject them or give

them high rates and exclusions. Sixty percent of large employers are self-insured and may require preemployment health checks to see whether potential employees are poor insurance risks; such employers could refuse to hire people with health problems, postpone coverage for 6 or 12 months, or delay paying for a chronic condition (53).

10. Job-linked health insurance, especially in the small business sector, is fraught with administrative and access nightmares. People without health insurance tend to be low paid and employed in small, high-turnover industries. Most employees without health insurance spend an average of 5 to 11 months on a given job. Between jobs they spend an average of $7^1/_2$ weeks unemployed. Under an EMHI plan, an employer would take a month or two to record the entitlement of a new employee to receive health insurance, and the employee would take a month or two to make arrangements with a health maintenance organization or other health care provider. By this time, the average newly insured employee would soon be leaving the job to be temporarily unemployed. The average unemployment period of $7^1/_2$ weeks would not be enough to establish Medicaid eligibility; nor would the former employee have sufficient funds to pay for the employer-sponsored plan to be converted to an individual private plan. After the average $7^1/_2$ weeks of unemployment, this typical high turnover worker would get another job, and would be subjected to the same bureaucratic treadmill all over again (54). EMHI is likely to sprout a "jungle of regulation," including checks on the compliance of businesses, regulation of insurance practices, oversight of the benefits offered, and monitoring the number of hours employees work, etc. (55).

11. Small-group insurance has high marketing and administrative costs (12). It makes no administrative sense to base insurance on groups of 10 or 20 people.

12. The mandating of health insurance benefits will substantially increase labor costs for small business, inevitably resulting in unemployment and business failures (see below). Not only will labor costs increase at the onset of EMHI, but health insurance costs are an open-ended employer expense, not subject to the control of the employer or the government that mandated the cost in the first place (50).

The Search for Funds in a Deficit-laden Society:
The Need to Combine Universal Access with Cost Control

From the 1960s to the 1980s, the federal budget deficit increased from about $5 billion to over $200 billion per year (49). States have been forced to finance a number of programs previously funded by the federal government. By 1990, state governments all over the nation were facing severe budgetary difficulties. In spite of an anti-tax political environment, federal and state taxes have increased substantially, particularly the social security tax, which hits hardest on lower- and middle-income families (56, 57). Voters have made it clear that they will not tolerate further large tax increases. In the health arena, insurance premiums have soared, and growing proportions of these premiums are being shifted from employers to employees, who also face rises in deductible payments (58). Thus neither employers nor individuals covered by private health insurance are in any mood to pay additional taxes for the care of other people (the uninsured). In this sense, the public-private relationship, which divides the population into the more-fortunate privately insured and the less-fortunate publicly insured (or uninsured), gives many people the impression that they are paying once for themselves and another time for someone else.

In such a climate, how might the insurance reforms discussed above fare in the political process? Dr. Gail Wilensky, director of the Health Care Financing Administration, has stated that neither the federal government nor the states have sufficient funds for Medicaid expansion (59). One might assume that such a statement would also apply to widespread public subsidies for the uninsured poor to purchase private health insurance. Only through an Oregon-type rationing program might Medicaid be extended, and even that program is in difficulty because it requires additional state funds. More state high-risk insurance pools could be established in this politico-economic atmosphere, but as noted above, they assist only a handful of people. Reinsurance pools for small-group insurance, as proposed by the HIAA, do not require significant government funds, but could require a government bailout guarantee, which politicians may not wish to offer during a climate in which bailing out financial institutions has turned into a giant albatross. The other insurance-sponsored reform, stripping down benefit packages, will almost certainly take place, but it is doubtful that this reform will reduce insurance premiums sufficiently to tempt many small businesses to cover uninsured employees (33). Pared-down health insurance offerings will simply create the negative effect of shifting more and more out-of-pocket costs to individuals and families, hurting lower-income people the most.

With the unlikelihood of significant new government spending, and the equal improbability of small business voluntarily providing health insurance even with incentives, EMHI appears as the only insurance reform that could work: it costs the government very little because it forces rather than cajoles small business to provide health insurance. But who pays for EMHI?

According to health economist Uwe Reinhardt (60):

> Mandated benefits are taxes in the sense that they coerce fiscal transfers among private entities in the economy. They are, alas, pseudo-taxes that permit the politician to exercise the government's power to tax without having to book these taxes as government revenue and, thus, without assuming accountability for the disposition of the implied tax revenue. It is the dream of any legislator who would use the government's power to achieve preferred social goals and, at the same time, appear as a fiscal conservative.

Reinhardt points out that the pseudo-tax of EMHI weighs heavily on small business owners and predicts that the tax will lead to substitution of labor saving capital equipment for the now more expensive labor: "At least some of the working uninsured may thus be transformed by mandated benefits into unemployed uninsured" (60). Blue Cross/Blue Shield executive Donald Cohodes concurs: "Mandating health insurance coverage for employees of small employers may be tantamount to mandating employer bankruptcy" (61). According to the business-oriented Partnership on Health Care and Employment, a national EMHI plan could cause the loss of between 5.4 and 8.6 million jobs. The pro-EMHI Senate Human Resources Committee predicts a maximum job loss of 120,000 (62). The truth may lie somewhere in between. An estimate made for EMHI in Massachusetts alone, calculating that mandating health benefits will increase the cost of labor for small employers by 12 percent, predicts the elimination of between 60,000 and 180,000 jobs in that state (63). Small business has provided the bulk of new jobs created during the most recent economic expansion. Is it wise to saddle this entrepreneurial element in our society with a new tax plus the heavy bureaucratic burden of insuring people and demonstrating compliance to the government? (60)

Not only the least profitable employers, but also the lowest-paid employees, will bear the brunt of EMHI financing. Business owners will attempt to shift the mandated pseudo-tax by passing it on to employees through lower wages. Employers will likely freeze wages for several years following the imposition of the pseudo-tax, creating in effect a delayed wage cut. Since workers in small companies generally receive minimum-level wages, such a pay cut defines EMHI as a highly regressive tax, generating funds for the extension of health insurance from the lower rungs of the economic ladder (44).

Adding to its numerous problems, EMHI has little or no cost-control component. Traditionally, when more people obtain insurance, costs go up. Massachusetts provides an example. As mentioned above, the Massachusetts plan allowed hospitals to receive substantially higher reimbursements for their already insured patients, with the result that hospital costs have inflated. By mid-1990, over 90 percent of the costs of the plan had been spent in paying hospitals higher rates for already insured patients rather than in extending access to the uninsured. Between 1989 and 1992, the plan will likely spend only 30 percent of what was originally expected in improving access to care for the uninsured (38, 64, 65). The program is in deep trouble because it costs too much for the Massachusetts budget to fund (40). The moral of the Massachusetts story is: if one does not solve the cost and access crises together, one will solve neither.

New York's UNYcare proposal purports to link cost control to increased access, and its single payer feature is likely to keep health inflation under better control (41). But inflation control is only one aspect of the health cost problem; the other piece of the puzzle is the necessity in a deficit-laden society to fund the start-up costs of extending health insurance by reducing existing unnecessary health system expenditures. UNYcare fails to do this, and its start-up costs are likely to be so great that the program can never get off the ground (66, 67).

To summarize, the health cost crisis has two aspects: the problem of inflation and the problem of financing the extension of health insurance to everyone. In an era of austerity, it is impossible to find additional billions to finance insurance coverage for the uninsured. The extension of health insurance must be financed by savings elsewhere in the system, and a strong inflation-control mechanism must be put into place to prevent future costs from careening out of control.

How can we locate funds currently spent on health care that could be shifted to pay for insurance for the uninsured? Three ideas come to mind. First is to ration care overtly, as Oregon has proposed, thereby achieving savings by denying coverage for costly medical interventions judged to be of low cost-effectiveness. The problem with the Oregon approach is that it applies a somewhat crude methodology to a highly complex reality in which each illness of each patient requires the weighing of multiple factors. In essence this approach removes an area of clinical decision-making from the physician and grants it to a legislative body whose primary concern is budgetary (68, 69).

A second way to free up existing health care expenditures is to reduce the volume of unnecessary and inappropriate health care currently delivered. This alternative is attractive since perhaps 30 percent of health costs are spent on unnecessary care (70). The difficulty comes in determining which interventions are unnecessary and in eliminating those and those alone. Thus far, our system of utilization review has failed to distinguish accurately between needed and unneeded care (71), and as fast as outcomes research provides an assessment for a particular intervention, new interventions mushroom to replace those that may be judged to be inappropriate. An additional problem is to capture such savings and utilize them to insure the uninsured.

The third and the only practical method of using existing expenditures as start-up money for universal insurance requires a fundamental change in health financing— the creation of a single health insurance mechanism that allows multibillion dollar reductions in health care's administrative costs and that permits these dollars to be captured immediately and utilized for the start-up costs of insuring the uninsured.

THE SOCIAL INSURANCE ALTERNATIVE

We have now discussed three basic problems left unsolved by current health insurance reform proposals: the inequities of the underwriting principle, the difficulties inherent in the linkage of employment and health insurance, and the need to find start-up costs for universal health insurance while slowing the rate of health cost inflation.

What is the alternative to the public-private philosophy that characterizes insurance reform proposals? The alternative must be a program that (a) transcends the underwriting principle by which people least able to pay for health insurance are required to pay the most, (b) delinks health insurance from employment, and (c) finances health insurance for the uninsured from unneeded existing health funds and has a strong anti-inflation component.

The plan that fulfills these three requirements is a social insurance program that provides one insurance mechanism for everyone in society. Competitive commercial insurance, with its imperative to maximize earnings through underwriting, would be replaced by a new dynamic. Let us remember that in a competitive market, insurers who wish to survive must employ the underwriting principle that, by its very nature, discriminates against those who need care the most and cuts the poor—who cannot afford the premiums—out of the insurance process. The solutions of government subsidies and/or mandates are beset by these same difficulties, only in somewhat muted from.

The best way to guarantee fairness in health insurance is to place the entire population in one risk pool and to spread the risk from the disabled and elderly to the healthy and young. Such a system would benefit all Americans because most people (the exception being those who die rapidly from an acute illness or accident) or their close families will someday need the insurance protection they are paying for. The underwriting principle—that the sick and elderly pay more than the healthy and young—would be eliminated. Rather, all people would contribute, through some form of prepayment, to the health costs of the entire society. Young and healthy people would pay now so that they will be protected when they become sick later. In this way, social insurance does not carve up the population such that people paying their own premiums are also forced to pay taxes for someone else's health care; each person pays for him/herself and for everyone else as well (46).

Social insurance also delinks employment and health insurance. Whether the funds to support a social insurance program come from employer-employee payroll taxes or premiums, from general revenues, or from income-adjusted individual health premiums, everyone contributes. The poor, chronically unemployed population also pays; that income group is heavily taxed through the sales tax, property tax, and business taxes that are passed onto consumers through higher prices (72).

A social insurance program has the best chance to solve the cost and access crises simultaneously. To control the inevitable inflationary impact of extended access, a single public insurer can set fees and fix budgetary limits. Multiple private insurers, none of which handle a sufficient proportion of health care dollars, are far less able to contain costs (73). Even with the cost-control mechanisms of the 1980s—transferring risk to providers through diagnosis-related groups and health maintenance organizations and micromanagement of care through utilization review—costs in the 1980s rose as fast as in previous decades. With multiple payers, providers can always shift costs from one sector of the health system to another, and overall systemic cost control remains a mirage (74). The experience of other nations shows that a single insurer can succeed in controlling costs (75, 76).

Equally important, the creation of a single social insurance mechanism has the potential to capture tens of billions in unneeded health expenses to finance the extension of insurance to the uninsured. Public insurance has proved to have far lower administrative costs than private insurance, in part because the expensive processes of marketing and underwriting are eliminated (77). Administrative savings can be utilized to finance the start-up costs of a social health insurance system, covering all Americans without adding an extra dollar to total health care expenditures (78).

REFERENCES

1. Mathiessen, C. Unsurance. *Hippocrates* 3(6): 36–46, 1989.
2. Tuller, D., and Olszewski, L. New crisis in health insurance. *San Francisco Chronicle*, February 26, 1990.
3. Lurie, N., et al. Termination from Medi-Cal—Does it affect health? *N. Engl. J. Med.* 311: 480–484, 1984.
4. Annas, G. J. Your money or your life: 'Dumping' uninsured patients from hospital emergency wards. *Am. J. Public Health* 76: 74–77, 1986.
5. Levit, K. R., Freeland, M. S., and Waldo, D. R. National health care spending trends: 1988. *Health Aff.* 9(2): 171–184, 1990.
6. Etheredge, L. Ethics and the new insurance market. *Inquiry* 23: 308–315, 1986.
7. Voelker, R. Cost jump seen for employer-sponsored health care plans. *Am. Med. News*, February 24, 1989.
8. Business healthcare costs soared 20% in '89 to all-time high. *Physicians Financial News*, March 15, 1990.
9. Freudenheim, M. Health care a growing burden. *New York Times*, January 29, 1991.
10. Service Employees International Union. *Employer-Paid Health Insurance is Disappearing.* 1989.
11. Nexon, D. Senator Kennedy's proposal to guarantee basic health benefits for all Americans. *Henry Ford Hosp. Med. J.* 38: 110–113, 1990.
12. U.S. House of Representatives. Subcommittee on Antitrust, Impact of Deregulation, and Privatization of the Committee on Small Business. *State Efforts to Increase the Availability and Affordability of Health Insurance.* August 10, 1990.

13. Freudenheim, M. Insurers seek help for uninsured. *New York Times*, January 11, 1990.
14. Freudenheim, M. Health insurers, to reduce losses, blacklist dozens of occupations. *New York Times*, February 5, 1990.
15. Davis, J. E. National initiatives for care of the medically needy. *JAMA* 259: 3171–3173, 1988.
16. Delmar, D. State laws aimed at uninsured seen benefiting doctors. *Physicians Financial News*, November 30, 1990.
17. Freudenheim, M. Broader Medicaid: Who would pay? *New York Times*, June 27, 1990.
18. The Crisis in Health Insurance [special issue]. *Consumer Reports*, September 1990.
19. Ruggles, P. The poverty line—Too low for the 90's. *New York Times*, April 26, 1990.
20. Griss, B. Strategies for adapting health insurance systems to persons with disabilities. *Access to Health Care* 1: 1–91, 1988/89.
21. Lund, D. S. Oregon panel issues updated Medicaid priority treatment list. *Am. Med. News*, March 11, 1991.
22. Oregon Health Services Commission. *Prioritized Health Services List of February 20, 1991*. State of Oregon, 1991.
23. Reid, W. F. The basic health plan of the State of Washington. *Henry Ford Hosp. Med. J.* 38: 123–124, 1990.
24. Brown, E. R., and Dallek, G. State approaches to financing health care for the poor. *Annu. Rev. Public Health* 11: 377–400, 1990.
25. American Hospital Association. *Promoting Health Insurance in the Workplace: State and Local Initiatives to Increase Private Coverage*. Chicago, 1988.
26. Friedman, E. Are risk pools being oversold as a solution? *Hospitals*, November 5, 1988.
27. Cohodes, D. R. America: The home of the free, the land of the uninsured. *Inquiry* 23: 227–235, 1986.
28. Kloman, H. Finding a cure. Image problem just a symptom, not cause of industry ills. *Business Insurance*, July 10, 1989.
29. Welles, C., and Farrell, C. Insurers under siege. *Business Week*, August 21, 1989.
30. Freudenheim, M. Reshaping laws on insurance. *New York Times*, March 5, 1991.
31. Stevens, S. Insurance groups offer strategies to broaden coverage. *Physicians Financial News*, March 30, 1990.
32. Delmar, D. Insurers offer bare-bones coverage in effort to reduce uninsured ranks. *Physicians Financial News*, January 15, 1991.
33. Families USA Foundation. *Barebones Coverage: Health Insurance That Doesn't Insure*. Washington, D. C., 1991.
34. Wilensky, G. R. Filling the gaps in health insurance: Impact on competition. *Health Aff.* 7(3): 133–149, 1988.
35. Friedman, E. Hawaii adopts universal coverage. *Med. World News*, March 12, 1990.
36. Wong, T. *Health Access for the Uninsured*. Department of Health and Social Services, Madison, Wis., 1989.
37. U.S. House of Representatives. Subcommittee on Health, Committee on Ways and Means. *Health Insurance Options: Expanding Coverage under Medicare and Other Public Health Insurance Programs*. June 12, 1990.
38. Sager, A., and Socolar, D. *Advancing toward Health Care for All: Lessons for Illinois from Other States*. Boston University School of Public Health, Boston, Mass., 1990.
39. Families USA Foundation. *To the Rescue: Toward Solving America's Health Cost Crisis*. Washington, 1990.
40. Stevens, S. Debate continues on implementation of Mass. Universal Healthcare Law. *Physicians Financial News*, February 15, 1991.
41. Beauchamp, D. E., and Rouse, R. L. Universal New York Health Care. *N. Engl. J. Med.* 323: 640–644, 1990.

42. Page, L. New York's Universal Health Plan faces uphill battle with physicians. *Am. Med. News*, September 22/29, 1989.
43. Freudenheim, M. California plans divide insurers. *New York Times*, May 8, 1990.
44. Jones, S. B. Many will be hurt: Another view of mandating proposals. *Bull. N.Y. Acad. Med.* 66(1): 95–100, 1990.
45. Havighurst, C. C. The questionable cost-containment record of commercial health insurers. In *Health Care in America*, edited by H. E. Frech. Pacific Research Institute for Public Policy, San Francisco, 1988.
46. Bodenheimer, T. Should we abolish the private health insurance industry? *Int. J. Health Serv.* 20: 199–220, 1990.
47. Holtom, R. B. *Underwriting Principles and Practices*. The National Underwriter Company, Cincinnati, 1981.
48. Staples, C. L. The politics of employment-based insurance in the United States. *Int. J. Health Serv.* 19: 415–431, 1989.
49. Bodenheimer, T., and Gould, R. *Rollback! Right-Wing Power in U.S. Foreign Policy*. South End Press, Boston, 1989.
50. Swartz, K. Why requiring employers to provide health insurance is a bad idea. *J. Health Polit. Policy Law* 15: 779–792, 1990.
51. Sloane, L. But what about your insurance? *New York Times*, April 7, 1990.
52. U.S. Bipartisan Commission on Comprehensive Health Care? (The Pepper Commission). *A Call for Action*. U.S. Government Printing Office, Washington, D.C., 1990.
53. Freudenheim, M. Medical insurance and job mobility. *New York Times*, February 13, 1990.
54. Schorr, A. L. Job turnover—A problem with employer-based health care. *N. Engl. J. Med.* 323: 543–545, 1990.
55. Kinzer, D. M. The real-world issues in access to care. *Henry Ford Hosp. Med. J.* 38(2/3): 154–157, 1990.
56. Kies, K. J. The outlook for federal tax and budget policy in the 1990s. *Tax Notes*, January 22, 1990.
57. Pechman, J. A. *Federal Tax Policy*. The Brookings Institution, Washington, D.C., 1978.
58. Gabel, J., et al. Employer-sponsored health insurance. *Health Aff.* 9(3): 161–175, 1990.
59. HCFA head Wilensky rejects Medicaid expansions. *Nation's Health*, October 1990.
60. Reinhardt, U. E. Are mandated benefits the answer? *Health Management Q.* 10(1): 10–14, 1988.
61. Cohodes, D. R. Taking a wrong turn: Mandated employment-based health insurance. *Inquiry* 24(Spring): 5–6, 1987.
62. Bill no boon to business: Study. *Physicians Financial News*, November 30, 1990.
63. Passell, P. Paying for wider health insurance. *New York Times*, May 18, 1988.
64. Sager, A. *The Massachusetts Universal Health Insurance Law: The Record, the Future, and Lessons for Health Care Access and Cost Control*. Boston University School of Public Health, Boston, 1990.
65. Sager, A., Socolar, D., and Hiam, P. A bigger piece of the pie? *Industry* 55(January): 12–32, 1990.
66. Wessler, J. *Summary and Evaluation of the UNYCARE Proposal*. Community Service Society, New York, 1989.
67. Himmelstein, D. U., and Woolhandler, S. Patchwork not Perestroika: The promise and problems of UNYcare. *Health PAC Bull.*, Summer 1990, pp. 22–26.
58. Somerville, J. Economist notes flaws in Oregon plan. *Am. Med. News*, March 11, 1991.
59. Grumbach, K., and Bodenheimer, T. Reins or fences: A physician's view of cost containment. *Health Aff.* 9(4): 120–126, 1990.
70. Brook, R. H., and Lohr, K. N. Will we need to ration effective health care? *Issues Sci. Technol.* 3(Fall): 68–77, 1986.

71. Dippe, S. E., et al. A peer review of a peer review organization. *West. J. Med.* 151: 93–96, 1989.

72. Bodenheimer, T. Health care in the United States: Who pays? *Int. J. Health Serv.* 3: 427–434, 1973.

73. Evans, R. G. Finding the levers, finding the courage: Lessons from cost containment in North America. *J. Health Polit. Policy Law* 11: 585–615, 1986.

74. Berki, S. E. Approaches to financing care for the uninsured. *Henry Ford Hosp. Med. J.* 38(2/3): 119–122, 1990.

75. Pfaff, M. Differences in health care spending across countries: Statistical evidence. *J. Health Polit. Policy Law* 15: 1–24, 1990.

76. Bodenheimer, T. Payment mechanisms under a national health program. *Med. Care Rev.* 46(Spring): 3–43, 1989.

77. Himmelstein, D. U., and Woolhandler, S. Cost without benefit. *N. Engl. J. Med.* 314: 441–445, 1986.

78. Grumbach, K., et al. Liberal benefits, conservative spending: The Physicians for a National Health Program Proposal. *JAMA* 265: 2549–2554, 1991.

CHAPTER 8

An Analysis of the American Medical Association's Recommendations for Change in the Medical Care Sector of the United States

Vicente Navarro

The medical care sector of the United States is in a profound crisis—a much-used term, but one that I think is appropriate to the sorry state of our medical care nonsystem. Even President Nixon, not allied with the protesting forces in the United States, used the term "crisis" in 1974 to describe our house of medicine. And *Fortune* magazine, not generally accused of radicalism, described the U.S. medical care system as "chaotic" and "inefficient." In spite of spending almost 12 percent of our gross national product (GNP) on health care, 17.5 percent of the U.S. population under 65 years of age is still without any form of health benefits, a total of 36.8 million people (1). But the problem is much larger than the uninsured. It includes also the underinsured. Twenty-eight percent of Americans were without coverage for at least one month during a 24-month period (1986–1988) (2). And an astounding 57 percent of Americans have indicated that they have problems in paying for medical care (3). It is not surprising that the majority of Americans are just plain fed up with the funding and organization of U.S. medicine. Though they might like their own doctors, Americans profoundly dislike the medical system. No less than 89 percent of the U.S. population wants to see fundamental changes in the health care sector, with the majority of Americans, Democrats and Republicans, favoring a national health program supported by tax funds (4). Sixty-six percent prefer the Canadian model over the U.S. system. In no other industrialized nation are the people more dissatisfied with the system of funding and organizing health services (5).

This popular mood has the American Medical Association scared. In the last 12 months alone, the AMA has published three major documents calling for reform, mounting a major public relations campaign trying to show that the AMA indeed cares (6–8). A full-page advertisement in the *New York Times* (9) proclaimed that "The AMA

Originally published in the International Journal of Health Services, 21(4): 685–696, 1991.

Cares" and that a new consensus "is being established among groups as diverse as the AFL-CIO, the AMA, and the Pepper Commission, a bipartisan congressional commission on health care around ways to solve the medical care crisis."

Hoping that the AMA, at least once, would be the keeper of the public conscience, I read these documents with great interest. I was disappointed. The AMA continues to live in an Alice in Wonderland world, punctiliously avoiding any contamination with reality. Where else could one read in this day and age that "approximately 213 million or over 87 percent of all Americans today have private or public health insurance coverage providing them access to the highest quality of health care services of any country in the world" (7, p. 3)? The majority of Americans, with first-hand experience of this "highest quality" medical care system, would not agree with this self-congratulatory statement. They want the medical care system to change profoundly, as soon and as rapidly as possible.

Similar self-congratulatory celebration appears when the AMA defines its role in the U.S. medical care scene, describing itself as "leading the changes to assure that the patients in this country received the best care in the world" (6, p. 1). The sad reality is that since the early 1920s the AMA has fought tooth and nail against the acceptance and implementation of the principle stated in the United Nations Human Rights Charter that access to health care in time of need should be a human right. Until very recently, a constant in the AMA Presidential Addresses has been the claim that health care in this country should be not a right but a privilege. The clarity of this position was, no doubt, a reflection of the intensity with which that principle was held. Yet progress has been made. This longstanding position that health care is a privilege is not repeated in any of the three recent AMA documents. By accepting the principle of universality of benefits, the AMA seems to have finally admitted that access to health care is indeed a human right, and one that should be realized in the last industrialized country on earth (along with South Africa) where such a right does not yet exist. But it would be wrong to conclude that the AMA has, at last, decided to put the needs of patients first. The AMA's primary concern is to preempt the establishment of a much feared alternative—a national health program, as called for by the Physicians for a National Health Program (PNHP), that would assure publicly funded, comprehensive coverage of our entire population (10). Actually, on detailed reading, the AMA recommendations bode ill for all patients and potential patients, i.e., all citizens of the United States. But before discussing the AMA's recommendations, we should analyze the problems in the medical care sector as perceived by the AMA.

THE PROBLEMS OF THE MEDICAL CARE SYSTEM AS PERCEIVED BY THE AMA AND THE AMA'S RECOMMENDATIONS ON HOW TO SOLVE THEM

The AMA defines two major problems in the medical sector: the growth of expenditures, related in part to the escalation of costs, and the uninsured, which the AMA claims to be only 11 percent of the population.

Regarding the first of these problems, the AMA considers the root of the problem to be that the average American is overly insured and contributes too little to the costs incurred in providing health care. In its report, *Challenge for America: Background for the AMA Proposal to Improve Access to Affordable, Quality Health Care*, the AMA zeroes in on the problem (6, p. 5):

> What is unique about the health care sector? The answer must be that the method by which services are financed is unique. In what other industry do so many consume so much without directly paying for it themselves at the point of purchase? In what other industry does one find "third-party payors" paying the bills for those who consume the bulk of its output of goods and services? The way we structure the financing of health care is responsible for the peculiar problems of the industry.

Later on in the same report, the same point is made again (6, p. 5):

> In the United States, most consumers pay for health care indirectly through prepayment or "insurance"—implicit exchanges of wages for fringe benefits, and taxes—realizing only a fraction of the cost directly out-of-pocket at the point of purchase. When the financial burdens fall on employers whose principal objective is to survive in competitive markets, and on government which must allocate limited tax dollars to numerous competing social programs, the problem of "cost" comes to the forefront.

And again (6, p. 6):

> Much of medical care is not paid for by the patient at the point of purchase. Consequently, patients do not perceive the full cost of consuming the health care resources they demand and, therefore, may consume more than they would if they were spending their own money or paying the full price of medical care out of their own pockets. . . . In this way, payors hope to reduce or eliminate unnecessary, inappropriate, or otherwise wasteful consumption of health care by patients. They hope to assure themselves that they are not purchasing services that do not produce value for the money spent or are not needed by the patient.

In summary, according to the AMA, the key problem in the United States is that the buyer (the patient) and the payer (the insurer) are not the same person. The solution: *the patient should also be the payer*. From this analysis, the AMA derives the following recommendations:

1. Higher copayments, deductibles, and other forms of patient participation that would "encourage cost-consciousness decisions by patients." Insurance is accepted, but with a limited role (7, recommendation 9, p. 9).
2. A baseline of benefits for its proposed employer mandated coverage that is very meager. It excludes not only long-term care but also psychiatric care, large parts of hospital care, prescriptions, rehabilitation, and preventive services, among others (7, recommendation 2, pp. 5–6).
3. "State laws requiring insurance to include special benefits that add unnecessarily to the costs of health insurance should be repealed" (6, p. 9; 7, recommendation 14, p. 11).
4. Taxing the employer-employee contributions by placing "a limit on the amount of the employer-provided health insurance that is tax exempted by the employee" (7, recommendation 8, p. 9). The AMA, like Enthoven (whose plan the AMA sympathetically reviews), favors taxing a large part of the employer-employee contributions.

All these AMA recommendations will lead to a further limitation of health benefits coverage for the majority of our population, creating enormous pain, suffering, sickness and death among Americans. Currently available data show that lack of coverage or limited coverage discourages people who need care. Mortality rates are higher among the uninsured or underinsured than among the comprehensively insured (11).

But the proposed changes do not end here. Not satisfied with recommending further reduction of coverage, the AMA calls for higher prices in the medical care sector. Indeed, it considers that the U.S. population, besides being overly insured, consumes too much in the medical care market, stimulated by the "low prices" existing in this market. As one of the AMA reports puts it, "increases in the volume of services are explained by choice of consumers given the low prices they face and their income" (6, p. 11). According to the AMA, Americans now have a growing amount of disposable income, which they use to buy "more cars, televisions, radios . . . and medical care." The solution therefore is to raise the prices in the medical market and "encourage cost-consciousness decisions by patients" (6, p. 9; 7, recommendation 14, p. 11). The AMA dismisses the evidence of medical inflation (a 12.7 percent annual growth rate from 1980 to 1983, and 8.9 percent from 1983 to 1987) by referring (without documentation) to labor costs as the cause of this inflation (6, p. 10). In summary, according to the AMA, the problem of growth in expenditures is due to the enormous growth in demand, which results from low-priced, overly insured services. The growth in cost of these services is due primarily to labor costs.

To resolve the second problem, the uninsured, the AMA supports the alternative (employer mandated coverage) also recommended by the Kennedy–Waxman proposal, the Pepper Commission, the National Leadership Commission, and the Enthoven (the informal spokesperson for the insurance industry) proposal. The health care benefits proposed by the AMA are far more limited than those suggested by the other proponents, however. Indeed, the AMA's recommendation is to "repeal or override state-mandated benefit laws" to make those benefits less comprehensive; "individuals should be free to choose, at their own cost, additional coverages if desired but such coverages should not be mandated as part of all policies" (7, recommendation 14, p. 11). For the uninsured who cannot get insurance, the states should create state-level risk pools to provide coverage for the medically uninsurable and those for whom individual health insurance policies are too expensive and group coverage is not available. These state risk pools would be funded by either state tax funds or insurance contributions or by employers' contributions and/or tax-deductible premiums by the insured (7, recommendation 3).

Two other major changes are also recommended by the AMA. One amounts to the dismantling of Medicare, replacing it with "an actuarially sound prefunded program with a trust fund funded with employer-employee contributions." When the employee retires, the trust fund would provide the senior citizen with a voucher for purchase in the private sector of a health insurance policy meeting federal standards (7, recommendation 4). The other recommendation is to establish a nationwide standard of Medicaid benefits, with the expansion of health benefits (one of the few occasions on which the AMA has called for such an expansion) and levels of providers' reimbursement comparable to Medicare fees (7, recommendation 1, p. 1).

It is an intriguing step that the AMA, which has for so many years opposed the expansion of health benefits coverage to the whole population, has now come out in support of an expansion of these benefits for the Medicaid population, and has also recommended that the uninsured be given some limited form of coverage by mandating employers to provide such coverage and by stimulating states to provide state risk pools for the nonworking uninsured and the uninsurable. The primary motivation for this change, however, is to weaken the pressure for the establishment of a publicly funded national health program. Indeed, all the AMA reports are full of warnings against government interventions, which the AMA equates with rationing. In a rather manipulative way, for example, the AMA tries to discredit the PNHP proposal for a Canadian-style program by grouping this proposal with the highly unpopular Oregon reforms in which Medicaid patients are denied life-saving interventions by the state. As one report puts it, the AMA is against "centralized control of financing and resource allocation, such as the systems of the various provinces of Canada or the Oregon plan for rationing" (6, p. 14). In case the point was not clear enough, the AMA informed all physicians in the country in a 1989 fund-raising letter that "We need your support now. We need your help to continue reaching millions of Americans. We must tell them the facts about the hidden dangers in a Canadian-type of health care system—before it is too late."

THE PROBLEMS WITH THE AMA'S ANALYSIS
AND RECOMMENDATIONS

The AMA diagnosis of what ails our medical care system is wrong. There is plenty of evidence to show it. The problem is not that the American people are overinsured. This type of "victim blaming" ignores the enormous amount of empirical data accumulated during the last two decades. The problem is precisely the opposite: Americans are underinsured. In no other country do citizens pay as much in direct costs for medical care as in the United States. No less than 25 percent of all health care expenditures are still out-of-pocket expenditures, a percentage that increased rather than declined during the 1980s. In 1988, for example, direct out-of-pocket expenses increased 10 percent over the previous year (12). Even the elderly, whose benefits are supposed to be covered by Medicare, pay for about half of all their medical care (13, 14). In Sweden direct payments represent 8.4 percent, in Canada 19 percent, in the United Kingdom 5.8 percent, in Germany 12 percent, and in Italy 8 percent of all health expenditures (15). Given this easily available information, it is quite remarkable for the AMA to state that in the United States, "the patient pays *only token proportions*" in her or his utilization of health services (6, p. 6).

By international standards, patients in the United States pay too much, not too little. And they do not get what citizens of all other countries (except South Africa) get in return, i.e., comprehensive health benefits coverage. A comparison of the pattern of expenditures in the United States with those in other countries shows that while all other countries have public funding of health services, the United States has private funding. The U.S. government spends only 4 percent of the GNP in public funds for health services, compared with 6.2 percent in Canada, 5.3 percent in the United Kingdom, and 6.4 percent in Germany (16). Most of our health service funding is private, administered by over 1500 insurance companies, and even our public funds are administered through the insurance companies, acting as intermediaries. This private dominance in the funding and administration of health services is at the root of the problem of high costs and limited coverage. Fifteen hundred insurance companies with enormous overheads contract with half a million providers for the delivery of services paid by service, and now by diagnosis. The amount of bureaucracy and paper shuffling is overwhelming— consuming almost 25 percent of all health care expenses (17). If the United States were to adopt a Canadian-style health care system, we would save $115 billion per year, more than enough to cover the uninsured and provide comprehensive health benefits coverage to all of our population. The U.S. health care system is the most inefficient in the industrialized world. This inefficiency, with its enormous human costs, is attributable to the private system of funding and administration in which insurance companies and the medical, hospital, and drug industries reap enormous benefits, and patients get what's left. And physicians are increasingly harassed by paper shufflers whose only concern is the "bottom line." This administrative nightmare is getting worse. Administrative costs in the United States increased 37 percent between 1983 and 1987, whereas in Canada they declined. Nowhere does the AMA touch on these issues. It remains embarrassingly silent. Rather, the AMA puts the blame on patients who are supposedly overinsured and paying too little, and on a labor force that consumes too many funds in salaries and wages.

The reality is that patients pay too much, the medical services are too expensive, and the insurance companies' and the medical and hospital profits and overhead are far too large. An international comparison of medical fees shows that the ratio of U.S. fees to the average fee in Germany, France, and Japan (in comparable dollars) is 5.6 per first consultation, 6.2 per cholecystectomy, 6.7 per hysterectomy, 7.6 per appendectomy, 2.2 per colon radiology, 9.8 per bronchostomy, and 3.1 per electrocardiogram (18, p. 233). And labor costs are lower in the United States than in Germany and France and similar to those in Japan. Total labor compensation in France was 107 percent that in the United States, while in West Germany it was 112 percent and in Japan 89 percent (18, p. 265). In all these countries, where labor is better compensated, where people pay less in direct costs in health care, and where most health service funding is public, the overall health care expenditures are much lower and the level of health benefits is far more comprehensive than in the United States. And most importantly, the level of people's satisfaction with health care is much higher.

Actually we have already faced the reality of what the AMA is advocating. We have seen the future as the AMA would have it, and it does not work. During the 1980s, Americans paid higher direct expenditures for medical care, medical fees grew substantially, the level of insurance coverage declined, and employees' contributions increased. All these events are in line with the AMA's recommendations. The overall rate of growth of health care expenditures, however, increased rather than declined; this rate was much higher in the 1980s than in the 1970s. At the current rate of growth of health expenditures, 15 percent of the GNP will be spent in health care by the year 2000. This growth will add another $300 billion to national health spending in the year 2000, an amount equivalent to the current defense budget. The same growth occurred with costs and prices and medical inflation. The policy of further privatization of funding, as advocated by the AMA, has failed to reduce costs and provide coverage. In fact, it has done precisely the opposite. The dramatic increase in the numbers of uninsured and underinsured has also meant the enormous growth of rationing in America. No other industrialized nation has more rationing than the United States. The failure of millions of people to get care or to receive full care because they cannot pay for it is a form of rationing.

The implementation of the Canadian National Health Program meant a reduction of rationing of health services in Canada. When universal medical insurance was introduced in Quebec, there was a shift of access from higher to lower income persons. Also, the recent introduction of universal health programs in Canada and Australia was accompanied by an expansion rather than a reduction in utilization of services, allowing utilization by those whose care had been rationed before the implementation of the programs.

THE WEAKNESS OF EMPLOYER MANDATED COVERAGE

In the 1970s, employer-provided health benefits coverage was presented by President Nixon as an alternative to the national health program advocated by the labor movement and by the Democratic Party. Nixon did not want to make the provision of employment-based benefits mandatory, but rather voluntary through tax incentives. It was Alan Enthoven who first proposed making such provision mandatory. Enthoven was an assistant to Secretary McNamara (and as such was one of the main architects of the Vietnam fiasco) and later worked on health areas, advising the Thatcher government on the National Health Service (NHS) reforms. He was described by the *Economist* as one of the main architects of those reforms. Enthoven soon added to his Vietnam fiasco the Thatcher fiasco, being responsible for her departure from government due in part to the enormous unpopularity of the health service reforms. Only the hated poll tax was more unpopular than the Thatcher NHS reforms. Those of us who do not support Bush's health policies and would like to see him go should be encouraged by the recent news that the Bush administration has asked for Enthoven's advice.

The elements of Enthoven's proposals include, besides taxing the employer-employee contributions, encouraging employers to choose the most economic alternative for the health benefits coverage of their employees. Both Enthoven and the AMA favor this policy as a way of broadening choice. The issue, however, is choice for whom? In their proposals it is the employer, not the employee, who chooses, and the majority of adults are employees, not employers. The employer mandated coverage advocated by Enthoven and the AMA will reduce people's choice most significantly. According to polls, most Americans do not consider employers' interests to be the same as employees' interests. Quite to the contrary: frequently they are in conflict (19). And the choice of health care benefits is no exception. In a recent survey by the Employee Benefits Research Institute and the Gallup Organization, employees were asked to rate the health care chosen by their employers; 56 percent of the respondents characterized it as only "fair" or "poor." One of the major labor conflicts in the United States is over health benefits. In 1989, for example, 78 percent of all labor disputes involved health benefits. The employers, left unrestrained, will choose the cheapest alternatives, with higher copayments and deductibles for the employees. The experience of the 1980s confirms this. In a time and climate favorable to employers' interests, we witnessed increases in employees' copayments and deductibles and reductions in benefits. The employees' contributions increased from 20 to 30 percent on employment-based health insurance premiums, while the employers' contributions declined from 79 to 69 percent from 1980 to 1987 (18, p. 241). This is the trend favored by the AMA, but not by the majority of Americans.

There is yet another major problem in the employer mandated coverage, never mentioned by the AMA, the Kennedy–Waxman proposal, the Pepper Commission, and the National Leadership Commission: it is enormously regressive. The chairman of Bethlehem Steel Corporation, Mr. Wilson, makes $1.5 million a year. He pays the same health insurance premium, $3120, for himself and his family as the unskilled steel worker in the steel mills of Baltimore, who makes 40 times less money than Mr. Wilson. The funding of health services through employees is the most regressive funding of any of our social services, even worse than the highly regressive form of funding public schools (which has been declared unconstitutional by some courts). Actually, the much hated poll tax in Great Britain, which contributed to Thatcher's downfall, was a similar type of tax: everyone paid the same amount of money for municipal services, regardless of their income. The Labour Party successfully mobilized people's discontent against Thatcher, forcing her resignation. In the United States, not only the AMA but the Democratic Party leadership and the AFL-CIO are the leading proponents of broadening a similar form of poll tax. Quite a difference from the Labour Party of Great Britain. And most of the legislators whom the AMA names as introducing their proposals are Democrats. Is there any wonder that people are confused about the direction of the Democratic party, once the party of the New Deal?

THE DISMANTLING OF MEDICARE AND THE EXPANSION OF MEDICAID: MEANNESS WITH A CHARITABLE SOUL

We have in the United States two major federal health care programs. Medicare, an entitlement program administered by the Social Security Administration, is highly popular. Social Security and Medicare are among the most popular federal programs. The other program, Medicaid, is a rather unpopular program that is means tested. The AMA wants to expand and strengthen Medicaid and practically dismantle Medicare. Rather than the Medicare administration administering the health care benefits, the AMA would have the private insurance companies do so. The elderly would be provided with vouchers to buy their insurance. The administration of these benefits would be shifted from Social Security, the most popular insurance program, to private insurance, one of the least popular businesses in the country. According to polls, insurance agents are, with car salesmen, the most unpopular people in the United States. [Social Security is always rated in polls as very popular. Insurance salesmen, however, are the lowest rated people for honesty and ethical standards. Only 13 percent of Americans think positively of them (20, 21).]

The AMA's recommendations on Medicare are accompanied by a series of assertions that have already proven wrong. One is a repetition of the scare tactic of frightening the elderly by indicating that there is a problem in funding Medicare, i.e., too many elders and too few workers to support Medicare (7, p. 7). This assertion ignores several facts.

1. The demographic transition in our society—a growth in numbers of elderly and a decline in numbers of young people—favors rather than hinders the expansion of tax-funded public services. Although the elderly consume more health services than the young, the young consume far more tax-based services such as education, transport, and recreation. The social policy secretariat of the Organization for Economic Cooperation and Development recently estimated that savings due to the demographic transition

amount to 0.8 percent of GNP per year, more than enough to expand health benefits coverage for the elderly (22).

2. The employment transition, with higher participation of women in the labor force, has created more workers per dependent than in the last two decades, a situation that is likely to improve further in the United States. As yet, only 66 percent of American women participate in paid labor, compared with 80 percent in Sweden, 72 percent in Norway, and 78 percent in Denmark. This expansion of the labor force is likely to continue (23).

3. People of all generations are against reducing health care benefits to the elderly; the young and the elderly are equally opposed to reducing public funds for the elderly.

The Medicare Trust Fund is in trouble not because there are few workers but because of the enormous administrative waste and economic inefficiency in the health sector. If, for example, the program were to be directly administered through Medicare rather than through private insurance intermediaries, it would save $2 billion per year. The high-minded voices of those such as the AMA and the Oregon legislature that call for austerity always envision the sacrifices being made by others rather than themselves. If Oregon, for example, were to have a single payer to administer health care benefits directly rather than through insurance companies, thus controlling the overall levels of profits, overheads, and high payments, that state would save $10 billion, enough to provide comprehensive coverage to all Oregonians (24).

There is no reason to frighten our elderly. A single-payer system, publicly funded and administered by a public agency, can, as the Canadian system has proven, provide comprehensive coverage of all their needs at a lower cost to them than today.

FINAL THOUGHTS

This critique of the AMA's recommendations would not be complete without some further observations. First, let us look at how the recommendations were reported on the day they were released. Remember that there is not much popular support for the AMA's recommendations. The majority of Americans do not favor the type of reforms that the AMA is advocating. Actually, not even the majority of physicians in this country support such proposals (25). Both the majority of physicians and the over-whelming majority of Americans favor the establishment of a national health insurance, with most Americans preferring a Canadian-style national health program.

Nevertheless, the release of the AMA report was presented very sympathetically by all major television networks—ABC, CBS and NBC—as a major development. Only CBS mentioned in passing that another group of physicians—PNHP—criticized the AMA. ABC did not even mention the PNHP, although the PNHP proposal is far more popular and has more support than the AMA's.

A similar type of bias appears in our political institutions. In a recent hearing on the need for health reforms sponsored by the Ways and Means Committee of the House, the AMA, Enthoven, and all other proponents of employer mandated insurance took up most of the time in the two days of testimony. The PNHP proposal was allowed to be presented last and least. There is a constant bias in the media and political institutions against proposals that enjoy popular support but conflict with powerful interest groups. Why do the representatives of these interest groups have so much more influence in the media and the Congress than do the voice and opinion of the majority of Americans? An analysis of who pays for the media and for the members of Congress can answer this question. The insurance companies and professional trade associations, including the AMA, paid $7.7 million to the health-related congressional committees in the 1988 elections (26). This is the reason for people's enormous skepticism about our Congress. Seventy percent of Americans feel that the Congress does not respond to their needs, but rather to moneyed interests (27). This is why the struggle for major health care reforms requires enormous political reforms. To make our medical system more responsive to people's needs, we must make our political system more accountable. The elimination of moneyed influence in the political forums is a prerequisite for true health reforms in this country.

A second observation is that any mobilization for health care reforms along the lines favored by the people and supported by the PNHP will require a large coalition in which the labor movement must play an important role. Indeed, the labor movement has historically played a most positive role in advocating a national health program for the United States. Today, however, the labor movement is not providing that leadership. Quite to the contrary. We have witnessed the sorry spectacle of the leader of the AFL-CIO, Kirkland, in speaking to an AMA audience, referring to the AMA as "labor's allies." This is the same AMA that is in favor of taxing employer-employee benefits, reducing employee benefits, increasing copayments and deductibles, and calling for an expansion of the most regressive system of funding that any social service has ever had. The AFL-CIO leadership is confused and ill-advised. It should recover its historical role and ally itself with the PNHP rather than with the AMA and the insurance companies. The majority of the American people—working people—want to see profound changes. The AMA does not.

Finally, a call to U.S. physicians. The growing commercialization of medicine goes against the basis of the medical profession. Medicine should not be a business; medicine should be a call to serve. Legitimate concerns about working conditions, standards of living, and popular appreciation can and should be taken care of. Canadian physicians' level of income is comparable to that of U.S. physicians, and their working conditions— free of administrative hassles—are better than those faced by U.S. physicians. Physicians in the United States are not satisfied with their working conditions. We cannot ignore the malaise that now exists among medical doctors, particularly among the young. While the number of applicants to medical schools has been increasing in Canada, it has been declining in the United States. Physicians are advising their children not to study medicine. The root of the problem is the commodification of medicine, and the AMA's recommendations will worsen that situation. Consensus on this state of affairs is most likely what motivated the second largest medical association in the country, the American College of Physicians, to call for a national health program similar to that supported by the PNHP. We in the PNHP applaud our colleagues in their commitment to eliminate commercialization in medicine. The elimination of the business mentality in medicine will be best for our patients and best for thoughtful and dedicated physicians.

REFERENCES

1. Congressional Research Service. Number and Percent of the Population under Age 65 without Health Insurance. *Green Book, 1990*, p. 293. [Based on data from Current Population Surveys.]

2. Nelson, C., and Short, K. *Health Insurance Coverage 1986–88*. Current Population Reports, Household Economic Studies, Series P-70, No. 17. U.S. Government Printing Office, Washington, D.C., 1990.
3. Aday, L. A., Flemming, G. U., and Andersen, R. *Access to Medical Care in the U.S.: Who Has It, Who Doesn't*, p. 56. Pluribus Press, Chicago, 1984.
4. 74% of Democrats and 53% of Republicans favor a national health insurance financed by tax money. The voters' views. *New York Times*, November 4, 1990, p. 34.
5. Blendon, R., et al. Satisfaction with health systems in ten nations. *Health Aff.* Summer 1990, p. 185.
6. American Medical Association. *Challenge for America: Background for the AMA Proposal to Improve Access to Affordable, Quality Care*. Chicago, March 1990.
7. American Medical Association. *The AMA Proposal to Improve Access to Affordable, Quality Health Care*. Chicago, February, 1990.
8. Todd, J. S., et al. Health access America—Strengthening the U.S. health care system. *JAMA* 265: 2503, 1991.
9. *New York Times*, May 14, 1991, p. A5.
10. Himmelstein, D., and Woolhandler, S. A national health program for the U.S. *N. Engl. J. Med.* January 12, 1989, p. 102.
11. Lurie, N., et al. Termination of Medi-Cal benefits: A follow up study one year later. *N. Engl. J. Med.* 314: 1266–1268, 1986.
12. Levit, K. R., Treeland, M. S., and Waldo, D. R. National health care spending trends: 1988. *Health Aff.* Summer 1990, pp. 174–175.
13. Rice, T., and Gakel, J. Protecting the elderly against high health care costs. *Health Aff.* Winter 1986, p. 722.
14. Arendell, T., and Estes, C. L. Older women in the post-Reagan era. *Int. J. Health Serv.* 21(1): 59–73, 1991.
15. Maxwell, R. T. *Health and Wealth: An International Study of Health Care Spending*, Table 4-1, p. 61. Lexington Books, Lexington, Mass., 1981.
16. Organization for Economic Cooperation and Development. *Financing and Delivering Health Care: A Comparative Analysis of OECD Countries*, p. 11. OECD Papers. Paris, 1987.
17. Woolhandler, S., and Himmelstein, D. U. The deteriorating administrative efficiency of the U.S. health care system. *N. Engl. J. Med.* 324: 1253, 1991.
18. Mishel, L., and Frankel, D. M. *The State of Working America 1990–1991 Edition*. Economic Policy Institute, Sharp Inc., 1991.
19. Gallup polls on employees' attitudes. *Gallup Report*, 1988 and 1989.
20. Gallup Organization, February 8–11, 1990.
21. *The American Enterprise*, January/February 1991, p. 83.
22. OECD Report of Social Expenditures. Paris, 1989.
23. OECD in Figures. Paris, June/July 1990.
24. Hollander, I., et al. *Administrative Waste in the US Health Care System in 1991: The Costs to the Nation, the States, and the District of Columbia*. Public Citizens Research Group, Washington, D.C., 1991.
25. Colombotos, J., and Kishner, C. *Physicians and Social Change*. Oxford University Press, New York, 1986.
26. Brightbill, T. Political action committees: How much influence will $7.7 million buy? *Int. J. Health Serv.* 21: 285–290, 1991.
27. People's opinion on government. *New York Times*, November 4, 1990, p. A5.

CHAPTER 9

Political Action Committees: How Much Influence Will $7.7 Million Buy?

Tim Brightbill

Campaign contributions from the health care industry to congressional candidates reached a whopping $7.7 million during the 1990 election campaign. Drug companies, hospital chains, and trade associations sharply increased donations through their political action committees (PACs).

The American Medical Association (AMA) was the leading health care PAC (Table 1). The Chicago-based AMA, which controls the second-largest PAC in the United States, contributed $2.1 million to congressional candidates through September and reported total receipts of $4.7 million from its 65,000 members. The American Dental Association ranked second among health care PACs, with contributions of $762,022. The American Hospital Association (AHA) trailed, with donations of $451,689.

Key lawmakers on committees that handle health legislation received nearly $1.5 million from health-related companies and associations, according to an analysis of Federal Election Commission (FEC) data. Sixteen senators and representatives on these committees received more than $30,000 each from health care PAC contributors (Table 2).

This year (1990), the FEC reported a total of 783 trade, membership, and health care PACs, which together made $28 million in contributions to candidates. About 370 labor PACs gave $21 million in this period, while other corporate PACs kicked in nearly $40 million. Congressional candidates are increasingly dependent on these funds to fuel their campaigns. Overall, PAC contributions make up 38 percent of all political war chests in the House and 23 percent in the Senate, up from 31 percent and 16 percent in 1984. PAC gifts are targeted to committee members who can influence the outcome of legislation, observers said. The money "isn't about giving to the best candidate," said

Reprinted in the International Journal of Health Services, 21(2): 285–290, 1991. Originally published in *HealthWeek* 4(21): 1, November 5, 1990. Copyright © 1990 by CMP Publications, Inc., 600 Community Drive, Manhasset, NY 11030. Reprinted from *HealthWeek* with permission.

Table 1

Congressional PAC contributions[a]

	1989–90	1987–88
Professional and Trade Associations		
American Medical Association	$2,127,348	$2,133,033
American Dental Association	762,022	845,000
American Hospital Association	451,689	384,527
American Academy of Ophthalmology	412,566*	n/a
American Optometric Association	292,750	n/a
American Nurses Association	281,240	n/a
American Health Care Association	180,505	162,828
Federation of American Health Systems	165,550	112,967**
Health Insurance Association of America	151,275	141,325
National Association of Retail Druggists	141,310**	n/a
National Association of Private Psychiatric Hospitals	59,300	40,683
American Pharmaceutical Association	46,650	26,800
Pharmaceutical Manufacturers Association	42,483	36,038
Health Industry Manufacturers Association	40,435	39,106
National Association of Medical Equipment Suppliers	27,600	19,300
National Association of Home Care	21,650	19,600
Group Health Association of America	10,150	11,750
Health Industry Distributors Association	4,400	n/a
Group Practice Association of America	2,500	3,100
Osteopathic Hospital Association	1,250*	7,250
Total	5,222,673	3,983,307
Drug Industry		
Abbott Laboratories	$158,700	$151,227**
Eli Lilly and Co.	150,990	112,490
Pfizer Inc.	125,750	156,095
SmithKline Beecham Corp.[b]	120,600	89,150
Schering-Plough Corp.	115,525	71,383
Ciba-Geigy Corp.	106,425	62,480
Upjohn Co.	97,200	39,700
Merck & Co. Inc.	78,450	33,150
Bristol-Myers Squibb Co.[c]	59,600	64,475
American Home Products Corp.	57,875	28,250
Hoffmann-La Roche Inc.	57,500	43,500
Warner-Lambert Co.	49,450**	102,100
E. R. Squibb and Sons Inc.[c]	43,450	62,933
Genentech Inc.	31,600	20,600
Syntex Corp.	18,725**	1,000**
Burroughs Wellcome Co.	5,400	10,250**
Marion Merrell Dow Inc.[d]	400*	2,600**
Total	1,277,640	1,051,383

Table 1

(Continued)

	1989–90	1987–88
Insurance Industry		
Metropolitan Life Insurance Co.	$276,471	$244,600
Aetna Life and Casualty Co.	198,629	196,334
Prudential Insurance Company of America	188,970	169,862
Blue Cross and Blue Shield Association	160,068	117,767
Cigna Corp.	152,625	178,987
Mutual of Omaha Insurance Co.	29,295	36,425
Total	1,006,058	943,975
Medical Suppliers		
Johnson & Johnson	$60,425	$60,150
Baxter International	46,700	60,100
Cooper Industries Inc.	32,300*	19,659**
Medtronic Inc.	10,500	6,925
Puritan Bennett Corp.	750	400
Total	150,675	147,234
Hospital Chains		
Humana Inc.	$39,500	$18,200
Hospital Corporation of America	12,800	4,300
HealthTrust	10,500	n/a
American Medical International	10,000	4,350
Total	72,800	26,850
Grand total	$7,729,846	$6,152,749

[a]Source: Federal Election Commission and *HealthWeek* research. *Denotes filings through June; **denotes filings through August; n/a, not available.
[b]1990 data reflect merger of SmithKline Beckman and Beecham.
[c]1990 data reflect merger of Bristol-Myers and Squibb; Squibb's PAC terminated on June 25, 1990.
[d]1990 data reflect merger of Marion Laboratories and Merrell Dow.

Karen Hobert of Congress Watch, a Washington-based affiliate of the group Public Citizen. "It's about gaining access and influence."

HealthWeek analyzed the PACs of 32 health care companies and 20 trade associations, and their donations to four health-related committees in Congress. The survey included FEC reports from January 1, 1989, to September 30, 1990.

The AMA's total PAC spending held steady in 1990. The medical association gave ten senators and 51 House members the maximum $10,000 contribution. "More and more medical decisions are being made on a political basis," an AMA spokesman said. "That's why it's important for our members to gain a platform for their point of view." The AMA also subsidizes key congressional races by providing "independent support," such as association-sponsored polls, television commercials, and other activities. Although 1990 data were not available, the AMA said it spent $1.2 million independently for six races in 1988.

Table 2

Members of Congress on health care committees who received
the most health industry donations[a]

	Total	Drug industry	Profess. assoc.	Medical suppliers	Hospital chains	Insurance industry
U.S. Senate						
John D. Rockefeller IV, D-W.Va.	$127,000	$16,000	$70,650	$3,000	$10,000	$27,350
Dan Coats, R-Ind.	98,020	39,000	29,070	12,250	0	17,700
Max Baucus, D-Mont.	89,250	19,500	54,500	2,000	1,000	12,250
Bill Bradley, D-N.J.	55,800	28,000	20,300	6,000	0	1,500
Paul Simon, D-Ill.	50,000	1,000	43,500	0	2,000	3,500
Tom Harkin, D-Iowa	48,800	11,500	28,000	1,000	0	8,300
Strom Thurmond, R-S.C.	41,200	12,200	23,000	1,000	0	5,000
Thad Cochran, R-Miss.	34,650	10,000	15,650	1,500	0	7,500
David Pryor, D-Ark.	28,500	5,000	17,500	1,000	1,000	4,000
Thomas Daschle, D-S.D.	23,250	4,000	13,250	0	0	6,000
U.S. House						
Thomas Tauke, R-Iowa[b]	$75,750	$11,000	$42,750	$7,500	$0	$14,500
Henry Waxman, D-Calif.	50,500	5,000	45,000	0	500	0
Fortney "Pete" Stark, D-Calif.	37,500	1,500	27,500	2,000	2,000	4,500
Jim Moody, D-Wis.	37,050	5,150	22,400	1,000	0	8,500
Edward Madigan, R-Ill.	36,490	14,000	19,240	2,250	0	1,000
Terry Bruce, D-Ill.	32,781	8,700	19,881	1,700	0	500
Benjamin Cardin, D-Md.	32,550	5,100	21,150	0	0	6,300
Thomas Bliley, R-Va.	30,750	10,850	16,300	1,500	0	2,100
Nancy Johnson, R-Conn.	29,343	4,950	18,693	1,250	0	4,450
John Dingell, D-Mich.	29,000	7,000	13,000	1,000	0	8,000
J. Roy Rowland, D-Ga.	29,000	8,300	17,700	350	1,000	1,650

[a]Source: Federal Election Commission and *HealthWeek* research.
[b]Running for U.S. Senate against Tom Harkin.

The AHA boosted its congressional spending 17 percent for this year's election. The group's contributions ran more than two to one in favor of Democrats. For example, the AHA gave favorite son, Senator Paul Simon (Democrat, Illinois) a total of $12,000, including $2,000 to help retire debts from his failed 1988 presidential campaign. The association did not contribute to Representative Lynn Martin (Republican, Illinois), who is running against Simon.

Although their political battles are fought mainly at the state level, ophthalmologists and optometrists raised their spending on congressional elections to more than $700,000 this year. Both the American Academy of Ophthalmology and the American Optometric Association now rank among the nation's top 50 trade and health PACs, according to the FEC. "The receptiveness among our members has been tremendous," said Mike Roberts, director of the ophthalmologists' PAC, founded in 1986. "These are pocketbook issues for them."

PAC Money Flows Freely. Overall, professional and trade associations accounted for about two-thirds of all health care PAC money (Table 3). Several groups beefed up their PAC contributions in 1990, including the Federation of American Health Systems, up 47 percent; the National Association of Medical Equipment Suppliers, up 43 percent; and the American Pharmaceutical Association, up 74 percent.

While most associations give more money to Democratic candidates than to Republicans, some were particularly bold. The American Nurses Association (ANA) gave more than 90 percent of its PAC funds to Democrats. Defying convention, which favors incumbents, the ANA gave 40 percent of its Senate PAC money to challengers. "We've taken a lot of risks on non-incumbents," said Pat Ford-Roegner, ANA political director. "We're anxious to see new and different people in government. We're running against the old guard in a lot of ways." The ANA, which has a 97 percent female membership, closely watched incumbents' votes this year on such issues as child care and parental leave, Ford-Roegner said.

On the other hand, contributions from medical supply companies and pharmaceutical firms heavily favored Republicans and incumbents. Seventeen drug companies increased PAC contributions to $1.3 million in 1990, up 22 percent from the 1988 congressional elections. Four drug firms, including Merck & Co. Inc. and Upjohn Co., doubled their PAC spending in 1990.

Although their total donations were relatively small, three leading hospital chains also doubled their PAC contributions in 1990. Humana Inc. in Louisville, Kentucky, led all hospital PACs with $39,500 in donations to congressional races.

Of the $1.5 million donated to members of influential health committees in Congress, the money was nearly evenly split between House and Senate candidates. Senator John D. Rockefeller IV (Democrat, West Virginia) led all individuals: he received $127,000 from the 52 health PACs surveyed. As of June, Rockefeller had raised more than $1.1 million in PAC contributions, while his opponent had raised only $14,000 and taken no PAC money.

Putting Money on a Sure Thing. Two senators who accepted large PAC donations are running unopposed: Thad Cochran (Republican, Mississippi) and David Pryor (Democrat, Arkansas). Both have campaign war chests in excess of $1.1 million, according to FEC data. The two senators accepted $34,650 and $28,500, respectively, from health care PACs. Representative Thomas Tauke (Republican, Iowa) was the leading House recipient of health care PAC money. Tauke's contributions totaled

Table 3

Contributions of 52 leading health care PACs[a]

	Amount	Percent of total
Professional and trade associations	$5,200,000	67%
Drug companies	$1,300,000	17%
Insurance companies	$1,000,000	13%
Other	$223,000	3%

[a]Source: *HealthWeek* research.

$75,750, much of which came as part of his Senate campaign against Democrat Tom Harkin. Harkin raised $48,800 from health care PACs. The Republican challenger in Nebraska's Senate race, former Representative Hal Daub, has turned a new leaf, refusing all PAC contributions during his campaign against Democrat James Exon; in 1988, Daub took more than $40,000 from health care PACs.

Pharmaceutical firms and trade associations wrote most of their checks to members of the House Energy and Commerce Committee's health subcommittee, where the average Democrat received $370 and the average Republican $435 from each of the 52 PACs surveyed. Committee chairman Henry Waxman (Democrat, California) received $50,500 in contributions from health-related PACs, second among all House members, while Representative Edward Madigan (Republican, Illinois) the ranking Republican member, received $36,490.

Abstaining from PAC Largesse. The only exception on the committee was Mike Synar (Democrat, Oklahoma), who refuses PAC contributors. Other House members who refuse PAC money include Bill Archer (Republican, Texas) and Willis Gradison (Republican, Ohio), who both serve on the Ways and Means Committee. Representative Fortney "Pete" Stark (Democrat, California), who chairs the Ways and Means health subcommittee, accepts PAC funds but received no contributions from the AMA or the AHA.

HealthWeek's study did not include donations from state PACs or private individuals. However, ten state medical and dental associations rank among the top 50 trade and health care PACs nationwide. The biggest: the Texas Medical Association's PAC, which spent $1.3 million on state and federal elections through June 30.

SECTION III

Why There Is Not
a National Health Program

CHAPTER 10

Why Some Countries Have
National Health Insurance,
Others Have National Health Services,
and the United States Has Neither

Vicente Navarro

PREVALENT THEORETICAL POSITIONS TO ANSWER THESE QUESTIONS

The "Popular Choice" Theories

In the last two decades many articles have appeared in the health care literature that try to answer the question: why are there variations in the funding and organization of health services among countries with similar political traditions. A similar and related question addressed by many of these authors is why the United States is the only major western industrialized nation that does not have a comprehensive and universal government health program. These articles have enriched a growing body of literature that aims at understanding international differences and similarities in national health policies.

The answers provided by these studies to those two questions are varied. But it is possible to group them into three major types of explanations. One type, which I would call the "popular choice" explanation, traces the international diversity in the funding and organization of health services among countries to the sets of values held by their populations and the choices they make. This popular *choice* takes place through the realization of consumer choices in the marketplace and through the expression of the citizens' mandate in the political institutions of each country. Examples of these positions are many, but I will just mention a few.

Reprinted in the International Journal of Health Services, 19(3): 383–404, 1989. Originally published in Social Science and Medicine, Vol. 28, No. 9, © 1989, Pergamon Press PLC. Reprinted with permission.

Victor Fuchs, a major figure in the field of health economics in the United States, in his recent book on the U.S. health economy begins by referring to people's choice as the determinant of what does and does not happen in the U.S. health sector. Within this interpretation of our realities he concludes that the United States does not have a national health program (a universal and comprehensive government health care program) because the American people do not want it (1). Eli Ginzberg, another well-known economist in the United States, also begins his major book on health policy in the United States by indicating that "in the U.S. it is still the citizen who, through their voice in the marketplace and in the legislature, ultimately determines how their money will be allocated." Thus, he also concludes that we do not have a national health program in the United States because people do not want it (2). The well-known Canadian economist, Robert G. Evans, concludes a comparison between Canadian and U.S. health policies by attributing the absence of a comprehensive and universal U.S. health program and the current cuts in U.S. federal health expenditures to the popular mandate expressed through the U.S. economic and political institutions (3). Rashi Fein, an ex-supporter of a Federal Health Program for the United States, also explains that there is no national health program in the United States because it "runs counter to long-standing American attitudes towards government and deep-seated beliefs—made more explicit in the late 1970s—in the efficacy of market solutions to social problems" (4, p. 16). These are just a few examples of a hegemonic position prevalent in health policy circles in the United States. The types of funding and organization of health services in western democracies (including the United States) are understood as an expression of the wills and wants of their populations.

While the authors belonging to this "public choice" school have contributed considerably to the descriptive information about the health services in the United States and other countries, the analytical value of their explanations is limited, when not faulty. These explanations ignore the extensive body of empirical information that questions their three major assumptions: (a) that popular values (and the choices they determine) generate economic and political power (rather than the other way round), (b) that our political institutions are truly representative of popular wishes, and (c) that public policies respond to popular mandates. To claim that popular values explain reality is to beg the question of how those values appear and are reproduced in these societies. In other words, the first assumption these authors make is that there is a free market of ideas, all competing on an equal footing for the hearts and minds of our population. Focusing just on the United States, we can see that many studies of social, economic, and political power have shown the invalidity of this assumption. Social groups and classes (e.g., corporate America) have an enormous influence in the value-generating systems (the media and academia, among others) of our society. (For an analysis of how power is reproduced in major U.S. media, see references 5 and 6; for an analysis of how ideology is reproduced in the U.S. school system, see reference 7; for an analysis of the reproduction of power in U.S. academia, see reference 8.) Values are produced and reproduced within highly controlled political environments by the promotion of values favorable to the powerful and by repression of values perceived to be threatening to them. This interpretation is not equivalent, however, to holding the position that dominant influence is tantamount to full control. Indeed, people are exposed to whole sets of highly controlled messages coming from different powerful establishments, but these messages are contrasted with people's own daily practices, also bearers of messages. Thus, popular opinion and desires are a synthesis of a whole set of messages within a highly skewed matrix, in which some value systems are structurally more dominant than others because of their articulation with the political and economic establishments in our society.

In brief, some values and positions have far more chance than others to be exposed to and influence our citizenry. But dominance does not mean full control. People do not repeat mimetically what the major economic and political establishments want them to believe. This explains why one frequently sees popular positions that are in clear contradiction to the positions of the political, economic, and academic establishments.

Witness, for example, how the majority of the U.S. population is in favor of the government (*a*) establishing a universal and comprehensive health program even at the cost of paying higher taxes (75 percent of the U.S. population) (9), and (*b*) expanding rather than reducing its role in protecting the health of workers and consumers and protecting the environment (10–12). These popular wants occur at a time of implementation of federal health policies that go in opposite directions to what people want, and at a time when the discussion on the establishment of a national health program has been practically "silenced" in major U.S. health policy forums.[1] Fuchs, Ginzberg, Evans, and Fein are empirically wrong. *The majority of the U.S. population supports a national health program and has supported it for quite a while.* As early as the 1940s, the majority or plurality of Americans already expressed support for a national health program, even at a cost of paying higher taxes (13). If the United States does not have a national health program it is not because people do not want it: they do want it—but do not have it.[2]

This situation—the people wanting it but not getting a national health program—shows the faultiness of the second assumption (i.e., that the U.S. political institutions respond to the majority opinion). The list of programs and interventions that the majority of the U.S. public wants from its government and does not get is enormous.

---

[1] During the period 1980–86, more than 5,000 health policy articles were published in major health policy forums in the United States—*The New England Journal of Medicine, Health Affairs, Journal of Health Politics, Policy and Law,* and *Health and Society.* Only two articles were published in support of a national health program. The focus of the majority of articles was on explaining and frequently justifying the need to reduce health expenditures and to privatize health services.

[2] Many authors, such as R. Fein, explain the absence of a comprehensive and universal government health program (national health program) in the United States as resulting from the inability of the social reformers to convince and educate the U.S. public of the merits of such a program, and also as an outcome of the American Medical Association (AMA) opposition to such a proposal. However, this explanation ignores the fact that the AMA did support such a program in the early 1910s, and that support did not translate into implementation of such a program. It also ignores the fact that later, when the AMA opposed it, the majority or large plurality of Americans continued to support such a program. Since the institution of major opinion polls asking people's attitudes toward such a program, the majority or large pluralities have consistently supported it.

Since the 1940s (when U.S. citizens were first asked these questions), the U.S. public has believed, for example, that the government should assure that everyone in need of health care or looking for a job should get it. Government policy does not necessarily reflect the opinion of the majority of the population. Frequently it does not. This does not mean that government can ignore popular wishes. Popular opinion, will, and wants count, but they are not the only or even the major determinants in shaping government policies, including health policies. Government policy is determined by a whole matrix of influences, in which some classes' and groups' interests have far more influence than others (e.g., big business has more power to influence public policy than labor has). This skewed set of influences explains why public policies frequently are carried out even against the wishes of the majority. It has been shown, for example, how the current federal governmental health and social policies of austerity (assumed to be carried out in response to a popular mandate) do not enjoy popular support (10-12).

The "Power Group" Explanations of Health Policy

The awareness that public policy is the outcome of the different degrees of influence exerted by several groups and forces over the state has characterized many theories of health policy (primarily those of political scientists and sociologists). I refer to those as "power group" theories. In these theories public policies in the health sector are attributed to the different degrees of power and influence exercised by several power groups (e.g., medical profession, hospitals, academic centers, insurance companies, etc.) on the public decision-making process in the health sector. Representative U.S. authors in this scholarly tradition are Ted Marmor (14), O. Anderson (15), and P. Starr (16). (For a critique of Starr's position, see reference 17.) In the case of Anderson and Starr, this explanation is presented not in opposition to but rather complementing the "popular choice" explanations. Indeed, the competition among these interest groups is for the hearts and minds of the U.S. public, which is, in the last analysis, the main arbiter and determinant (through its public representatives) of national health policy. Thus, Starr explains the current austerity of federal health policies as responding to a popular mandate, and concludes his book by indicating that the future of U.S. medicine depends on "the choices that Americans have still to make" (16).[3]

---

[3] According to R. Fein and O. Anderson, government health policy decisions are reached by a form of social consensus that precedes the determination of that policy. Consequently, Fein (4) concludes his recent book by calling for a new consensus among Americans about the basis for the establishment of a new national health policy. Similarly, Anderson (18), in his explanation of the differences in health policies in the United States, United Kingdom, and Sweden, attributes those differences to the differences in social consensus that he assumes to exist in these societies. These explanations fail to take into account that these policies are not based on consensual processes or outcomes. Quite the contrary: these national health policies are the result of heartbreaking struggles, with winners and losers, the latter not necessarily part of a general agreement or consensus. For an empirical proof of that position in the case of the United Kingdom, see reference 19, and in the United States, reference 20.

These authors have contributed extensively to the health care literature, providing valuable descriptive information about our health services. But I find their explanatory and analytical value limited. Besides sharing the questionable assumptions of the popular choice theorists, these authors also face a methodological problem. By focusing on the visible actors or interest groups whose interplay is assumed to shape the nature of national health policies (finally approved by the American people), they do not seem to be aware of the nonvisible actors, who may in fact be more important than the visible actors in explaining those policies. The visible interest groups are parts of broader categories of power such as classes that give them an ideological cohesiveness that explains their basic agreements on the parameters upon which their interaction, power competition, and discourse take place. By focusing on the visible actors—interest groups—and not on the nonvisible actors—classes—that determine the parameters of what is possible, these authors are not fully explaining national health policies.

For example, the current debate about cost controls in the health sector takes place under a set of assumptions about what is "politically feasible" in the United States. However, to fully understand these cost-control policies, it is not sufficient to analyze the different degrees of power exercised by different interest groups (e.g., for-profit hospitals, insurance companies, medical associations, and others) over the State. One needs to ask why these types of cost controls are politically feasible and others are not. And the explanation cannot be found by focusing only on the power of those interest groups. As David Himmelstein and Steffie Woolhandler (21) have recently shown, the most effective cost-control measures would be interventions that act upon the overall systemic pattern of funding and organization of health services, such as the nationalization of the funding and/or organization of health services. These alternatives, however, are not even considered because they are held to be almost "un-American." But these interventions are considered un-American by the major political, medical, and communications establishments because they would conflict not only with the interests of such interest groups, but more importantly with the correlations of class forces that determine what is considered acceptable within the practices and discourses of those interest groups. To focus only on the interest groups is to give them an autonomy from those broader class forces that actually condition what can and cannot be done in the United States. This assumption of autonomy makes these explanations seriously limited.

The Theories of Convergence

A third group of explanations belongs to what can be called the "convergence" theories according to which all developed western societies, usually referred to as post-industrial societies, are converging toward similar patterns of funding and even organization of health services. The elements of similarity are presented as outweighing the differences. In these theories, politics tend to disappear. Instead the major determinants for change are supposedly the demographic transition and economic development: the more developed a society is, the larger the percentage of elderly people living in it, the larger the popular demand for health services, and the larger the amount of resources available to respond to that demand. The best empirical proof of this position is the positive correlation assumed to exist between economic development (usually measured by gross domestic product (GDP) per capita) and percentage of the GDP spent on health services. Thus, all health services are perceived as evolving toward maturity, a stage of health care development defined as having reached "public health expenditure saturation" (22). Within this scenario, the current policies of austerity (which include the privatization of health services and the reduction of public expenditures) of many industrialized nations are explained as the result of these countries having transcended the level of maturity and gone beyond the saturation level.

The problems with these types of explanations are many. First, they are empirically wrong. As I will show in this article the level and type of health funding (and I could add organization) are primarily determined by political rather than biological and/or nonpolitical managerial-technological forces. Also, these explanations beg the question not only of what is a mature health service (i.e., how do we recognize one when we see one) and when are the services saturated, but equally important who defines maturity and saturation. These are indeed political factors that vary from country to country and determine the different levels and types of funding that we witness today in western industrialized nations.

CLASS POWER AS AN EXPLANATORY VARIABLE FOR THE FUNDING AND ORGANIZATION OF HEALTH SERVICES

Thus far I have summarized some of the major theoretical positions presented in the social science literature to explain the diversity in the types of funding and organization of the health services in the western industrialized nations. All these positions have provided valuable descriptive information about different health services. For the reasons I have summarized, however, I find them limited or faulty in their analytical value. They do not satisfactorily explain the reason for the diversity.

I postulate in this article that in order to understand the causes for this diversity, we have to shift our analytical paradigm: (a) we must look at the forest (the powers in society) rather than the trees (the different visible actors within the institutions of medicine); and (b) we must realize that power is not only distributed according to region, race, gender, or professional and interest groups, but also and primarily according to class. Thus the starting point for an analysis of the diversity in the systems of funding and organization of health services in different societies has to be based on an understanding of class relations in those societies, i.e., the class structure, class formation, class alliances, and class interests, as well as the behavior of the political and economic instruments of those classes. It is primarily through an analysis of those class instruments (parties, unions, chambers of commerce, fraternities, etc.) and their influence in the policy-making bodies that one can understand the development of national health policies. Thus, the explanation of "why some countries have national health insurance, others have national health services, and the United States has neither" has to be found in an understanding of how classes have historically realized the pursuit of their class interests in each of those countries. And in capitalist developed societies[4] I consider the capitalist and working classes as the two major classes whose instruments (e.g., parties, unions, chambers of commerce, fraternities, etc.) have played a key role in shaping the nature of the health services. It is in fact the thesis of this article that the working class and its labor movement have played a critical role in the development of both the welfare state and national health programs. Thus, in order to provide the explanation suggested by the title of this article, we have to start by understanding the historical position of the labor movement and its major political parties—socialist, social democrat, and communist parties—toward health policy.

The Health Policy of the International Labor Movements

The major health policy concerns of the labor movement in developed capitalist countries have historically been (a) universalization of health benefits, (b) control by and/or participation of the labor movement in the direction of the health care system, (c) state responsibility for the management of funds, and (d) support of the health care system by a progressive system of taxation.[5] These components of a national health policy have been part of labor movement demand for a welfare state that would (a) grant entitlements outside market relations, (b) institutionalize collective political responsibility for individuals' living standards, and (c) redistribute income and resources from the capitalist class to the working class, and provide goods and services outside the cash nexus (27).

The principle of *universality* was of paramount importance to the working class. It assured the key principle of labor, class solidarity whose opposite, class fragmentation, would weaken the working class. Thus, from the very beginning the labor movement was against the provision of benefits according to wages or to economic sectors of the labor force, i.e., the corporatization of health benefits. It was also against the means-test programs and the poor-law legislation and programs. Thus, the labor movement fought against stratification and corporatization of benefits, and for entitlement

---

[4] In the remainder of this article, I use the term "developed capitalist societies" rather than the most common term, "industrialized countries," because it is more rigorous a term. Industry, either as percentage of gross national product or employment, is not the largest activity in the so-called industrialized countries; the private ownership of the means of production, however, is a common characteristic in all western industrialized nations.

[5] For an historical analysis of the labor movement's evolving position on social (including health) programs, see the excellent article by G. Therborn (23) (particularly Section I, "Once upon a time there was a working class"). The labor position that has changed most from the 19th to the 20th centuries has been the state responsibility for the management of funds. In the 19th century, labor developed the Friendly Societies or Voluntary Sickness Funds, which assured the continuation of income during workers' sickness and the provision of medical care. Unions and Workers Parties used those funds to attract new members to the labor movement. (For an expansion of this position, see reference 24.) As labor became more powerful and influential over the state, it shifted the focus of its demands on the state. In the United States at the beginning of the 20th century, labor was divided in its demands for a universal and comprehensive governmental health program. Samuel Gompers, president of the American Federation of Labor (AFL) (the majority of craft unions), was against a national health program, while J. B. Lennon and J. O'Connel, the Vice-President and Treasurer, respectively, of the AFL, supported it. The Confederation of Industrial Organization (CIO) (the majority of industrial unions) supported it. The AFL also supported the national health program after Gompers retired (25). For a historical evolution of U.S. labor, see reference 26.

to benefits without economic conditions, i.e., without means tests (27, p. 229). Consequently, one of the first measures taken by socialist parties (in this article, I use the term "socialist parties" to define the social democratic, socialist, labor, and communist parties historically rooted in the I, II, III, and IV Internationals) in northern European countries, in Germany, and in Austria was the elimination and/or reduction of means testing, assigning very low priority to poor relief types of programs. Table 1 shows how means-test programs, as a percentage of all social (including health) programs, declined most substantially during periods in which socialist parties were in power in these countries.

As part of the struggle for universalism, the labor movement fought not only for the establishment of uniform levels of benefits but also for the coordination and even integration of the different publicly administered or licensed insurance funds that provided insurance health benefits for several sectors of the working population. Also, and as part of the process of disengaging the levels of benefits from the labor market, the labor movement fought to shift the sources of funding from payroll taxes to general revenue taxes, based on progressive taxation. The capitalist class, however, opposed each of these labor demands. It opposed any measures that could strengthen the working class. And critical to this opposition was the breaking of working class solidarity by the favoring of *stratification and individualization of benefits and the introduction of means tests*. Thus, the capitalist class preferred private health insurance with occupational-related health benefits since these programs strengthen both the wage earner's attachment to the labor market and to the employer, and the existing inequalities and differentials among wage earners, favoring the strongest over the weakest. As Gosta Esping-Andersen has indicated "By explicitly targeting legislation to workers and by promoting sharp status distinctions, the political aim was to build and consolidate status cleavages among the wage-earner population. The strategy, in other words, was to thwart broader class formation" (28, p. 231).

Class Power as Explanation of National Health Policy

The degree to which either the capitalist or the working class reached the aforementioned objectives depended on the power of each class to influence public policy

Table 1

Selected welfare state characteristics in Scandinavia, Austria, and Germany during the post-war period: Means-tested social (including health) expenditures as a percentage of total social security expenditures[a,b]

Years	Denmark	Norway	Sweden	Austria	Germany
1950	13.2	11.0	11.8	10.1	15.4
1974–75	1.0	2.1	1	2.8	4.9

[a]Source: adapted from reference 28, Table B2, p. 198.
[b]In all these countries socialist parties increased their political following and were in power for the whole or parts of this period.

in each country. In the case of the working class its power depended on six conditions:

1. The degree of unionization among the labor force: the higher the level of unionization the stronger the labor movement would be.
2. The type of union organization: industrial unionism provides more class power than craft unionism, and a close coordination of unions within a strong central union federation (that would be responsible for the collective bargaining agreements for the whole labor force rather than for the different sectors) allows for stronger labor positions than does a highly decentralized sectoral bargaining process.
3. The unity of the union movement, without division into confessional (e.g., Christian and lay unions) or political (e.g., socialist, social democratic, or communist) led unions.
4. A close organic linkage between the labor movement and a political party that historically has primarily represented the interests of the working class and allied popular forces.
5. The absence of major political divisions within the working class with different parties competing for similar constituencies.
6. The electoral following of such working-class parties, and time spent in power either alone in government or in coalition with other parties. (For a further elaboration of working class power, see references 28 and 29.)

These six conditions determine the power of the instruments of the working class (parties and unions) to reach the class aims mentioned earlier. Power, however, is a relationship phenomenon. By this I mean that the power of the working class also depends on another two factors:

1. The power to establish alliances with other classes such as farmers and middle strata. For example, in Sweden, the early commitment to a comprehensive and universal health program, as well as other components of the welfare state, was made possible primarily by the alliance of the working-class Social Democratic Party with the Farmers' Party. Such an alliance was not established in France and Italy, explaining the much later development of similar programs in those countries. Similarly, the highly popular New Deal programs (the basis of the U.S. welfare state) were primarily the outcome of the alliance of the working-class northeastern urban centers with southern farmers. (For the establishment of the Swedish welfare state, see reference 30; for the establishment of the New Deal, see reference 26.)

2. The power and unity or disunity of the capitalist class. When the capitalist class is divided into different parties such as in Sweden (the different conservative parties are self-named the bourgeoisie's parties), the possibility for change stimulated by the united working-class parties is larger than when the capitalist class is united into a major party (as in Austria and Italy).[6]

---

[6] Working-class political parties are those that traditionally have been founded and supported by the majority of working-class organizations such as unions. Capitalist political parties are those that traditionally have been founded and/or supported by the majority of capitalist associations (29). The U.S. Democratic Party is a multiclass party since, at least until recently, both working-class organizations and some capitalist class organizations have supported it (26).

Having indicated the differing historical aims of the different classes (primarily the capitalist and working classes) and having elaborated on the meaning of class power, let me now put forward my positions:

1. *The establishment of a national health program in any country is related primarily to the establishment and influence of the labor movement in that country, realized through labor's economic (unions) and political (parties) instruments.*
2. *The different types of funding and organization of health services are explained primarily by the degree to which the differing class aims in the health sector (as described earlier) have been achieved through the realization of class power relations.*

In support of the first position we can see in Table 2 a clear relationship between the time when the major working-class parties were organized, the time when the major trade union federations were organized, and the time when the first social insurance programs (including health insurance programs) were established. These historical data show that the most important force behind the social security schemes was the politically organized working class. It is worth stressing this point in the light of historical interpretations of social security that root its development primarily in the process of industrialization, which created the insecurity problems that social security schemes were supposed to resolve. If this indeed were the case, Belgium and Great Britain—the first two countries to become industrialized—would have been the first countries to have social security. They were not; in these countries the working class did not develop its own political party until later. The craft nature of the labor movement in both countries explains the rather late development of a class party such as the Labour Party.

Table 2

Timing of establishment of working-class socialist parties, major trade union federations, and first social (including health) insurance scheme[a]

	Socialist party	Trade union	Social insurance
Germany	1875	1868	1883
Austria	1888–89	1893	1888
Denmark	1878	1898	1891
Norway	1887	1877	1894
France	1905	1895	1898
Belgium	1889	1910	1900
Netherlands	1894	1905	1901
Britain	1900	1868	1908
Switzerland	1888	1880	1911
Sweden	1889	1898	1913
Italy	1892	1906	1914

[a]Source: reference 23, p. 10.

In brief, *the critical force in the birth of health and other social insurance schemes was the political and economic strength of the working class.* Whether a country had or did not have a national health program depended on the correlation of class forces in that country. This correlation of class forces also explains the evolution of the different types of funding and organization of health services, and very much in particular, the corporate and the liberal models.

The Corporate Model

The corporate model appears in countries such as Germany, Austria, France, and Italy where the capitalist classes were rather weak and unable to break with the feudal order. As a consequence, the capitalist classes had to ally themselves with the feudal aristocracies against the rising growth of the working classes. The Absolutist State was the outcome of those alliances. The church played an ideologically cohesive role in the power block that dominated the state and its public policies, including social and health policies. These policies were aimed at (*a*) dividing the working class by strengthening status differentials in the levels of health benefits (making them dependent on work-related contributions) within that class, and (*b*) directing class loyalties away from the universalist appeals of socialism and toward the employer. These policies were aimed at the privileged sectors of the working class, establishing a gradation of benefits in which those at the bottom—the poor—would be taken care of by charity under religious auspices.

Germany was the first country to develop this model. The conservative and social-Christian forces in Germany were the elements of the dominant power block threatened by a growing working class, organized in the Social Democratic Party. That threat was responsible for the establishment of the first Health Security Act of 1888. The specific event that triggered that Act was the Paris Commune of 1871, in which the Parisian working class had taken over Paris in the first-ever workers' state. The Paris Commune had an enormous impact on Bismarck and his closest social policy advisors, including Hermann Wagener who had been an eye witness to the Paris events. Bismarck's major concern was to avoid a similar occurrence in Germany. Consequently, the Absolutist State under his leadership developed a policy that included repression (the stick) against the Social Democratic Party leadership, as well as the establishment of a health insurance program (the carrot). As indicated by Bismarck (23, p. 2):

> We already, in February of this year, expressed our conviction that social depreda-
> tion cannot be expressed simply by the repression of Social Democratic excesses,
> but that this must be accompanied by the positive enhancement of the workers. . . .
> To this end a revision of the Bill on workers' insurance introduced by the Federal
> Government in the previous session will be submitted. . . . A more intimate connec-
> tion with the real forces of the life of the people and their concentration in the form
> of corporate associations under State protection and with state encouragement will,
> we hope, also render possible a solution to the tasks which the State Administration
> alone would be unable to handle to the same degree.

This quote refers not only to the motivation of the Health Security Act but also to its administration. The insurance programs were to be administered by several funds covering different types of workers and providing different levels of benefits. These funds would be licensed, supervised, and administered by different branches of the state.

It is worth stressing that while the threat posed to the social order by the working class political party was the stimulus for the Act, the way in which the Act was developed, organized, and administered responded to the capitalist class aims of dividing the workers and weakening the class solidarity within the working class. By providing levels of benefits according to status and type of employment, and by having the state (in which the capitalist-aristocratic power block was the dominant force) administer the different health insurance programs, the capitalist and aristocratic classes tried to divide and control the working class. Indeed, as Goran Therborn (23) has indicated, the primary purpose of the state response was to regulate the class relations within a power matrix in which the capitalist and aristocratic classes continued to be dominant. Indeed, if the objective of the insurance program had been the protection of the worker against social risks, the insurance program could have been administered as any other form of insurance (e.g., property insurance) through private means. The goal of social and health insurance was different, however: it was the need to regulate class power relations that motivated the granting of those programs. Having said this, let me now clarify a critical point.

It is frequently stated by Sigerist (31) and many other historians that such health and social reforms coopted the working class into avoiding the realization of its revolutionary potential. But this assumes that revolutions are fought by a revolutionary working class asking for revolution. Historical evidence shows these assumptions to be wrong. From the Bolshevik Revolution to the Nicaraguan Revolution, history shows that revolutions are fought by masses of people who ask for specific reforms and social changes (e.g., peace with Germany, social security and land in the Bolshevik Revolution, freedom and end of repression in Nicaragua, and so on). Whether or not a revolution occurs depends on the ability and/or willingness of the dominant classes to provide those reforms, as well as on the strength of the popular forces asking for those changes. In Germany, the working-class threat was the stimulus for the health and other reforms, but in the way those reforms were granted by the Absolutist State they divided that class. While strengthening some sectors of the working class they weakened its solidarity. The working class was not coopted— rather it was weakened by the specific form in which the health and social programs were established and administered. This point merits attention because of the overabundance of opinions, particularly within the U.S. radical tradition, that social reform is a way of coopting the working class and a form of legitimation of the social order, i.e., that it generates consensus and social acceptance of the status quo. This position denies the possibility that (a) social reforms can strengthen rather than weaken the dominated classes; (b) the absence of social rebellion is not necessarily an outcome of cooptation but rather a division of those classes, achieved by the specific ways of implementing those social reforms; and (c) although the working class may not be in consensus and the social order may not be perceived as legitimate, still the working class may not rebel because it does not see any alternative to the current order or it does not see itself as having the power to transcend the social order. (For a further expansion of this point, see reference 32.)

A second point that needs to be stressed (and will be expanded in the next section) is that as the working class regained strength in all those countries in which the corporate model was established, the socialist parties have fought for (a) universalism, aimed at making benefits independent of work related wages; (*b*) state centralization and uniformity of the different sickness funds; and (*c*) shifting of medical care funds from payroll taxes to general revenues. The degree to which these objectives were met depended, again, on the correlation of class forces within each country. In those countries where the working class was a dominant force in the political institutions (as in northern Europe), these objectives were better met than in those countries where that dominance was more spotty, limited, or nonexistent (as in southern Europe).

The Liberal Model: Welfare Market Capitalism

The liberal model appears in the "New World" societies in which the capitalist class did not need to establish alliances with a feudal aristocracy. In these societies, such as the United States, Canada, Australia, and New Zealand, social and health policies have reflected primarily the aims of the capitalist class, as defined earlier. Health policies have been characterized by (*a*) a reliance on the market with its attachment for private contractual health insurance and fringe benefits and (*b*) a strong commitment to means-testing as a way of distinguishing the "deserving" from the nondeserving and as a means of securing optimal help at a minimum cost. (For a representative position, see reference 33.) The reliance on the market emphasizes voluntary membership and individualistic actuarialism, with benefits closely connected to previous contributions and performance, and with comparatively meager public benefits and standards so as to encourage private insurance alternatives that complement the limited public programs.

In those countries with welfare market capitalism, the working class organizations have been traditionally weak and divided, largely owing to the role of ethnicity and race. All of these countries are "immigrant" countries in which the working class is divided according to ethnic or racial groupings, and thus its articulation within the economic and social system has been through channels in which working-class instruments (parties and unions) are weak or nonexistent. In the United States, for example, there is no working-class mass-based party (social democratic, socialist, or communist) that represents the interests of that class. Historically the working-class interests have been channeled through political instruments such as the Democratic Party in which the working class has not had a dominant leadership role. Nor in the United States is there a centralized bargaining process, with a central labor federation defending the economic interests of the whole class rather than of its different sectors. The bargaining process does not take place centrally; it occurs in a decentralized way, sector by sector of the labor force. Still, it is worth repeating that the working class in the United States has not been silent. The genesis of the U.S. welfare state, the New Deal, was the outcome of labor mobilization and class alliances (of the northeastern urban industrial centers with the southern farmers), forcing the establishment of universal programs such as Social Security, the most popular program in the U.S. welfare state.

This active mobilization of major sectors of the working class was the main stimulus for the New Deal. An atmosphere of crisis appeared in which the major capitalist class instruments were antagonistic to the changes that were occurring and to the speed with which they were taking place. But the primary concern of the Roosevelt administration was "about the offensive against his administration, not from those who thought it was doing too much, but from those who thought it was doing too little" (4, p. 228). And foremost among those were the militant sectors of labor: they wanted more and they wanted it soon. Never before had labor been so strong, but it was not strong enough to force the passage of the unfinished business of the New Deal—the establishment of a national health program. Health benefits coverage continued to be provided and administered primarily by the employers, and only for a very small sector of the laboring population. This limited coverage expanded somewhat during World War II. The war, however, had an enormous impact on the U.S. population: it was an antifascist war, won with the promise of a better world. It heightened enormously popular expectations. Labor was militant and called again for a national health program. Both the industrial unions of the CIO and the craft unions of the AFL called for such a program. As the President of the AFL, Mr. William Green, put it "Facts and logic are on the side of a national health insurance . . . sooner or later the program for which labor pleads will be enacted" (34).

The capitalist class strongly opposed those demands, and it triggered a response in all ideological, political, and economic fronts directed at weakening the working class. Through its enormous influence in the U.S. Congress, the capitalist class was able to pass the Taft-Hartley Act (bitterly opposed by labor), which forbade the working class to act as a class; for example, a steel worker could not (and still cannot) strike in support of a coal miner. No other capitalist developed country has such legislation. This legislation (sponsored by Senator Taft, who also opposed a national health program) weakened the working class enormously. Consequently, health benefits continued to be covered by collective bargaining agreements, sector by sector of the labor force, agreement by agreement. Thus, 85 percent of health benefits in the United States are work related, strengthening inequalities and differentials among wage earners, favoring the strongest (the sector of labor with strongest muscle at the bargaining table) and discriminating against and/or excluding the weakest (35). This unevenness in health coverage in the United States has been based on "interest group" rather than class behavior, as imposed by law. It has undermined class solidarity toward the welfare state, since those groups within the working class that command a privileged position in the private market are less likely to support and identify with public programs.

It is important to stress that, contrary to Starr's claims, the Taft-Hartley Act was a defeat not a victory for the U.S. working class, and that the right to struggle for health benefits coverage at the bargaining table was not a sign of strength but of weakness of U.S. labor (16, p. 313). It was an indicator of defeat of labor demands for a national health program. At the time that the Taft-Hartley Act was passed, even George Meany, the rather moderate leader of the AFL, was asking for a national health program (25).

In summary, it is the weakness of the U.S. working class (unparalleled in the western developed capitalist world), with the absence of a mass-based socialist party and with very low levels of unionization, together with the strength of the U.S. capitalist class (unequaled in any other western capitalist country) that explain the absence of a comprehensive and universal health program in the United States. In the other "New World" societies such as Canada, Australia, and New Zealand, there are mass-based socialist parties, which have been responsible for establishing national health programs within the parameters of welfare capitalism. In the case of Canada, the socialist party (the NDP) was instrumental in establishing a comprehensive and universal health insurance system in the province of Saskatchewan and in its later expansion to the rest of the nation (36).

DEVELOPMENTS IN THE HEALTH SECTOR AFTER WORLD WAR II

In the foregoing sections I have tried to show how the origins of the differences in funding and organization of the health services in major western developed capitalist countries are historically rooted in the different relations of class forces in each country. It is interesting to note that, while the basis for the welfare state (and for the basic structure of the funding and organization of health services) was established prior to, during, or immediately after World War II, the actual development of the welfare state and of its health services took place primarily in the postwar period, during the 1950s, 1960s, and 1970s. Measured in terms of either employment or expenditures (total expenditure, percentage of overall government expenditures, or percentage of the GDP), the public funds for health services grew significantly in all the countries considered thus far. Table 3 shows how the expenditure of public funds (as percentage of GDP) on health services has grown in all developed capitalist countries, with Sweden (where the working class is strongest) showing the highest and the United States (where the working class is weakest) showing the lowest expenditure.

During this same period, although these countries continued to differ in their forms of organization and funding, some elements of commonality appeared. In all of these countries (with the exception of the United States, there was the *establishment of*

Table 3

Public funds spent on health, as percentage of GDP, 1960–83[a]

	1960	1970	1980	1983
Sweden	3.4	6.2	8.8	8.8
United Kingdom	3.4	3.9	5.2	5.5
West Germany	3.2	4.2	6.5	6.6
France	2.5	4.3	6.1	6.6
Italy	3.2	4.8	6.0	6.2
Spain	1.4	2.3	4.3	4.4
Greece	1.7	2.2	3.5	—
Portugal	0.9	1.9	4.2	3.9
Austria	2.9	3.4	4.5	4.6
Australia	2.4	3.2	4.7	4.9
New Zealand	3.3	3.5	4.7	5.3
Canada	2.4	5.1	5.4	6.2
United States	1.3	2.8	4.1	4.5

[a]Source: reference 37, Table 2, p. 12.

universalism, with a tendency toward increasing health benefits coverage. Tables 4 and 5 show how, during these years, the percentage of the population eligible for hospital care and ambulatory care under a public scheme has increased to cover the whole of, or the overwhelming majority of, the population. In countries with national health insurance, there has also been a tendency toward increasing health benefits, equalizing benefits regardless of wage differentials, and centralizing the different public insurance funds. Even in the United States there has been a growth of coverage of the population by both public and private insurance programs, although that growth has not reached universalism or comprehensiveness.

A primary reason for the expansion of health coverage with the advancement of universalism has been the growing strength of the working class in these countries and the realization of its class aims as defined earlier. Particularly in the late 1960s, the 1970s, and early 1980s we saw the full development of working-class political parties. Table 6 shows that working-class parties reached political maturity in many western European countries during this period. At the same time, in other western capitalist countries the parties of the labor movement gained popularity. For the first time in history, the representatives of the socialist parties became the largest voting block within the European Parliament in the middle 1980s (38). Prior to that time many of these parties had been in power in coalition with other parties representing other classes. In the United States, labor gained strength until the middle 1970s in part because of shortage of manpower. Similarly, unionization increased in 18 of the top 23 OECD (Organization for Economic Cooperation and Development) countries, reaching an all time high (with the exception of France and the United States) in the late 1970s (39, p. 9). It is the growth of the labor movement that is behind the achievement of universalism and comprehensiveness, a growth that has not been

Table 4

Public protection against hospital care risks, expressed as percentage of population eligible for hospital care under a public scheme, 1960-83[a]

	1960	1970	1980	1983
Sweden	100	100	100	100
United Kingdom	100	100	100	100
West Germany	86	93	95	95
France	85	96	100	100
Italy	87	93	100	100
Spain	50	61	83	87
Greece	30	91	98	98
Portugal	16	52	100	100
Austria	78	92	99	99
Australia	77	79	100	100
New Zealand	100	100	100	100
Canada	68	100	100	100
United States	22	40	40	40

[a] Source: reference 37, Table 1, p. 68.

Table 5

Public protection of ambulatory care services, expressed as percentage of population eligible for ambulatory care under a public scheme, 1980–83[a]

	1960	1970	1980	1983
Sweden	100	100	100	100
United Kingdom	100	100	100	100
West Germany	87	90	92	92
France	85	96	99	99
Italy	87	93	100	100
Spain	50	61	83	87
Greece	75	90	97	98
Portugal	18	52	100	100
Austria	78	92	99	99
Australia	78	76	100	100
New Zealand	100	100	100	100
Canada	2	95	100	100
United States	6	24	25	25

[a] Source: reference 37, Table 2, p. 69.

stopped or slowed down even when conservative forces have regained power. This is due to (a) the great popularity of the principle of universalism and comprehensiveness in health coverage among the western populations (including in the United States) and (b) the existence of socialist parties competing for popular electoral support. For example, President Reagan has been more successful than Prime Minister Thatcher in reducing public expenditures in the health sector not because Americans have been less supportive of those expenditures than the British population—the U.K. (40) and the U.S. (10) populations have been against health cuts—but because the Conservative

Table 6

Countries where the labor movement has topped 50 percent of the vote in national parliamentary elections since 1965[a]

Country	Election year(s)
Austria	1971, 1975, 1979
France	1981
Finland	1966
Greece	1981
Sweden	1968, 1970, 1982
Norway	1969
Spain	1982, 1986
Portugal	1976

[a] Source: reference 39, p. 8.

Party in the United Kingdom had to compete with a working-class Labour Party committed to an expansion rather than reduction of health expenditures, while the Republican Party did not have to compete with a working-class party opposition. The health cuts were done with the support of the Democratic leadership. As the Democratic Senator Moynihan put it in voting in 1981 for the most dramatic cuts to social expenditures that the U.S. Congress ever passed, "we have undone thirty years of social legislation in three days" (quoted in reference 41).

It is also important to indicate that the growth of the welfare state, related to the strength of the labor movement, has been characterized by government interventions not only in the realm of distribution of the national product but also in the world of production. In a perceptive analysis of legislative practices in western Europe, Leo Panitch (42) concludes that the primary focus of legislative reform during the 1970s was in the sphere of production rather than distribution. For instance, the major unions and the Social Democratic (SPD) government in West Germany turned toward investment planning, and management and workers codetermination was extended beyond the iron and coal industry. In Sweden, this change was evident in the famous Meidner Plan and in the mid-1970s legislation providing a legal framework for union challenges to managerial prerogatives on the shop floor and for workers participation schemes on work councils and company boards. Similarly, Great Britain witnessed the Bullock Inquiry proposals for industrial democracy, as well as the Planning Agreements and the National Enterprise Board of the Labour Party of 1973. France witnessed the emphasis on workers' control and nationalizations in the Common Programme. The list could go on (42). Similarly, in the health sector of developed capitalist countries, we saw, in the 1970s, the rise of national health policies that intervene both in the funding and in the organization of health services. Most developed capitalist countries, including the United States, saw not only the expansion of government coverage of health benefits, but also the establishment of health planning and regulatory programs aimed at guiding and/or directing the reorganization of health services. During this same period, there was also a growth of occupational and environmental legislation in the majority of developed capitalist countries, with active government interventions at the workplace and in the environment that reduced and constrained some of management's prerogatives.

In brief, it was during this period, and particularly in the 1960s and 1970s, that labor strengthened its power, putting the capitalist class on the defensive. This situation explains the strong reaction of the capitalist class in the 1980s, including antiwelfare state policies as key elements of their austerity measures. As one of the best known spokesmen for the "new" conservative party of the United Kingdom wrote recently, "Old fashioned Tories say there isn't class war. New Tories make no bones about it; we are class warriors and we expect to be victorious" (quoted in reference 43). In a similar fashion, the head of Kaiser Aluminum Corporation, Chairman Cornell Maier, one of the major supporters of current federal policies in the United States, declared, "This is war. The battle is not over our economic system. The battle is over our political system" (quoted in reference 44), a battle carried out by the most antilabor administration since 1920. These antiwelfare and anti-working-class policies have been most successful where the working class is weakest, as in the United States.

This survey of national health policies should not lead to the conclusion that all western European countries have evolved in a similar form toward identical goals, i.e., the establishment of a welfare state in which a national health program is a key component. The elements of commonality—universalism and growing comprehensiveness—should not be confused with identity of experience, far from it. The experiences in the northern European countries have been very different from those in southern Europe: industrialization took place in the north much earlier than in the south. Consequently, the working classes were better developed and organized politically in the north than in the south of Europe. The union movements in the north were, and continue to be, strong and for the most part united. (The degree of unionization of the labor force in Sweden or Austria is 70 to 80 percent, in West Germany or Britain is 40 to 50 percent, and in France is less than 20 percent.) In the northern countries, the socialist parties were rooted in the labor unions, which were the main force behind them. To use a Gramscian expression, the parties were and are the organic instruments of the unions. It was the early strength of the labor movement that explains the more highly developed nature of the welfare state in the northern European countries.

Since industrialism appeared much later in southern Europe, the working class was weaker, and a different balance of class forces resulted. On the one hand, the southern working class tended to generate more revolutionary traditions than did the reformist north—initially anarchists, subsequently communists. But these forces were not majority forces within a working class that remained divided at the union and political levels (45). The working class was and continues to be weaker in the south than in the north of Europe. On the other hand, the dominant political block in southern European countries, until recently, was profoundly conservative—and even on occasions, as in Greece and Spain, and in Italy (prior to World War II), fascist. The state in those societies was highly centralized, grossly unreconstructed, and bureaucratic, and had strong military-police apparatuses and functions. This situation (which differed from that in northern Europe) had two consequences for national health policy. First, as Table 2 shows, public expenditures in the health services in the post-World War II period were lower in southern than in northern European countries. Second, the main discourse and practice of the southern Socialist parties, once in power, has involved the modernizing and democratizing of the state apparatuses rather than the expansion of social expenditures. In two of these countries (Greece and Spain), the establishment of national health services occurred when socialist governments first gained power. In Italy, the establishment of a national health service was the outcome of a historical compromise between the Communist Party and the Christian Democratic Party. In France, the major focus of health policy during the Socialist-Communist Government was not only on expanding the social expenditures but also on decentralizing the state. In all these countries, the welfare state is still less developed than in the northern European countries.

Another important observation about changes in health policies in the postwar period is that, while the working class has been the major force behind these changes, it has not been the only force. This explains why there is not a one-to-one correlation between the strength of the working class and the nature of those changes. Variations do exist, which can be attributed to other factors and forces as well. The emphasis on class forces in this article aims at remedying the current "silence" on this topic in current literature that attempts to explain policy; it does not aim at denying the importance of other factors. Another point of clarification is that the electoral success of the working-class parties was largely due to their identification with the interests of the majority of the wage earners, including white-collar employees and the middle strata of technical-professional workers. This alliance has not been an easy one. For example, these sectors have been willing to join the working class in support of comprehensiveness and universality in health coverage in times of economic security and growth, but in times of economic austerity, these same sectors may resent the equalization of benefits and become more receptive to the capitalist class message of linking benefits to wages. These tensions are appearing in most developed capitalist countries today.

CONCLUSION: WILL THE UNITED STATES HAVE A NATIONAL HEALTH PROGRAM?

The major conclusion of this article is that the development of the welfare state and one of its main components, a universal and comprehensive government health program, is directly related to the strength of the working class and its political and economic instruments. The United States is the only major capitalist developed country without a national health program, and without a mass-based socialist party. It is also one of the countries with weaker unions, which is to a large degree responsible for the lack of a mass-based working-class party. Consequently, the possibilities for the establishment of a national health program are dependent on the possibility of strengthening the labor movement in the United States. Without a stronger labor movement the possibilities for a national health program are greatly diminished, and have been further weakened during the current period of strong antilabor policies of the U.S. government.

The awareness of this weakness has motivated some changes within the labor movement, which, however timid, could change the orientation of that movement and strengthen its political and economic influences. These changes include recent AFL–CIO recommendations for (a) centralization of the bargaining process, (b) avoidance of union competition, and (c) involvement not only in work-related issues but also in issues that are relevant for the majority of the population (46). Also, and as a step toward gaining political influence, the AFL–CIO has decided to actively intervene in the primary process of selection of the Democratic Party Presidential candidate, a move aimed at forcing that Party to be more receptive to labor's position.

These steps, which some have defined as the "Europeanization" of U.S. labor, have been accompanied by an increasing class polarization of U.S. politics, with the upper class and upper middle class voting Republican and the lower middle class and working class voting Democrat (47). If this trend continues, it is likely that we could also see the Europeanization of U.S. politics. The possible strengthening of the labor movement could then provide the basis and conditions for the establishment of a national health program. Whether this possibility will become a reality depends on the correlation of class forces in the United States.

REFERENCES

1. Fuchs, V. R. *The Health Economy*, p. 269. Harvard University Press, Cambridge, Mass., 1986.
2. Ginzberg, E. *The Limits of Health Reform: The Search for Realism*, p. 3. Basic Books, New York, 1977.
3. Evans, R. G. Illusions of necessity: Evading responsibility for choice in health care. *J. Health Polit. Policy, Law*, Fall 1985, pp. 439–465.
4. Fein, R. *Medical Care Medical Costs: The Search for a Health Insurance Policy*. Harvard University Press, Cambridge, Mass., 1986.
5. Parenti, M. *Inventing Reality. The Politics of the Mass Media*. St. Martin's Press, New York, 1986.
6. Bagdikian, B. H. *The Media Monopoly*. Beacon Press, Boston, 1983.
7. Bowles, S., and Girtis, H. *Schooling in Capitalist America*. Basic Books, New York, 1976.
8. Smith, D. N. *Who Rules the Universities. An Essay in Class Analysis*. Monthly Review Press, New York, 1971.
9. Schneider, W. Public ready for real changes in health care. *National J.*, March 23, 1985, p. 665.
10. Navarro, V. Where is the popular mandate? *N. Engl. J. Med.* 307: 1516–1518, 1982.
11. Navarro, V. The 1984 election and the New Deal: An alternative interpretation. *Social Policy*, Spring 1985, pp. 3–17.
12. Ferguson, T., and Rogers, J. The myth of the American public's turn to the right. In *The Decline of the Democrats and the Future of American Politics*, pp. 3–39. Hill and Wang, New York, 1986.
13. Coughlin, R. *Ideology, Public Policy and Welfare Policy. Attitudes Toward Taxes and Spending in Industrialized Societies*, p. 77. Research Series No. 42. Institute of International Studies, University of California, Berkeley, Cal., 1980.
14. Marmor, T. *Political Analysis and American Medical Care Essays*. Cambridge University Press, New York, 1983.
15. Anderson, O. W. *Health Services in the United States. A Growth Enterprise since 1875*. Health Administration Press, Michigan, 1985.
16. Starr, P. *Social Transformation of American Medicine*. Basic Books, New York, 1983.
17. Navarro, V. Medical history as justification rather than explanation. *Int. J. Health Serv.* 14(4): 511–527, 1984.
18. Anderson, O. *Health Care: Can There Be Equity? The United States, Sweden, and England*. J. Wiley, New York, 1972.
19. Navarro, V. *Class Struggle, the State and Medicine. A Historical and Contemporary Analysis of the Medical Sector in Great Britain*. Robertson, London, 1978.
20. Navarro, V. *Medicine under Capitalism*. N. Watson, New York, 1976.
21. Himmelstein, D., and Woolhandler, S. Socialized medicine: A solution to the cost crisis in health care in the United States. *Int. J. Health Serv.* 16(3): 339–354, 1986.
22. Schieber, G. T., and Poullier, T. P. International health care spending. *Health Affairs*, Fall 1986, pp. 112–122.
23. Therborn, G. When, How, and Why Does a State Become a Welfare State? Paper presented at the ECPR Workshop on Comparative Study of Distribution and Social Policy in Advanced Industrialized Nations, Freiburg, March 20–25, 1983.
24. Immergut, E. Between state and worker. Sickness benefits and social control. In *Public/Private Interplay in Social Protection: A Comparative Study*, edited by M. Rein and L. Rainwater, pp. 57–98. Sharpe, White Plains, N.Y., 1986.
25. AFL backs national health plan. *Mich. CIO News* 15: 2, January 1, 1953.
26. Davis, M. *Prisoners of the American Dream*. Verso, London, 1986.
27. Esping-Andersen, G. Power and distributional regimes. *Politics and Society* 14(2): 223–256, 1985.
28. Esping-Andersen, G., and Korpi, W. Social policy as class politics in post-war capitalism: Scandinavia, Austria, and Germany. In *Order and Conflict in Contemporary Capitalism*, edited by J. H. Gadthorpe. Oxford University Press, New York, 1984.
29. Korpi, N. *The Democratic Class Struggle*. Routledge and Kegan Paul, Boston, 1983.
30. Esping-Andersen, G. *Politics against Markets: The Social Democratic Road to Power*. Princeton University Press, Princeton, N.J., 1985.
31. Sigerist, H. E. From Bismarck to Beveridge: Developments and trends in social security legislation. *Bull. Hist. Med.* 8: 365–388, 1943.

32. Navarro, V. Radicalism, Marxism, and medicine. *Int. J. Health Serv.* 13(2): 179–202, 1983.
33. Meyer, J. A., and Levin, M. E. Poverty and social welfare: An agenda for change. *Inquiry* 23(2): 122–133, 1986.
34. Green, W. A national health program for a stronger America. *American Federalist* 59: 6, February 1952.
35. Navarro, V., and Renner, C. The macro-economic changes in the United States and their implications in health coverage. *Int. J. Health Serv.*, in press.
36. Taylor, M. G. *Health Insurance and Canadian Public Policy*. McGill University Press, Montreal, 1978.
37. Organization for Economic Cooperation and Development. *Measuring Health Care 1960–1983. Expenditures, Costs and Performance*. OECD Social Policy Studies No. 2, 1985.
38. A left majority in the EEC. *New Socialist* 33: 4, December 1985.
39. Therborn, G. The prospects of labour and the transformation of advanced capitalism. *New Left Rev.* 145, 1984.
40. Newsnight poll, February 10. *Guardian* February 11, 1986. Cited in *Marxism Today*, March 1986.
41. Edsall, T. B. *The New Politics of Inequality*. Norton, New York, 1984.
42. Panitch, L. *Working Class Politics in Crisis*, p. 7. Verso, London, 1986.
43. Wood, E. M. *The Retreat from Class*, p. 182. Verso, London, 1986.
44. Pertschuck, M. *Revolt Against Regulation*, p. 57. University of California Press, Berkeley, Cal., 1982.
45. Anderson, P. European social democracy. *Against the Current* 1(6): 21–28, 1986.
46. AFL-CIO. *The Changing Situation of Workers and their Unions*. A report of the AFL-CIO Committee on the Evolution of Work, February 1983.
47. Edsall, T. B. Growing party allegiance by income. *N.Y. Rev. Books*, April 24, 1986.

SECTION IV

The Struggle

CHAPTER 11

The Rediscovery of the National Health Program by the Democratic Party of the United States: A Chronicle of the Jesse Jackson 1988 Campaign

Vicente Navarro

On Tuesday, July 19, 1988, at 5:47 p.m., the delegates to the Democratic Party Convention in Atlanta, Georgia, passed by acclamation the Jesse Jackson amendment to the platform of the Democratic Party calling for the establishment during the coming Democratic administration of a national health program that, under federal leadership, will guarantee comprehensive health benefits coverage to all Americans. On the floor of the convention, Frank Clemente, the issues director of the Jackson campaign, and I hugged each other with great joy. It was the end of the first step in a long and tough struggle that began for me four years ago when Jesse Jackson asked me to help him define the health policies of the Rainbow Coalition. The next day, the major media, as usual, reported only on the three Jackson amendments to the platform of the Democratic Party that were not accepted. They did not report on the other ten Jackson amendments that were accepted, one of which was the call for a national health program.

This amendment was a very important first step. It committed the Democratic Party to a project it had abandoned almost ten years ago. In its move to the right, the Democratic Party in the 1980s had reproduced too uncritically many of the Republican arguments that we in the United States, the wealthiest country in the world, could not afford to make access to health care a human right. Mondale's Democratic platform in 1984, for example, did not call for a national health program. Rather, it spoke of the need to reduce government intervention in people's lives (1). Candidate Mondale, in his acceptance speech in San Francisco, indicated that, "We have to learn the lesson of the 1980 elections. People want government off their backs." The one exception was Jesse Jackson. In 1984, he was the only candidate who called

Originally published in the International Journal of Health Services, 19(1): 1–18, 1989.

for the establishment of a national health program. His candidacy was dismissed by the Democratic establishment, however, as a nuisance, or, in the words of Mondale's health advisor, Professor Ted Marmor, as a spoiler (2). Jesse's views were dismissed as irrelevant, and his call for a national health program put aside. For all these nightmarish Reagan years, the name of the game has been austerity without gloves. Cost controls and cost reductions have been the major trademarks of federal health policies.

Jesse's 1988 campaign has changed all this. It has raised people's expectations, and his views cannot be dismissed again. By the end of the primaries, Jesse had received only 16 percent less of the popular vote than the leading Democratic contender, Michael Dukakis. Jesse now had 7 million primary and caucus votes (more than Mondale in 1984) and had won in 13 primaries and caucuses: Virginia (46 percent), South Carolina (54 percent), Georgia (40 percent), Alabama (44 percent), Mississippi (46 percent), Louisiana (37 percent), Alaska (36 percent), Puerto Rico (32 percent), Michigan (55 percent), Virgin Islands (86 percent), Delaware (46 percent), District of Columbia (80 percent), and Texas (leader in delegates). Jesse had finished first or second in 46 of 54 races—more than any other candidate, winning 1200 delegates as well as the majority of all voters 18 to 44 years of age. He also won in the largest cities in the country, including New York, Chicago, Detroit, San Francisco, Milwaukee, Birmingham, Atlanta, Indianapolis, Topeka, Louisville, New Orleans, Baltimore, Minneapolis, St. Louis, Newark, Miami, Cleveland, Philadelphia, Hartford, Washington, D.C., Charleston, Houston, Richmond, Denver, Seattle, Portland, Oregon, and many others. Jackson and the Rainbow have become a major force in the Democratic Party and in the country. His views and the positions of his campaign cannot be ignored. Critical elements of Jesse's positions, such as the need for a national health program, have been incorporated into the platform of the Democratic Party. Even the starting paragraph of the platform is a verbatim copy of the Jackson position paper calling for justice and solidarity in the United States.

How did this change—from 1984 when we were ignored to 1988 when we were recognized—come about? Answering this question is the purpose of this article. It has been my experience that the history of the United States is frequently written by the hired pens of the powerful who redefine the interpretation of events in ways that serve their interests. The powerless and those who oppose the establishment usually do not have their history written. To the degree that I am able, I would like to correct this situation. While events are fresh in my mind, I will write my recollection of these important events. As usual, to explain these events we have to put them into a historical perspective and understand the historical forces that shape them.

But, first, let me add a personal note and explain how I came to be part of this splendid campaign. I have had the enormous privilege of being the health advisor to Jesse Jackson and his 1988 campaign, and one of his representatives on the Democratic Party Platform Committee. I have been and continue to be part of the Jackson movement, which has been defined by *The New York Times* as a political earthquake that has profoundly changed the terms of politics in the United States. How did I come to be part of that movement?

Along with millions of Americans, I had been increasingly angry and frustrated with the Democratic Party's move to the right since 1978. Promise after promise had been abandoned on the basis of a nonexistent move to the right by the American public. The abandonment of the Democratic Party's long-term commitment to make health care a human right in the United States had been explained and justified by an assumed antigovernment mood of the American public. The evidence shows otherwise, however. Poll after poll shows that no other U.S. government project has consistently enjoyed such popular support as the establishment of a national health program. Since 1945, the American public, by large majorities or pluralities, has repeatedly favored such a program. Reflecting on our political establishment's responsiveness to moneyed interests and its unresponsiveness to popular desires, this popular demand has joined the long list of things and projects people want from their government but don't get. This failure has been further accentuated during the past eight years when Democrats joined the Republican Administration to, as Senator Moynihan recognized (quoted in reference 3), further reduce the limited social network that the federal government provides to its citizens.

In government and academia, only a very few voices have kept asking for a national health program, voices usually dismissed as oddities from the past. The makers of the conventional wisdom have worked overtime to silence these voices. I have been one of these voices stressing that such a project is feasible and desired by our people.

In 1984, I shared my frustration with a much-valued friend who has been the voice of reason and common sense in the U.S. health scene, Dr. Quentin Young. Quentin, as Jesse Jackson's doctor, spoke to Jesse about my frustration and our concerns. The next day, I received a call from Carolyn Kazdin, staff to Jesse Jackson (and later a key element in the campaign, in charge of labor and farmer relations), asking me to come and talk with Reverend Jackson. We met and had extensive conversations about the need for a national health program. I will always remember our first conversation. Knowing of his presidential aspirations, I approached him in a rather predictable fashion: with a whole set of polls showing the popularity of such a program. Thoughtfully but surely, he dismissed such an approach. "Dr. Navarro," he said, "even if it would not be popular, we should ask for such a program on the basis that is the right thing to do." I was humbled. I had approached him as I had approached many other U.S. politicans during my 22 years here, encouraging them to join the very few political voices that keep asking for a national health program. Jesse was different. His very first consideration was of the morality of the issues involved. He reminded me of the leaders of the Spanish anti-fascist underground that I was a member of in the 1950s. They, like Jesse, had gone through enormous sacrifices in their struggle for justice and freedom. They were deeply moral persons whose struggles had most profoundly shaped their outlook on life. Jesse approached the issue of pain and suffering due to lack of comprehensive health care coverage as it should be approached—on moral grounds. The United States should not be the only major country other than South Africa that does not guarantee health care as a human right. He asked me why we do not have a national health program that could assure comprehensive health benefits coverage to our people. I assured him that, contrary to what is usually said, the root of the problem is not money—we in the United States could indeed afford to have such a national health program. Nor is the problem that people do not want a national health program—they do. The problem is the enormous power of moneyed interests—the insurance and medical complexes—that oppose such a program. The political establishment, many times paid by such interests (I did not need to remind Jesse that we have the best Congress money can buy), has not dared to challenge those interests. Jesse agreed and felt that he dared to take on what he called "the barracudas eating the little fish." At the end of a half day of discussion, he asked me to be his health advisor. I agreed. This is how I became part of his team. With the assistance of another extraordinary human being, Jack O'Dell (a trusted friend and advisor to Jesse), I founded and chaired the National Health Commission of the National Rainbow Coalition. This Commission had the responsibility of advising the National Board of the Rainbow Coalition in matters of health policy. Later, when Reverend Jackson decided to run for President of the United States, he asked me to be his health advisor in the campaign as well.

THE MAIN CHARACTERISTICS OF JESSE JACKSON'S 1988 CAMPAIGN

A main characteristic of the Jackson 1988 campaign has been the awareness of the importance of class as well as race in understanding our realities and reaching our constituencies. I was involved in the Jackson 1984 campaign at the local level. At that time, the campaign was the political maturation of the civil rights movement allied to other social movements. This movement, however, grew and changed to emphasize class as well as race in 1988. Jesse realized better than any other major political figure that the enormous power of the U.S. establishment has been and continues to be reproduced by dividing the working people. Divide and conquer works well in the United States. Racism is stimulated to make the white worker believe that his or her enemy is the black worker. It is not paradoxical that the Reagan Administration, the most pro-business administration this country has had since Coolidge, is also the most racist. The latter is a consequence of the former. Jesse had understood this better than any other major political leader. His typical discourse, as printed in his basic speech of January 19, 1988, in *The New York Times* (4), aims at establishing the linkages among the working people of this country, united by the common needs to liberate themselves from the *economic violence* they suffer. As the perceptive (and class-conscious) conservative *The Economist* warned its readers, Jackson is speaking of class. He speaks to the workers and farmers of America as no other leader has. He speaks in class terms about the need to unite workers in this country and abroad. No other major political leader in the United States since Henry Wallace has said that "workers of the world must unite because slave labor anywhere is a threat to organized labor everywhere." Jesse's commitment to the farmers and to the working men and women of this country is the main trademark of his campaign. His is a call for an alliance of labor and farmers with all other disenfranchised forces and social movements, such as peace activists, feminists, environmentalists, gays and lesbians, and others. As Andrew Kopkind observed in *The Nation*, "Jackson is running that unspeakable anomaly, that horror of all horrors, a class campaign" (5). *The Wall Street Journal* warned that "the substance of Mr. Jackson's message . . . might best be described as the politics of socialist joy. His economic and defense programs, in particular, make Mr. Jackson not merely 'the most liberal' Democrat but an authentic radical voice. It is a voice more typical of the British Labour Party than of American politics." Although this statement had a nice sense of flattery for the British Labour Party, it contained an element of truth. Jesse's campaign was atypical and outside the liberal discourse. It was a class message and a class campaign. Careful of detail, Jesse first announced his intention to run for President at a labor rally during the Labor Day Weekend of 1987. And the person who introduced his nomination to be President of the United States during the Democratic Convention was a labor leader, Winpisinger, head of the machinists union and member of the Executive Committee of the AFL-CIO, and one of the few labor leaders who defines himself as a socialist.

The popularity of this strategy during the campaign led to mimetic behavior by all the other Democratic candidates. The American working class, presumably long gone in middle-class America, was rediscovered during the primaries by establishment politicians, such as Gephart, who suddenly wanted to parade as champions of the working men and women of America. And Senator Biden even plagiarized a speech by Kinnock, the leader of the British Labour Party.

Jesse Jackson's campaign strategy to reach and unite working people led to the call for programs such as full employment and a national health program to benefit the majority of working people in the United States. Programs for people with special needs needed to be built upon programs that benefit the majority of Americans. Compassion needed to be accompanied by a call for class solidarity.

A third characteristic of the Jackson 1988 campaign was to address the enormous maldistribution of economic and political power in the United States and the need to change its unjust distribution by empowering the majority of working men and women whose hopes and expectations have been greatly diminished as an outcome of so many broken promises. The Jackson campaign wanted to show that many problems that we face in the United States are the outcome not of scarcity of resources but rather of skewed and unjust control over those resources. For example, the fact that the United States does not have a national health program is not because we could not afford it. We already spend more on health care than any other country on earth. Money is not the issue. The issue is the control over the channels that these funds go through, i.e., the system of funding and organization that benefits the few—the medical-industrial complex—rather than the many—people in need of health care. In Jesse's words, the problem is the barracudas who keep eating the little fish. And there are indeed a lot of barracudas in the health sector.

The Jackson 1988 campaign showed that we could indeed afford a national health program. Our position was that we could afford universal and comprehensive health care coverage at lower costs than we as a nation are now paying for health services. We deliberately referred to Canada's health system as a point of reference. We stressed repeatedly that, until 1966, Canada and the U.S. had similar levels of health expenditures and similar health indicators. In 1966, the Canadians established a national health program. Since then, their health expenditures have grown at a slower pace than ours while expanding rather than reducing health benefits coverage, and their health indicators have improved much faster than ours. If Canadians can do it, why cannot we? We in the Jackson 1988 campaign wanted to focus the debate not so much on the question of how much the national health program will cost but rather on who will control the funding and organization of health services. The latter will determine the former. In our proposal, we wanted to emphasize the power of the federal purse to change and reorganize the private delivery of health services to make them more efficient, comprehensive, and cost-effective. We outlined in our internal position papers where the savings would come from. We showed that a health care system similar to the Canadian one would save $70 billion a year while providing comprehensive health care coverage to all our people. [See the following article "The Jackson National Health Program" (6).]

These were the main objectives that guided all health and other positions of the Jackson campaign. The purpose of our proposals was to unite our working people, empower them, and help them to question the prevalent pattern of class, race, and gender control over the institutions that affected their lives. Change could and should take place; hope had to be kept alive.

THE BEGINNING OF THE JESSE JACKSON 1988 CAMPAIGN: THE HEALTH PLATFORM

The Jackson 1988 campaign prepared positions on many health areas from the very beginning. We were the only campaign that prepared a detailed set of positions on how to face some of the major health problems in the United States, such as the lack of comprehensive health care coverage, drugs, acquired immune deficiency syndrome (AIDS), environmental issues, occupational health and safety, alcoholism, gun control, and others. The formal introduction of the major health positions took place in a major presentation by Jesse in November 1987 at the annual convention of the American Public Health Association (APHA), a splendid professional association that has distinguished itself by offering continuing leadership in assuring public health in the United States. The preparation of that speech became a pattern for writing later speeches. I prepared the basic draft of the speech; Frank Clemente improved it considerably and added the unique Jackson style. Others were also called upon to provide ideas and suggestions. And finally, Jesse himself went over it line by line, changing it, editing it, and finally approving it. For Jesse, however, the speech is only a signal on a road, not the road itself. Jesse rarely sticks precisely to a written text.

The speech stressed as a major point the need to establish a universal and comprehensive national health care program that would be federally funded and administered, equitably financed, with active popular participation, and public accountability of the public and private institutions. It received a standing ovation from the 10,000 members attending the New Orleans APHA convention. The convention had to cancel all other activities because everyone attended Jesse's speech. Jesse addressed with characteristic eloquence the major concerns of the APHA, and put forward a program that was close to APHA's major positions. The audience loved it. The standing ovation lasted five minutes. At the end, something happened that showed the attention to human detail and thoughtfulness that is so typical of Jesse. It was his personal touch. I had had my 50th birthday one week earlier. Upon arriving in New Orleans, I had disclosed this event to David Himmelstein, a close friend with whom I had shared many of the joys and frustrations of the campaign. I asked him not to pass the word around. I have always felt very uncomfortable with social events and birthday parties.

When Jesse ended the session, he told the audience that I, who was chairing the session, had achieved 50 years and started singing "Happy Birthday" with the huge crowd. Moreover, the television and press were there and recorded the singing. For several days, I could not go anywhere in New Orleans without people wishing me happy birthday. I liked it. It taught me two lessons. One was not to trust David to keep a secret. I am sure that David told Jesse about my getting into middle age. The other lesson was something I already knew—that Jesse was a person thoughtful of details.

The New Orleans APHA speech became the guideline for the health policy platform of the campaign (7). Shortly after the APHA speech, the Jackson 1988 Campaign released the major position papers on the national health program (which I prepared with the collaboration of David Himmelstein and Steffie Woolhandler, both from Harvard University) (8); AIDS (prepared by Nancy Krieger, a member of the National Health Commission of the National Rainbow Coalition) (9); drugs (prepared by Frank Clemente, Director of Issues in the Jackson campaign) (10); occupational health (prepared by Polly Hoppin, a member of the National Health Commission of the National Rainbow Coalition, and Jim Weeks from the United Mine Workers) (11); the environment (prepared by Barry Commoner, well-known environmentalist) (12); gun control (prepared by Steve Teret, Professor of Injury Control at The Johns Hopkins University) (13); alcoholism (prepared by Bob Laforge from Brown University) (14); smoking (prepared by Andrew McGuire from San Francisco General Hospital) (15); care of the elderly (prepared by Meredith Minkler from the University of California, Berkeley) (16); long-term care (prepared by Charlene Harrington from the University of California, San Francisco) (17); and others (18).

Besides these position papers, the Jackson 1988 campaign received approximately 80 questionnaires from journals, associations, and private institutions asking for our health positions on practically every health topic under the sun. For most of them, Frank Clemente and Steve Coates (also from the issues department) would ask me to draft an answer, which Frank would then change and approve.

As a result of this process, three major events took place. One was that the Jackson campaign took positions on most health problems that the country faces. Put together, I believe that these positions represent the most progressive agenda in the health sector in the United States.

Second, a network of health professionals was established that helped the Jackson 1988 campaign enormously in defining our positions. Some of these positions had already been prepared by the National Health Commission of the Rainbow, but many others had not. This network was possible because of the excellent response I always received. It was to the great credit of the enthusiasm raised by Jesse and his campaign that everyone whom I approached on behalf of the campaign went to great lengths to meet our requirements, including our crazy and hectic deadlines. I want to thank them for all they did. Their collaboration was superb.

Third was the excellent working relationship I developed not only with the issues department but also with the whole leadership of the Jackson campaign. I have never found in the United States more committed individuals than the staff of the Jackson campaign headquarters. I was delighted to work with them. Among them Frank Clemente is an extraordinary individual. We developed from the very beginning a very good and close working partnership. And he soon became my main ally within the campaign. Under his direction, we were able to put forward a progressive agenda in the health field. It was always a great joy to work with Frank—even when he frequently called me at 11:00 o'clock at night to prepare a 20-page report for 8:00 o'clock the next morning.

THE CAMPAIGN: PRIMARIES UNTIL MICHIGAN

Until Michigan, Jesse was the only candidate who called for a national health program. His remark, "We are the only major country, other than South Africa, that does not have a national health program. We have to change company," soon became a trademark of his presentations. And Jesse's calls for drug control programs and AIDS programs became main topics of his campaign. He broke many taboos and questioned many myths. He attended the major gay and lesbian demonstration in U.S. history. He touched on the roots of the drug problem, including the political connections of the drug trade. He touched on the major issues that have a bearing on health: wealth and income redistribution, housing, full employment, education, and peace became parts of the health agenda. All these positions were part of a strategy of mobilizing the working people of this country, the majority of the United States. In this period of the campaign, the establishment media tried to marginalize Jesse by presenting him as simply a black leader, a presentation that was frequently reproduced even in left-wing circles. Jesse was indeed a black leader, a civil rights leader who appealed to the great majority of blacks. But Jesse was also a class leader (or, in U.S. terminology, a populist). He was calling on the working class and its different components—black, brown, yellow, and white, women and men, young and old. Jackson had already received more than 15 percent of the white votes in the Democratic primaries and caucuses through the end of May. He increased his white support in the later primaries. He received 35 percent of the white vote in Oregon, 21 percent in Connecticut, 23 percent in Wisconsin, and 28 percent in California. Also, he scored very well among whites in caucus states such as Alaska, Maine, Colorado, Minnesota, and Michigan. In Michigan, he would have won even if the congressional districts in Detroit, which are predominantly black, had not been counted. In toto, Jesse received 4.4 million black votes and 2 million white votes. Almost one-third of Jesse's primary votes were white. Still the press kept referring to him primarily as a black leader. Blackness was the main emphasis in the presentation. Otherwise, Jesse was presented as one more of the "seven dwarfs." Jesse's positions were presented as similar to those of the other six. The only difference was his color. He was the *black* candidate. During this period, the establishment media, for the most part, ignored his positions. Just one example: when Jesse called for a national health program at the APHA convention in New Orleans, the major press did not report this event. Instead, they reported that he had asked for campaign money during the convention. Since the Jackson campaign did not get funds from corporate America, it needed to get money directly from people. Thus, Jesse usually asked for money from those in his audiences who supported his positions. The establishment press reported this as a sign of the campaign's desperation. Meanwhile, no one in the press reported on his call for a national health program.

This attitude of ignorance of our positions or token attention also appeared in liberal circles. For example, the Villers Foundation prepared a widely circulated documentary about the Democratic and Republican candidates' positions on health in general and long-term care in particular. Jesse was presented last and least as a perfunctory footnote, with the same space given to Pat Robertson. Liberals in the United States usually have an uneasiness, sometimes bordering on contempt, for those voices that out-left them.

THE PRIMARIES AFTER MICHIGAN

Michigan, however, changed that position. It was a political earthquake. Jesse won an overwhelming victory, winning the majority of white and black votes. Michigan has been one of the hardest-hit states in the country. Auto makers, steel workers, construction workers, as well as farmers, voted in droves for Jesse. Jesse could become the Democratic Presidential candidate after all.

All types of forces were called to arms to stop that possibility. The term used was the need to "scrutinize" Jesse. The assumption was that Jesse had had an easy ride up to this point because he was black. As Geraldine Ferraro put it, "If Jesse Jackson were not black, he would not be in the race." In this scenario, the racist argument was advanced that black people are not victims of discrimination but the recipients of "special treatment." Mayor Koch also claimed that Jackson was escaping criticism because he was black. Jesse, however, had not been treated fairly or given special treatment. Quite to the contrary. In a profoundly racist way, his positions were either ignored or brutally distorted. In the March/April issue of *Extra!*, there was a detailed survey of the major media, comparing the media's treatment of Reagan and Jackson. The article noted, among other things, that "nearly every significant piece on Jesse Jackson has contained the word 'anti-Semitism,'" whereas it is hard to find a profile of Reagan with the word "racism," even though he long opposed civil rights laws, once accused blacks who moved into whites-only neighborhoods of trying "only to cause trouble," and blamed Martin Luther King's assassination partly on his civil disobedience. The media had similar memory lapses when it came to Koch. He wasn't constantly reminded that he once said he felt most black people were anti-Semitic or that he once donned an Afro wig for a party with the press and sang, "Ain't Nobody's Business What I Do."

After Michigan, these attacks grew fiercer. The call to arms was the need to "scrutinize" Jesse: to show that his programs would ruin the country and that he did not have any political credibility, i.e., did not know what he was talking about. He had to be presented as one more demagogue who should be shown for what he was, a charlatan.

The New York Times published a series of articles in early April which stated that Jackson's demands—such as the establishment of a national health program—would ruin the country. In the words of *The New York Times* (19), the country could not afford such a program. That same position was reproduced in the major U.S. media: CBS, ABC, NBC, *The Boston Globe, The Baltimore Sun, The Los Angeles Times,* and *The Chicago Tribune,* among others. As Jesse Jackson's health advisor, I responded to *The New York Times,* indicating that we could indeed afford a national health program and showing how the Jackson National Health Program, while providing comprehensive and universal health care coverage, would cost the nation less than what we now spend in health care. I also tried to inform the readers of *The New York Times* that until 1966, the United States and Canada spent the same percentage of their gross national product (GNP) in health care and had similar health indicators, but since 1966, when it established a federally run national health program, Canada has been better able to control the growth of health expenditures (in 1987, the United States spent 11.2 percent of the GNP in health care while Canada spent only 8.9 percent), while expanding rather than reducing health care coverage. Moreover, Canadian health indicators are better than ours. I showed that the United States can indeed afford the provision of universal and comprehensive health care. What we cannot afford is not to have it. *The New York Times* did not publish my letter. Nor did the other papers that had dutifully parroted *The New York Times* line that Jesse would indeed bankrupt the country. The only difference between Koch ("Jesse will destroy the country in three weeks") and *The New York Times* was the form, not the substance. That message has indeed become the "conventional wisdom" of the U.S. establishment.

The other strategy of the U.S. media to discredit Jackson has been to show that he lacks credibility. *The New Republic* spearheaded this campaign immediately after the Michigan primary with an article by Fred Barnes (20) in which he denounced Jesse's manipulation of facts. According to Barnes, Jesse was abusive to an extreme in the utilization of facts—his list was extensive. This became the most quoted article in the major U.S. media at that time. *The Economist, The Baltimore Sun*, and many others quoted Barnes extensively. And for a few days Barnes was the guest on many shows, such as ABC's "Nightline," in charge of scrutinizing Jesse's positions. My colleagues in the Jackson Campaign sent a detailed reply showing that it was Barnes rather than Jackson who got his facts wrong. Independently, I also sent a letter to *The New Republic* correcting Barnes. He claimed, for example, that federal expenditures in prenatal care have not declined as Jackson said, but rather have increased. Barnes reached this conclusion by looking at the federal Women, Infants and Children program, which he wrongly defined as the main government prenatal program. As I indicated in my letter, Medicaid is the major government prenatal care program; it is the largest public health program for mothers and children. During the Reagan era, the percentage of poor mothers and children receiving Medicaid benefits has been declining, partly due to deep cuts in Medicaid in 1981 and 1982. Between 1981 and 1983, Medicaid enrollees decreased by 1.1 million instead of increasing by an estimated 635,000 to reflect higher unemployment. Congress has partially restored some of these cuts, but it has been unable to undo many of the Reagan Administration's restrictions to the program, which have made Medicaid less accessible to poor women and children. Other programs—Title V Maternal and Child Health Block Grants, Community and Migrant Health Centers, Family Planning, and Immunization—that benefit poor women, including poor pregnant women, also received large cuts. Congress has tried to restore some of these cuts, but the FY 1985 appropriations levels for these programs were less than their FY 1981 levels in constant service dollars. Largely because of these cuts, the percentage of babies born to women who had received adequate prenatal care, which had increased from 1970 to 1980, declined from 1980 to 1985. Also, and partly because of these cuts, infant mortality has stopped declining at the same rate as in the previous 20 years.

In my letter to *The New Republic*, I also showed that Barnes got his facts equally wrong regarding federal child care programs. He criticized Jackson for saying that these programs have been cut. Barnes admitted that there has been a decline, but he accused Jackson of exaggerating. Barnes referred to a "slight" decline in federal expenditures. In fact, budget cuts and inflation have reduced the value of the most important federal program for child care for low-income families (Title XX) to *one-half* (in real terms) of what it was a decade ago. In 1982, the Reagan Administration cut $75 million earmarked for training of child care and other service providers and administrators. Subsequent minor boosts in the Title XX appropriations have failed to restore these cuts. Meanwhile, the number of children living in poverty, even though their parents are working, has increased substantially. Even before the 1982 cuts, Title XX child care programs served only 472,000 of the 3.4 million poor children under six years of age. By 1984, there were 4.9 million poor children under six years of age, and less money to serve them. The states have not, as Barnes claimed, compensated for these cuts. Only 15 states are serving more children now than before the cuts; 23 states are serving fewer. As the FY 1988 Children's Defense Fund budget indicates, "By and large the states have not closed the gap created by federal cutbacks."

Like *The New York Times, The New Republic* never published the Campaign's detailed response or my letter. The editors told me, in response to my queries, that they will publish the Campaign's detailed answer or parts of it. When I stressed the need to publish it right away to correct the damage, they laughed: "Dr. Navarro, please be patient. We have many letters to publish." They never published the detailed answer from the Campaign or my letter to them. These are just a few examples of how undemocratic our "democratic" press can become under stress. I wrote an article based on that experience and submitted it to *The Nation* for publication. They did not publish it (21). Meanwhile, these attacks had an effect. Exit polls in the New York primary revealed that one-third of Dukakis's votes came from people who were voting to "stop another candidate."

DUKAKIS CALLS FOR A UNIVERSAL HEALTH PROGRAM: DIFFERENCES BETWEEN THE DUKAKIS AND JACKSON PROGRAMS

Another effect of the Michigan victory was that all other candidates further stressed their populist tone addressing the issues of the working class. And Dukakis, for the first time, started calling for what he called a universal health program. He kept referring to the need to assure that everyone should have basic health coverage. Dukakis stole our slogan but not our position. While he was calling for universal health insurance coverage, his campaign literature and his health advisor, Dr. David Blumenthal, kept clarifying that the Governor was only commited to the Kennedy-Weicker employer-mandated health benefits coverage and, pending the resolution of the federal deficit, an expansion of Medicare and Medicaid. Moreover, an internal document of Dukakis's campaign, never released, spoke of comprehensive coverage as a long-term goal (22). His short-term ends were far more limited: to expand some areas of coverage based on federal subsidization of the private sector.

Dukakis's message gained further credibility when the State of Massachusetts passed a health plan assuring universal health care coverage. He kept referring to the establishment of such a program as a sign of his commitment to make access to health care in time of need a human right in the United States. In the Dukakis–Jackson debates in New York and Michigan, Dukakis referred twice to the need for a univeral health program. Once, he referred to AIDS and pointed to the need for a universal health program to take care of people with AIDS. In his summary statement, he also called for universal health insurance. Similarly, in his debates in Pittsburgh and Philadelphia, he called for universal health insurance.

Dukakis's oral statements, however, contradicted the positions of his campaign, which continued to call for support for the employer-mandated coverage and expansion of Medicare and Medicaid. I wrote extensive documents to the Jackson campaign showing the disparity between Dukakis's general call for universal health coverage and the specific proposals put forward by the Dukakis campaign (23-25). Jesse referred to this disparity in one of his debates with Dukakis.

Still, the fact that Dukakis kept referring to his Massachusetts plan gave great credibility to his commitment to universal health care coverage. He was able to retain that credibility partly because of the uncritical reporting by the major press of the Massachusetts program. Many times, the media reporting was not only uncritical but grossly biased. *The New York Times*, for example, referred to a Massachusetts referendum calling for a universal and comprehensive health care program that had been overwhelmingly approved by a three to one vote as proof of the popularity of the Massachusetts health plan. The only problem with that information is that the referendum approved in Massachusetts called for a national health program like the one proposed by Jackson rather than the one put forward by Dukakis. This important distinction was not mentioned in *The New York Times*.

David Himmelstein, Steffie Woolhandler, and I prepared a detailed critique presenting major flaws in the Massachusetts program. We stressed that the Massachusetts program is not universal (a lot of people would still remain uncovered after the plan is implemented in 1992) or comprehensive (major benefits such as long-term care, responsible for the personal bankruptcy of many elderly in this country, were not included in the Massachusetts plan). [These differences between the Dukakis and Jackson national health proposals are discussed in the following article (6).] Moreover, the Massachusetts plan is extremely expensive. It will continue to rely on the private insurance companies for the administration of the system. This was the root of Dukakis's problem. His Massachusetts plan had not touched the enormous power of the insurance industry and of the medical-industrial complex. Unless this power is touched, we cannot provide comprehensive coverage. I sent a message to Jesse that concluded with the following statement (26):

> I can assure you that under a Dukakis administration the U.S. will not have a universal and comprehensive health program; neither will Massachusetts in 1992 when his program is supposed to be established. The reason is simple. Dukakis leaves the enormous power of the insurance companies (and the medical-industrial complex that they have created) unmolested. The problem is rooted in this basic fact. Not only is the U.S. the only country (besides South Africa) that does not provide a national health program, it is also the only country in the industrialized world that relies on private insurance companies for the provision of health benefits

coverage. The latter explains the former. We cannot provide federally funded coverage that is comprehensive and universal and rely on the private insurance companies to administer the program. It is like trying to square a circle. Dukakis seems to admit this by calling for a universal but not a comprehensive program. Only the Jackson program can provide a comprehensive and universal program. And it does that by daring to challenge the huge power of the barracudas in the health sector. This is why I believe that we in the campaign should continue to struggle to make health care a human right in the U.S. Your movement is the only force that can do it. Health and being healthy are the most important gifts people can get. When health fails, everything else crumbles. This is why people put access to health care in time of need at the top of their list of concerns. Whether they will get it or not, however, depends on how strong our movement is. This is why I suggest further strengthening the already splendid movement that you have started by pushing forward in all platforms we have access to—including the National Platform Committee and the National Democratic Convention—the need for a universal, comprehensive, federally funded and administered, equitably financed national health program.

I believe that these documents had an effect. Three days later, in an interview with *The Wall Street Journal*, Jesse said that the need for a national health program was one of the issues we would fight for in the Democratic Party Platform Committee. The campaign recouped the issue of a national health program, and Jesse made extensive references to the need for a national health program.

THE NEED FOR SPECIFICITY: THE JACKSON BUDGET

One of the areas in which the Jackson campaign was criticized was that we were asking for too much. Mayor Koch's remark that Jesse would ruin and destroy our country was a gross oversimplification of what the establishment was thinking. This situation forced the campaign to do what no other campaign in U.S. history has ever done: to prepare a budget to show that the issue was not the resources but rather the priorities in the allocation of those resources. We showed how we could indeed pay for our dreams (27). It had an enormous impact since it strengthened the focus of the campaign in the area that we had been hammering at: the issue of priorities. The response was generally positive, and leading economists, such as James Tobin (Nobel prize winner in economics), supported it.

In the health sector, the budget repeated the principles upon which the national health program would be paid, primarily by earmarked taxes going to a national health trust fund separate from the general federal budget. The budget also called for the establishment of a Presidential commission to implement a national health program based on the principles defined in our health position paper. I was against this approach. It made us vulnerable to the criticism that in the health sector we have avoided the specificity of detailing where revenues will come from and where expenditures will go. Our budget only included the short-term growth of already existing programs. But in the key area of the health platform, the establishment of a national health program, the budget only called for the establishment of a commission to study how to pay for it. As I expected, Dukakis used that vulnerability in the San Francisco debate. When Jesse criticized Dukakis's lack of specificity, Dukakis answered by referring to his Massachusetts health plan, while Jesse was merely asking for a commission. It was the only area where Jesse was not specific enough. And, as I had predicted, Dukakis used it.

A major problem in the Jackson campaign was the reluctance to release an internal document that I had prepared in collaboration with David Himmelstein and Steffie Woolhandler. This 30-page document (reprinted following this article) detailed the sources of revenue for the national health program (6). It went through several drafts. Elements within the Jackson campaign leadership were uneasy. This document was sent to 15 individuals outside the campaign, whose responses were mixed. Quentin Young had the difficult task of summarizing the reviewers' comments. Some were enthusiastic, others less keen. The primary concern expressed by the latter was that while the proposal was in tune with the 1970s, it was not attuned to the Reaganomics of the 1980s. They saw it as too ambitious. A whole set of discussions took place within the campaign as to when and how to release it. I stressed that what we were asking was not so new. The Kennedy-Griffith proposal, put forward in 1969, was similar to ours. The major difference was that we were calling for earmarked taxes, rather than general revenue or payroll taxes, because of the popularity of such a program.

The campaign prepared a major speech for the annual convention of the American Federation of State, Council and Municipal Employees, where Jesse detailed our proposals, our differences with Dukakis, and how we would pay for them (28). At that time, our position paper was finally released in a modified form (29). *The New York Times* reported it as a major event. Unfortunately, the primaries were practically over.

June 7 ended the first stage of our campaign. Jesse had received 7 million votes, 16 percent less than Dukakis. This had been achieved in spite of the enormous scarcity of resources for the campaign. Never before in the history of the United States had a second runner come closer to the winner. The unfair campaign rules explain why the Dukakis delegate count was far larger than deserved. A key element was the 800 superdelegates. Had it not been for them, Dukakis would have entered the Atlanta convention without the magic number of over 2000 delegates needed to win the nomination. This is why Jesse refused to accept Dukakis's victory. To accept that victory would have meant accepting the unfair rules that gave Dukakis such an advantage.

Jesse did not give up. He decided to go all the way to the convention and continue the struggle for the causes that the campaign fought for from the very beginning. An important step was the battle of the platform.

THE BATTLE OF THE PLATFORM: THE CALL FOR A NATIONAL HEALTH PROGRAM

The campaign had ended one stage and was entering into a new one in which it was important to have people in the leadership who knew the modus operandi of the Democratic Party apparatus, with its baroque set of rules and committees that are always skewed in favor of the status quo and stability. The majority of the Democratic Party National Committee, neutral in principle, was clearly pro-Dukakis. Jesse appointed Harold Brown (convention manager), Eleanor Norton (head of the Jackson campaign in the Platform Committee, and Carter Administration official in charge of civil rights), and Ann Lewis (well-known Democrat and past director of ADA), who were party regulars and who knew well the workings of the party apparatus. Some of them were latecomers to the movement and practically unknown to the Rainbow. Except for Eleanor Norton, the majority of Jackson representatives on the Platform Committee were elected by the Jackson state delegates and were individuals who had been in the campaign from the very beginning. Assisting the committee was an impressive group of staffers—Bob Borosage, Frank Clemente, Mark Spitz, and Carol O'Cleireacain. Linda Green was asked to serve as assistant to Eleanor Norton.

The staff prepared an excellent draft of our positions. It was the best manifesto of professive forces in the country (30, 31). It was later modified to include some suggestions made by the members of the initial group of staffers, advisors, and Jackson members of the Platform Committee, a group that *The Washington Post* had referred to as the "kitchen cabinet of the campaign." I made two suggestions: one, that the draft be changed to ask for "a national health program, federally funded and administered and equitably financed," and second, that recognition of Cuba be added. Both became part of the Jackson proposals for the platform. The recognition of Cuba was dropped in subsequent drafts. It was considered too hot an issue, one that could distract from other topics considered to be more urgent, such as the Palestinian question. Needless to say, we knew that we would not get our platform approved by the whole Democratic Party Platform Committee. But still, it was our position. The struggle was to get as many of our positions as possible within a set of priorities set up by Jesse. The reversal of Reaganomics—taxing the rich, freezing the military budget—were among the top priorities.

The first meeting took place in Michigan. In a place described by Ann Lewis as the preppiest place in the United States, the Platform Drafting Committee met to discuss the first draft of the platform proposed by Ted Sorensen, a relic of the Kennedy era. It was a vacuous and meaningless statement. Both camps, Jackson's and Dukakis's, agreed that there was a need to be more specific while being concise. The Jackson camp was in a clear minority of five of 15 members of the drafting committee. The other ten consisted of five pro-Dukakis members appointed by the Democratic National Committee and five appointed by Dukakis. As a token gesture, the chairmanship was given to Congressman Gray, who had supported Jackson in the Pennsylvania primary. It was difficult to see Gray as a Rainbow type, however. A few days before, he had voted against Congressman Pepper's long-term care proposal, which had been supported by the Jackson campaign, with the argument that we could not afford it. Gray operated as a scrupulously neutral chairman. The final draft to be submitted to the whole Democratic Party Platform Committee in Denver, Colorado, on June 25-26, 1988, was rather disappointing (32). The majority of Jackson delegates felt quite negative and expressed their disappointment to Eleanor Norton and to the leadership of the committee. In the health field, the platform called for the right to have universal and comprehensive coverage as a long-term objective without specifying how that would take place and under whose leadership. The only specificity was the call for gradualism and expansion of already existing programs.

A long process of bargaining took place. The Dukakis forces accepted several modifications to the platform. But they did not give up one inch in 13 major areas that we considered to be critically important. One of these was our amendment calling for a national health program under federal leadership (33). Jesse decided to present all of them to the Atlanta Democratic convention as minority planks (34). It was quite clear that Dukakis's forces were going to resist the call for a national health program that, under federal leadership, would guarantee comprehensive health care coverage to all Americans (35). The most the Dukakis camp was willing to accept was the call for the right of all Americans to have basic health insurance, without specifying what level of government would guarantee that right or the extent of "basic." It seemed to imply that the Dukakis program would assure that the uninsured would have access to basic insurance (the Kennedy-Weicker proposal), but from our standpoint, that was not enough. In defense of our amendment, I tried to make the members of the committee aware that the problem we faced was not only the 38 million who did not have insurance. The problem was also the insufficient coverage of the majority of Americans. *The New England Journal of Medicine* had just published an article showing that the majority of working Americans still have major problems of coverage. I did not seem to convince many Dukakis supporters. With a remarkable party discipline, they turned us down on amendment after amendment.

I left Colorado with major misgivings. We had won important victories that the press chose to ignore (36). But we had also lost in important areas. Dukakis was still within the Reaganomics frame. He did not dare to reverse Reaganomics. He was going to follow Reagan's policies of austerity in softer terms. In the health sector, he was going to support the employer-mandated coverage proposed by Senators Kennedy and Weicker. But not much more.

Jesse, however, did not give up. He kept campaigning, showing that we were a major force in the Democratic Party. And indeed we were. Ours was a long-term strategy, not merely an electoral one. We were building a movement that was not going to be taken for granted. Jesse did not want to be disruptive, however. He instructed Eleanor Norton to keep meeting with Mike Barnes, Dukakis's representative in the Platform Committee, to continue exploring a compromise that would enable us to go to Atlanta with a sense of unity and agreement on the major purposes of the campaign. To get rid of the Reagan era was not enough. We needed to reverse Reaganomics as well.

As always occurs with liberals, Dukakis took Jesse for granted. His primary concern was to attract the right. His choice of Bentsen as Vice-Presidential candidate was not only a geographical but a political balance. The Democratic Party was going to have a moderate-conservative ticket. Not only that choice but the insensitive way in which it was made showed that Dukakis had not fully realized that a new force—the progressive wing of the party—had appeared and would not be taken for granted. Jesse was disappointed, and his followers angry. It almost seemed that Dukakis had followed a confrontational line. The Jackson campaign was ready to give a fight and let the delegates to the convention decide on the nature of the ticket and the platform. Whether the convention was going to be divisive or united would depend on the Dukakis camp. He had to take the initiative since he had created the problem. Meanwhile, Jesse instructed Eleanor Norton to discontinue all contacts with the Dukakis camp and avoid further compromises.

Concerned about the image that disunity would create in the country, Dukakis responded to several of the campaign demands. On the morning of Monday, July 18, ten hours before the convention began, the Dukakis camp agreed, as a part of the need to reach unity, that we could present ten amendments, to be referred to as the Jackson amendments, to the floor of the convention with their tacit support and approval (33). One of them was a modified version of our amendment that called for a national health program under federal leadership. We had given up on equitably financed. But the call for a national health program under federal leadership was one of our contributions to the platform. Forty-eight hours later, the convention approved the amendments by acclamation. We had succeeded.

Needless to say, a platform is only a platform. But it represents a commitment and a promise to the American people. The coming Democratic Administration cannot ignore it without paying a high political cost. Jesse and the Rainbow will continue to press for the major causes we have struggled for and been identified with, including the call for a national health program. We will be there.

This ends a brief personal account of some of the experiences I had in the Jesse Jackson 1988 campaign, and touches on only a small part of the whole splendid experience. It is only the tip of the iceberg. The whole movement would not have occurred without Jesse, who led and inspired all of us and, even more important, without the mobilization of millions of people who felt they could make a difference. I was honored to be able to be one among many who struggled to make this land, as Guthrie told us once, our land. During this journey, I met many people. But two persons specially impressed me. They were representative of the level of commitment of our Rainbow people. One was a woman, an employee of a hospital in Baltimore, black, aged, still working. She reminded me of the women Jesse usually refers to in his speeches—the workers who clean up the bedpans of the sick, wipe the sweat of fever off their foreheads, change their clothes—and when they get sick can't lie on the beds they make up every day. She, Mary, did not have insurance. She came every morning at 5:30 to work for the campaign for two hours before going to the hospital at 7:30 a.m. She did this for three months. She would take the kids afterward to a neighbor and come back and work from 8:00 p.m. until 11:00 or 12:00. She had never before registered, voted, or cared about politics. She did it for the first time. She believed that the campaign's cause was her cause. She rarely spoke in our meetings. She usually sat with John, a white steelworker who voted for Reagan in 1980, did not vote in 1984, and ran as a Jackson delegate in 1988. John also worked day and night in the campaign. Mary and John never realized—and they would have felt embarrassed if I had told them—that, for me, they had been the most important source of inspiration in the whole campaign. It was an honor to serve them and millions of people like them. To them, I dedicate this report of a personal journey.

REFERENCES

1. Text of the 1984 Democratic Party Platform. *1984 Congressional Quarterly Almanac*, 1984, p. 23.
2. Marmor, R. T. The lessons of Mondale's defeat: Reflections on the 1984 presidential campaign. *Political Q.*, April 1985, pp. 7–21.
3. Esdall, T. B. *The New Politics of Inequality*, p. 17. W. W. Norton Company, New York, 1984.
4. Jesse Jackson's basic speech: From a tradition of marching for jobs and rights. *The New York Times*, January 9, 1988, p. 8.
5. Kopkind, A. The Jackson campaign. *The Nation*, April 2, 1988, p. 1.
6. Navarro, V., Himmelstein, D., and Woolhandler, S. *The Jackson National Health Program.* Internal document of the Jesse Jackson 1988 Campaign.

7. Jackson, J. Enough of Bandaids: The Need for a National Health Program. Speech to the Annual Convention of the American Public Health Association, Atlanta, Georgia, October 19, 1987. Released as official document of the Jesse Jackson 1988 Campaign.
8. Meeting All Our Health Care Needs. Position paper of the Jesse Jackson 1988 Campaign.
9. Dealing with the AIDS crisis. Position paper of the Jesse Jackson 1988 Campaign.
10. Meeting the Real Threat to Our National Security: Jesse Jackson's Anti-Drug Program. Position paper of the Jesse Jackson 1988 Campaign.
11. Protecting the Health and Safety of Our Workers. Position paper of the Jesse Jackson 1988 Campaign.
12. Protecting Our Environment. Position paper of the Jesse Jackson 1988 Campaign.
13. Ending the Terrorism of Guns. Position paper of the Jesse Jackson 1988 Campaign.
14. Ending Alcoholism. Position paper of the Jesse Jackson 1988 Campaign.
15. The Need to Stop Smoking. Position paper of the Jesse Jackson 1988 Campaign.
16. Meeting the Needs of Our Elderly. Position paper of the Jesse Jackson 1988 Campaign.
17. Solving the Long-Term Care Problem. Position paper of the Jesse Jackson 1988 Campaign.
18. Ending Hunger in America. Position paper of the Jesse Jackson 1988 Campaign.
19. *The New York Times*, April 4, 1988, p. 3.
20. Barnes, F. Jesse's words. *The New Republic* 3: 820, 1988.
21. Navarro, V. Scrutinizing Jesse. The undemocratic tics of our "democratic" press. Letter not published in *The Nation*.
22. Health care: Shaping a better future. Internal document of the Michael Dukakis 1988 Campaign.
23. Navarro, V. Dukakis is stealing the health issue from us. Internal memorandum of the Jesse Jackson 1988 Campaign, April 13, 1988.
24. Navarro, V. Dukakis is stealing our slogan but not our program. Internal memorandum of the Jesse Jackson 1988 Campaign, April 22, 1988.
25. Navarro, V. Evaluation of the Jackson-Dukakis Philadelphia and Pittsburgh debates. Internal memorandum of the Jesse Jackson 1988 Campaign, April 25, 1988.
26. Navarro, V. Letter to Reverend Jackson, June 13, 1988.
27. Paying for Our Dreams: A Budget Plan for Jobs, Peace and Justice. Position paper of the Jesse Jackson 1988 Campaign.
28. Jackson, J. A National Health Program for the Needy, Not for the Greedy. Speech to the Annual Convention of the American Federation of State, County and Municipal Employees, June 22, 1988.
29. The Jackson National Health Program. Position paper of the Jesse Jackson 1988 Campaign.
30. Draft Platform Issues. Internal document of the Jesse Jackson 1988 Campaign.
31. Borosage, R. L. Draft Jackson 88 Platform.
32. The Restoration of Competence and Hope. Drafting Committee Proposal for the 1988 Democratic Party Platform.
33. Jackson Amendments or Planks to Draft Platform Document. Meeting of the Democratic Party Platform Committee, Denver, Colorado, June 24–26, 1988.
34. The Minority Report to the 1988 Democratic Platform. Democratic National Convention, Atlanta, Georgia, July 18–21, 1988.
35. The Restoration of Competence and the Revival of Hope. Majority Report to the 1988 Democratic Platform. Democratic National Convention, Atlanta, Georgia, July 18–21, 1988.
36. Preliminary List of Jackson Wins in Denver Session. Internal document of the Jesse Jackson 1988 Campaign.

CHAPTER 12

The Jackson National Health Program

Vicente Navarro, David U. Himmelstein, and Steffie Woolhandler

INTRODUCTION: HEALTH IS NOT A HUMAN RIGHT
IN TODAY'S UNITED STATES

Health is not a human right in today's United States. Millions of Americans do not receive the care they need because they cannot pay for it. Among Western industrialized nations, only our country and South Africa lack a National Health Program that makes access to health care a basic right for all.

The President and the U.S. Congress frequently claim that we have neither the resources nor the popular will to make health a human right in this country. They are wrong. As one of the wealthiest countries ever known, we have the resources to make sure that everyone who needs care receives it. We already spend more on medical care than any other nation on earth. Nevertheless, no other industrialized nation except South Africa faces our combined problems of wrong priorities, high costs of health care, and poor health coverage. Americans are aware of these problems. They want major changes in the way we organize and pay for health care. Two-thirds of Americans feel that our medical care system requires major changes; and 72 percent favor the establishment of a federal comprehensive and universal health care program that would assure the right to receive health care. Americans have favored such a program, even at the cost of paying higher taxes, for more than 20 years. Responding to this popular demand, the Democratic Party's platform called for a National Health Program in 1972, in 1976, and again in 1980. In 1984, the Democratic Party gave up on that demand; going along with political fashions and expediency, it joined the Republican Party in calling for reduction of government programs. During the 1984 Democratic primaries, Jesse Jackson was the only candidate to call for a National Health Program.

Originally published in the International Journal of Health Services, 19(1): 19–44, 1989.

During these years under the Republican Administration, federal health expenditures have received unprecedented cuts. Consequently, the percentage of the poor receiving Medicaid has declined during the Reagan years, and the out-of-pocket and direct expenditures of the elderly have increased. Medicare, which represents 7 percent of all federal expenditures, has received 12 percent of all federal cuts. Thus, the percentage of federal expenditures going to the care of the elderly and disabled has declined from 7.6 to 7.1 percent, while the percentage for defense has increased from 22 to 26 percent. Also, during these years of Republican regime, we have seen a weakening of government interventions to protect the health and safety of workers, farmers, and consumers, and the safety of the environment.

In the private sector, health insurance premiums of working Americans have increased at unprecedented rates, with further growth of the amount of money people have to pay as copayments and deductibles.

All these policies have had a devastating effect on the health of our people. From 1980 to 1985, more U.S. children died of poverty, hunger, and malnutrition than the total number of U.S. battle deaths in the Vietnam War. Today, a child from a low-income family (black or white) is twice as likely to die in the first year of life as a child from a higher income family. Infant mortality—a good indicator of the health status of a population—is no longer declining at the rate it did in the last 20 years. We are 19th in the infant mortality league. Even some underdeveloped countries, such as Singapore, have lower infant mortality than we do.

Recently, some new proposals have been put forward by the U.S. Congress that would expand the rather limited health benefits coverage of our population. These new proposals are necessary, but insufficient to solve our major problems. The Catastrophic Health Care Bill for the elderly, for example, will still leave our elderly without coverage for major health care expenditures; they will continue to pay a large percentage of their health expenses, with our low-income senior citizens spending 25 percent of their income on medical care. Similarly, the employer-mandated health care coverage proposal put forward by Senators Kennedy and Weicker—the Minimum Essential Health Care Act—will still leave 14 million Americans uninsured and 25 million underinsured.

We cannot continue with this patchwork approach to health care. We need bold leadership and a new direction.

THE PROBLEMS WITH OUR CURRENT SYSTEM

Inadequate Coverage and Lack of Coverage

In 1986, 38 million Americans did not have any form of health insurance coverage, public or private; 36 percent of them were children. In 1984, 35 million people were underinsured, and 55 percent of poor or near-poor blacks and 63 percent of Hispanics were uninsured for all or part of the year. In 1986, more than a third of black women and more than a fifth of white women received inadequate prenatal care. Problems of coverage affect not only the minorities, but the majority of Americans. People have to pay higher out-of-pocket expenses for medical care in the United States than in any other industrialized nation.

The situation has been worsening during this Republican Administration. The number of people without health coverage increased by 5 million from 1982 to 1984. The average out-of-pocket expenditures for the average American have increased, and the percentage of Americans who do not have a regular source of care has increased by 65 percent. Our elders have seen their Medicare premiums increased by 38 percent. People are paying more and getting less coverage.

Excessive Costs

We spend more on health care than any other society: 11.2 percent of our gross national product (GNP). And the rate of growth of these expenditures (8.9 percent per annum in 1987) is higher than the rate of growth of our GNP. Medical care expenditures are among the fastest growing expenditures in our economy. A major reason for the growth of these health expenditures is the very fast growth of health care costs.

The President and the U.S. Congress have tried to control the enormous growth of these costs by stimulating "competition" in the medical care sector. By having hospitals and other providers competing for patients, the price and overall costs of health services would supposedly decline. They have not. The market does not work in medical care. The providers, such as hospitals, nursing homes, physicians, and insurance companies, have enormous influence in shaping prices, costs, and expenditures. Recent studies have shown that competition has exacerbated the problem of high costs and large expenditures. The rate of growth of national health expenditures (corrected for the overall inflation rate) has been larger in the 1980s (the "competitive" years) than in the 1970s. Costs have increased, as have out-of-pocket expenditures for the average American. In 1985, high costs of health care were considered by the majority of Americans to be among their top five concerns in the health sector. Also, 73 percent of Americans thought that medical and hospital fees rose too high, and 20 percent feared that they would not have been able to pay for necessary health care. As a consequence of this large growth of prices and costs, health benefits coverage has further declined.

"Competition" has not only increased costs and reduced health care benefits coverage, it has also stimulated an economic behavior among providers in which patients are evaluated for their profitability. Many providers are selecting "profitable" cases and discharging prematurely or refusing "unprofitable" cases (such as AIDS (acquired immune deficiency syndrome) patients, whose average cost per case is $120,000). Examples are many. Seventy-eight percent of admitting physicians report pressure from their hospitals to discharge patients. A major nursing home chain—Manor Care—refuses to serve unprofitable Medicaid patients at its 147 nursing homes, preferring wealthy and lucrative patients. In Austin, Texas, Hospital Corporation of America purchased a hospital and closed the rehabilitation unit that served about 400 severely impaired patients—the only such unit in the city—because the unit was not profitable. The list could go on and on.

Crisis Intervention Rather Than Prevention

The World Health Organization defines health as "the physical, mental, and social well-being of mankind, not just the absence of disease." The road to good health is not only through health care services, but through improvement of living and working conditions. And the goal of the health care system should be not only to cure but, most importantly, to prevent the acquisition of disease and disability and promote the full development of a joyful and healthy life. These goals and the roads to achieve them require major changes in our priorities, both in our society and in our approach to medical care.

1. Poverty is a major cause of poor health, disease, and death. Today, on average, one child dies of poverty, hunger, and malnutrition every 50 minutes in the United States. The medical care system tries to solve this problem with high-technology interventions. North Carolina, for example, has about the same number of babies born per year as Sweden, but has twice as many low birth weight babies and neonatal deaths, due to poverty and malnutrition. North Carolina, however, has twice as many highly expensive ventilator-equipped neonatal intensive care unit beds as Sweden, with further expansion proposed. It would be much more humane and cost-effective to provide food, social services, and prenatal care to expectant mothers. The Neonatal Intensive Care Unit costs more than $1,000 per day, often amounting to $100,000 per infant, while adequate prenatal care costs only $800 per infant.

2. The 4 million major injuries per annum at the work place, whose economic costs (in care payments) amount to $982 million, could be prevented at much lower cost by improving safety and working conditions.

3. Relatively low expenditures for prevention of AIDS, in programs of education aimed at the general population and at populations at risk, could have saved much of the $40 billion likely to be spent on the care of AIDS patients by the year 1991.

4. Many patients are wrongly hospitalized: it has been estimated that 20 percent of inpatients in highly technological hospitals could be taken care of in less expensive, less technologically oriented, and more humane institutions.

These are examples of wrong priorities in our society and in our medical care system, which place more emphasis on curative, high-technology medicine than on preventive health care that is cheaper and more humane.

Privatization/Medical Lobbies/Excessive Profits

Not only does the United States spend the most money on health care, but it is also the country in which most health care funds come from the private sector. Of all the Western industrialized nations, the United States spends the least public funds in the health sector (4.5 percent of the GNP compared with 8.8 percent in Sweden, 6.6 percent in West Germany, 6.6 percent in France, and 6.2 percent in Canada). Of all industrialized nations, the United States spends most on defense and least on health. The health statistics show the consequences of this gap. The United States has the highest infant mortality rate among the top 19 industrialized nations. In many inner cities, the health indicators are similar to those in underdeveloped countries. While the President and the U.S. Congress keep referring to the need to close the military gap, we should speak of the enormous urgency to close the health gap, which is due in part to the gap in public expenditures on health between the United States and other industrialized nations.

Another characteristic of U.S. medical care is that most of the funds—private and public—are spent on private institutions and providers. Less than 10 percent of overall health expenditures are spent in the public sector. Since 1965, the federal government has spent more than a trillion dollars on health care in the private sector, has provided more than $40 billion for private hospital capital spending, fueled the creation of the $80 billion per year private health administrative apparatus, and virtually guaranteed the profits of drug companies, equipment manufacturers, hospital and nursing home chains, and other profit-making health enterprises. Yet government exercises little real control over the enormous health care industry that it funds. Private providers have been given license to dominate health care, and excused from the burden of responsibility for the health of the population. This is the root of the problems of high costs and poor health benefits coverage. Private providers, whether for-profit or nominally nonprofit, have tailored services to financial rather than health needs. While the private sector has rushed to accept government payments for covered services, it has proven unwilling to provide needed services for which compensation is not available, even though most of its buildings and equipment were bought with government money. As a result, the first person most patients see on entering a hospital or clinic is a billing clerk who collects the information needed to separate lucrative from nonlucrative patients. Two hundred thousand people are refused care each year at private hospital emergency rooms because they cannot pay and are uninsured, emergency rooms most often constructed with public funds. Another 800,000 families are denied nonemergent care each year. Some of these people forego care completely. Others rely on the chronically underfunded and often distant public hospitals and clinics.

While government revenues have paid for the massive expansion of private health care, public hospitals have been left as pitiful remnants of their former selves, housed in aging buildings, equipped with outdated machines, serving largely those uninsured patients who are unprofitable for private hospitals. Since 1965, six of 19 public hospitals in New York City have been closed, as have 29 of California's 66 county hospitals and the only public hospitals serving Detroit and Philadelphia. Meanwhile, since the founding of the first for-profit hospital chain in 1960, the number of for-profit hospitals has grown to more than 1,000. By 1982, Hospital Corporation of America controlled 351 hospitals with more than 50,000 beds and total revenues of $3.5 billion, much of it from government sources.

The emphasis on "competition" under Reagan has exacerbated the problems of privatization and profit-making. Hospitals and health maintenance organizations (HMOs) have reaped enormous financial rewards by successfully "beating" the system. They have excluded the uninsured and very sick while encouraging the well-insured and not very sick to use their facilities. As a result, average hospital profits on Medicare patients have more than doubled, while many inner city and rural hospitals serving people most in need of care have experienced an increasing financial crisis, and the maldistribution of health facilities grows ever worse—rich hospitals in already well-served communities have the cash to expand, while communities most in need are threatened with the loss of the few remaining providers.

The irrationality of privatization and competition is emphasized by the fact that financial success has little to do with efficiency, and nothing whatsoever to do with meeting medical needs. For-profit hospitals make profits because they charge more, give less nursing care, and exclude the uninsured. They have higher administrative costs than nonprofit hospitals. Hospitals affiliated with multi-hospital systems charge 19 percent more than free-standing hospitals, and for-profit chain hospitals charge 36 percent more than free-standing ones. While the number of people without insurance and unable to gain access to care has skyrocketed, so have the profits of hospitals and other health care firms. Indeed, even the Peer Review Organizations, which contract with the federal government to monitor the Medicare program for abuse, are enjoying record profits. According to the Inspector General, 38 Peer Review Organizations made profits of $27.5 million on their initial two-year contracts. In the most extreme cases, "competitive" incentives have led to criminal behavior in search of profits. International Medical Centers (IMC), the largest HMO in the Medicare program, signed up thousands of elderly patients and then refused to pay for their care—a sure-fire way to make money. The IMC president was indicted for fraud after protracted investigations that revealed the hiring of nine ex-Reagan Administration officials by IMC to smooth the way with the government.

In summary, it is this for-profit motivation in the health sector that shapes the priorities to optimize revenues rather than respond to human needs. Profits before people. During the Reagan Administration, the profits of the hospital industry have increased. Four out of five hospitals in 1985 had a profit margin of 14 percent, several times higher than the 3.3 percent after-tax margin reported by *Business Week* for the services industry as a whole. From 1981 to 1986, the average net income of physicians increased from $90,000 to $120,000, while the income of the average wage earner declined. Also during this period, hospital corporation executives remained among the highest paid in the nation. David Jones of Humana makes $21 million per year, placing him at the top of the corporate heap; $21 million is enough to give 1,750 families a poverty-level income. National Medical Enterprise's Leonard Cohen and Richard Eamer are the two highest paid executives in the Los Angeles area, making $9.7 million and $7.9 million, respectively. According to the General Accounting Office, for-profit takeovers of nonprofit hospitals have resulted in a doubling of capital costs per patient discharged (much of which is paid by government). The new for-profit owners paid inflated prices, borrowed heavily, and then passed the interest costs along to patients and government.

There is too much greed in the health sector. Too much profit is being made by the greedy at the cost of the needy. These powerful medical, insurance, hospital, and corporate interest groups have enormous influence in the U.S. Congress and White House. The current Republican Administration is crowded with individuals who worked for and were part of these business interest groups. Starting from the top: President Reagan used to work for General Electric—a major hospital supplier—appearing in advertisements opposing Medicare, the program responsible for a decline of 2 percent per year in the mortality rate among our senior citizens. Vice-President Bush used to be a director of Lilly, one of the largest and most profitable drug and medical equipment companies. The list could go on.

These interest groups are also very powerful in the U.S. Congress. It is difficult for people to win when corporate political action committees, responding to the health industry, gave the candidates running for federal office in the last two elections 14 times as much money as did political action committees favoring national health coverage. This situation cannot go on. We must change it.

THE JACKSON NATIONAL HEALTH PROGRAM

These major problems must be resolved. We need a new direction to assure that health is indeed a human right in the United States. In order to achieve this, we call for a National Health Program with the following characteristics.

Coverage: Universal and Comprehensive

The National Health Program (NHP) will provide comprehensive health care coverage and will ensure access to quality health care to all citizens and residents of the United States, regardless of income, race, class, gender, or sexual preference. The health benefits will include the provision of and access to acute, rehabilitative, chronic, long-term, and home care; mental health and dental care; prescription drugs and medical supplies; and preventive and public health measures.

The program will be universal. All citizens and residents of the United States will be provided with a blue, white, and red American health card giving them access to health care providers of their choice. Copayments and deductibles will be eliminated. As in Canada, alternative insurance coverage for services included under the NHP will be eliminated.

Universal coverage will solve the gravest problem in health care by eliminating financial barriers to care for the uninsured and underinsured. A single comprehensive program is necessary not only to assure equal access, but also to minimize the complexity and expense of billing and administration. Mandating public administration of the insurance funds will save tens of billions of dollars. The more than 1,500 private health insurers currently consume about 10 percent of their revenues for overhead, while both the Canadian NHP and the U.S. Medicare program have overhead costs of only 2 to 3 percent. The complexity of our current insurance system, with its multiplicity of payers, forces U.S. hospitals to spend more than twice as much as their Canadian counterparts on billing and administration, and U.S. physicians to spend about 10 percent of their gross incomes on excess billing costs. Failure to eliminate alternative insurance coverage for included services would require the continuation of the costly excess bureaucracy.

Copayments and deductibles endanger the health of the sick poor, decrease the use of vital inpatient services as much as the use of unnecessary ones, particularly discourage the use of preventive care, and are unwieldy and expensive to administer. The Canadian experience suggests that out-of-pocket charges are not necessary for cost containment. Canada has eliminated most such charges, yet health costs are lower than in the United States and have risen slowly. Increases in copayments and deductibles have failed to moderate cost escalation in the United States.

Funding

Federal Administration of the NHP Funds: Progressive Rather Than Regressive. The funds for the NHP will come from the same sources that they come from today: government, individuals, and corporations. And the amounts coming from each source will be similar to the amounts collected today from each source, except in the case of individuals. Individuals will be paying less and getting more because the federal government will be the primary administrator of health care funds and will use its purchasing power to stimulate a far more efficient delivery of services, which will continue to take place primarily in the private sector. The current system of funding health care, which relies very heavily on premiums, payroll taxes, and fees-for-service, is highly regressive: it is unfair to the middle- and low-income families who pay for the majority of health services in the United States.

Also, the current system of health benefits coverage, which relates the type and size of health benefits to people's jobs, produces enormous inequities in the distribution of health benefits. For 80 percent of our people, health benefits coverage is provided at the workplace. Where the unions are strong, as in manufacturing, health benefits coverage is much more extensive than in those sectors where unions are weak, such as services and sales. Thus, the type of health benefits that families or individuals get depends on the type of work and bargaining power. A sales worker has, on average, 53 percent less coverage than a manufacturing worker.

This diversity and inequality of health benefits is detrimental not only to the majority of workers who are not in manufacturing, but also to workers in manufacturing. Manufacturing workers are very vulnerable to corporate employers' decisions to reduce benefits, increase copayments and deductibles, or establish two tiers of benefits, one for the old timers and another (with fewer benefits) for new entrants to the workplace. Relating health benefits to type of job is wrong. It divides people in different types of employment and divides the employed and the unemployed. Moreover, it creates an enormous fear of job loss or the risk of changing jobs because health benefits may be lost or reduced in a new situation. Seventy-five percent of workers over 45 years of age who lost their jobs in the 1982 recession lost their health insurance as well. The provision of health care should be based on need rather than on ability to pay or ability to bargain.

A further problem of relating health benefits coverage to the workplace is that the current shift of employment in the United States from manufacturing (high benefits coverage) to retail and service jobs (low coverage), the increase in part-time employment (low coverage), and the high number of newly created low-wage jobs (low coverage) lead to an increased number of underinsured, uninsured, and uninsurable workers. Between 1982 and 1984, for example, 5.5 million jobs were added to the workplace, but the number of workers with employer-paid health benefits coverage fell by 1 million.

Sources of Revenue. Revenues for the NHP will come from several sources:

1. Federal, state, and local governments will contribute to the NHP Trust Fund in the same percentages that they currently contribute to the health sector. *Federal revenues will remain the same*, since the NHP will not require extra federal revenues. Therefore, the federal deficit will not be affected by the establishment of an NHP.

2. Corporations will contribute to medical care, on average, the same amount they pay today. Rather than paying through group insurance packages for their employees, they will pay the same amounts to the NHP Trust Fund as earmarked taxes.

3. Individuals will pay less than under the current system of individual premiums, copayments, deductibles, and fees. Rather than paying the insurance companies or providers, they will pay a lesser amount to the NHP Trust Fund through earmarked health taxes based on personal income taxes. General income taxation retains some (limited) measure of progressivity (in spite of the recent "tax reform" packages that sharply reduced taxes on the wealthy) and provides the broadest and fairest base on which to fund the NHP. Collecting funds through taxes is both fairer and cheaper than collecting individual premiums, copayments, deductibles, and fees. Individuals will pay earmarked health taxes that will be, on average, less than they pay now through the private sector; savings will be $9.5 billion in just one year, 1989. Because of the savings incurred and more efficient administration of the NHP, individuals will get far more comprehensive care than they currently receive. Practically all health care needs will be covered, without copayments, deductibles, or any other expense, and individuals will have free choice of provider. Public opinion polls, as well as the 1986 Massachusetts NHP referendum, indicate that the American people would welcome such a system.

Payments to Providers. The system of payment to providers will minimize financial incentives for both overcare and undercare. Hospitals will be shifted from their current fee-for-service reimbursement basis to an annually budgeted basis. The federal government, operating through state and local authorities, will negotiate annual operating budgets with each hospital, based on the size and health care needs of the population served by the hospital. (The federal government has shown in a number of other programs, in health care as well as in employment and other fields, that it can perform such an allocation based upon a variety of statistical indicators). The hospitals will then know what staff they should hire and will plan their service delivery in the most sensible and cost-efficient way. By eliminating billing and much of the attendant internal cost accounting, such annual budgeting could save the 10 percent of total hospital spending now devoted to such activities. (On average, U.S. hospitals spend more than 18 percent of total revenues for billing and administration, while Canadian hospitals spend only 8 percent because of simplification of billing.)

Capital funds for expanding or replacing health care facilities will be allocated by state and local authorities, and handled separately from operating budgets. (Canada has shown that this is an effective and workable scheme for ensuring that there is equitable access to health care facilities for the entire population of the country.)

Physicians will be paid by a combination of salary, capitation, and fee-for-service. Physicians accepting payment from the NHP will not receive additional payment from individuals for covered services. Payments to providers will be made by the NHP Trust Fund directly, or indirectly through private administrative agencies (such as employer-employee trust funds or insurance companies) that can administer the provision of benefits as efficiently as the NHP, without prior selection of beneficiaries. In such a case, the NHP will contract with these agencies for the administration of benefits.

Savings and Other Benefits

A National Health Program will assure universal access to comprehensive medical care with no out-of-pocket charges, copayments, or deductibles. The resulting increased utilization of health services can most reliably be estimated based on the findings of the Rand Corporation's massive five-year health insurance experiment. Overall utilization will increase by 14.6 percent. Death rates will drop by 0.45 deaths per 1,000 population per year, averting about 106,000 deaths annually in the United States.

Since the United States currently has a surplus of hospital beds and an impending excess of physicians, the 14.6 percent increase in utilization could easily be accommodated by existing resources at modest cost. For instance, a patient hospitalized in an otherwise empty hospital bed costs only 64.5 percent of current hospital charges, since fixed costs for buildings and equipment can then be spread over a larger number of patients. Similarly, physicians' office expenses will rise little if patients fill appointment slots that now are empty. Overall, the 14.6 percent increase in utilization of services will result in a 9.4 percent increase in costs if no other changes are made in the health care delivery system.

However, an NHP will also reorganize the administrative structure of health care and greatly streamline the health bureaucracy. The resulting savings will more than offset the cost increases due to increased utilization. Since all will be covered, there will be no need for the costly efforts currently expended to determine insurance eligibility and to market competing insurance plans. Since hospitals will be paid on a lump sum basis, they will no longer send millions of bills, keep track of the enormous welter of detail required to attribute costs to individual patients, nor perform the many other administrative tasks required by the current reimbursement system. Similarly, doctors' billing will be greatly simplified. Administrative and billing costs for nursing homes, home care agencies, and other providers will also be greatly reduced. Currently, health administration costs in the United States amount to 22.7 percent of total health spending. In contrast, administration in the Canadian NHP accounts for only 12 percent of health spending. Thus, an NHP similar to the Canadian system will result in annual administrative savings of 10.7 percent of health spending, $69.3 billion in 1989. Tables 1 to 4 show the savings on administration, marketing, and profits under the Jackson NHP in 1989, 1990, 1991, and 1992. Table 5 shows the savings for the whole period 1989–92, $314.4 billion. These savings will be partially offset by the expected increase in the utilization of health services, due to the expansion of health care usage stimulated by the establishment of the Jackson NHP. Therefore, the net savings (Tables 6 to 10) will be lower than the ones presented in Tables 1 to 5. The total savings for 1989 will be $9.5 billion and for the period 1989–92, $43.5 billion. These savings will enable the Jackson National Health Program to diminish substantially individual contributions to the NHP.

At present, government pays for about 40 percent of all health care. Another 25 percent is paid by corporate employers, while the remaining 35 percent is paid by individuals for insurance policies and out-of-pocket expenses. Under the Jackson NHP, the out-of-pocket expenses and the insurance premiums will be practically eliminated. The Jackson NHP will cover the overwhelming majority of health care benefits. Only

Table 1

Savings on administration, marketing, and profits under the Jackson National
Health Program, 1989

Category of expenditure	Projected cost under current system ($billions)	Projected cost under NHP ($billions)	Savings under NHP ($billions)
Insurance overhead and central program administration	31.7	14.8	16.9
Hospital administration	41.8	18.3	23.5
Nursing home administration	7.2	4.0	3.2
Physicians' office overhead and billing	54.4	43.5	10.9
Hospital and health care advertising	6.5	0	6.5
Health industry profits	22.5	14.2	8.3
Total	164.1	94.8	69.3

Table 2

Savings on administration, marketing, and profits under the Jackson National
Health Program, 1990

Category of expenditure	Projected cost under current system ($billions)	Projected cost under NHP ($billions)	Savings under NHP ($billions)
Insurance overhead and central program administration	34.6	16.2	18.4
Hospital administration	45.8	20.0	25.8
Nursing home administration	7.8	4.4	3.4
Physicians' office overhead and billing	59.7	47.7	12.0
Hospital and health care advertising	7.1	0	7.1
Health industry profits	24.6	15.5	9.1
Total	179.6	103.8	75.8

Table 3

Savings on administration, marketing, and profits under the Jackson National
Health Program, 1991

Category of expenditure	Projected cost under current system ($billions)	Projected cost under NHP ($billions)	Savings under NHP ($billions)
Insurance overhead and central program administration	36.3	17.7	18.6
Hospital administration	50.3	22.0	28.3
Nursing home administration	8.6	4.8	3.8
Physicians' office overhead and billing	65.6	52.5	13.1
Hospital and health care advertising	7.8	0	7.8
Health industry profits	26.9	17.0	9.9
Total	195.5	114.0	81.5

Table 4

Savings on administration, marketing, and profits under the Jackson National
Health Program, 1992

Category of expenditure	Projected cost under current system ($billions)	Projected cost under NHP ($billions)	Savings under NHP ($billions)
Insurance overhead and central program administration	38.2	19.3	18.9
Hospital administration	55.1	24.1	31.0
Nursing home administration	9.4	5.2	4.2
Physicians' office overhead and billing	72.1	57.7	14.4
Hospital and health care advertising	8.5	0	8.5
Health industry profits	29.4	18.6	10.8
Total	212.7	124.9	87.8

Table 5

Savings on administration, marketing, and profits under the Jackson National
Health Program, 1989–92

Category of expenditure	Projected cost under current system ($billions)	Projected cost under NHP ($billions)	Savings under NHP ($billions)
Insurance overhead and central program administration	140.8	68.0	72.8
Hospital administration	193.0	84.4	108.6
Nursing home administration	33.0	18.4	14.6
Physicians' office overhead and billing	251.8	201.4	50.4
Hospital and health care advertising	29.9	0	29.9
Health industry profits	103.4	65.3	38.1
Total	751.9	437.5	314.4

some forms of elective care, such as some types of plastic surgery, will not be covered. Because of the savings detailed before, individuals will pay much less and will get much more. Just in 1989, individuals will pay $9.5 billion less than they would have to pay under the current system. Individuals' contributions will be made to the NHP by paying earmarked health taxes on personal income.

Corporate costs will remain unchanged, but will be paid as taxes into the NHP. In the long term, their contributions will decline. Government contributions to the NHP (the Federal Health Trust Fund) will be similar to the contributions under current arrangements. Tables 6 to 10 show the health spending under the current health system and under the Jackson NHP by sources of funds for 1989, 1990, 1991, 1992, and for the whole period 1989–92.

Administration

1. The program will be federally administered. We have learned from the last 20 years that an NHP must be funded and guided by the federal government in order to assure adequate funding in poorer areas, to prevent regressive state governments from blocking effective implementation of an NHP, and to assure that all Americans have the same chance to get good care.

In effect, since 1965 we have been conducting two experiments in National Health Programs. One, Medicare, provides health insurance for the elderly under the auspices of the federal government. The other, Medicaid, provides health insurance for the poor through a program funded jointly by the federal and state governments, and

Table 6

Health spending in 1989 under the current health system and under the
Jackson National Health Program, by source of funds

Source of funds	Projected spending under current system ($billions)	Projected spending under Jackson NHP ($billions)	Savings under Jackson NHP ($billions)
Government			
Federal	176.4		
State and local	68.0	Same	—
Total	244.5		
Corporations	147.8	Same	—
Individuals	198.8	189.3	9.5
Total	591.1	581.6	9.5

Table 7

Health spending in 1990 under the current health system and under the
Jackson National Health Program, by source of funds

Source of funds	Projected spending under current system ($billions)	Projected spending under Jackson NHP ($billions)	Savings under Jackson NHP ($billions)
Government			
Federal	195.5		
State and local	73.6	Same	—
Total	269.0		
Corporations	161.8	Same	—
Individuals	216.5	206.1	10.4
Total	647.3	636.9	10.4

Table 8

Health spending in 1991 under the current health system and under the
Jackson National Health Program, by source of funds

Source of funds	Projected spending under current system ($billions)	Projected spending under Jackson NHP ($billions)	Savings under Jackson NHP ($billions)
Government			
Federal	216.0		
State and local	79.3	Same	—
Total	295.4		
Corporations	177.0	Same	—
Individuals	235.7	224.4	11.3
Total	708.1	696.8	11.3

Table 9

Health spending in 1992 under the current health system and under the
Jackson National Health Program, by source of funds

Source of funds	Projected spending under current system ($billions)	Projected spending under Jackson NHP ($billions)	Savings under Jackson NHP ($billions)
Government			
Federal	238.3		
State and local	85.4	Same	—
Total	323.7		
Corporations	193.2	Same	—
Individuals	256.1	243.7	12.4
Total	773.0	760.6	12.4

Table 10

Health spending, 1989–92, under the current health system and under the
Jackson National Health Program, by source of funds

Source of funds	Projected spending under current system ($billions)	Projected spending under Jackson NHP ($billions)	Savings under Jackson NHP ($billions)
Government			
Federal	826.2	Same	–
State and local	306.3		
Total	1132.6		
Corporations	679.8	Same	–
Individuals	907.1	863.6	43.5
Total	2719.5	2676.0	43.5

administered by the states. Although Medicare has a number of defects, especially
failure to cover all of an individual's health care bills, the program has been efficiently
managed and popular with both patients and providers. The administrative costs are
much lower for this highly popular federal program than for similar programs in the
private sector.

Medicaid, on the other hand, suffers from limitations placed on it by different
states, reflecting biases against minorities and the poor as well as the fiscal condition
of each state's budget. Many states have demeaning eligibility tests, poor quality care
for Medicaid recipients, and inadequate access to many Medicaid-covered services for
qualified recipients (due, in part, to low reimbursement rates set by the states, with
consequent reluctance by providers to provide Medicaid-covered services).

We believe that decent health care must be established as a right for all, and that
this right, like our other constitutional rights, must be guaranteed at the federal level.

2. While the federal government will have the responsibility of administering the
NHP (through a National Trust Fund and a National Health Board) and assuring the
provision of comprehensive health coverage to the population, the states and local
authorities (counties and municipalities) will be responsible for the planning of health
services in their states and local areas. Thus, operating budgets and capital expenditures will have to be approved at the state and local authority levels. State and local
plans will have to be developed and approved by the State and Local Health Boards.
These plans will have to meet the federal guidelines approved by the National Health
Board.

3. The health institutions, such as hospitals and nursing homes, that receive
government funds will be governed by boards of trustees that are publicly accountable
and representative of the communities they serve. Today, 53 percent of hospital funds
and 83 percent of nursing home funds are already tax funds, but the Boards of
Trustees—the top authorities in each institution—are highly unrepresentative of the

population they serve. There is a perverse quota system in which the trustees come only from the top 5 percent (in income) of our population. This situation has to change. Community participation must be made a meaningful and not token reality in our country. In no other area is community participation more important than in the health sector.

4. The Executive and Legislative branches of the federal government will appoint a National Health Board to be in charge of directing the NHP. At the state and local authority levels, the executive and legislative branches of each level of government will appoint the Health Boards, the top planning authorities at each level of government.

5. The National Health Policy Guidelines will aim at changing the orientation of the system, shifting toward a greater emphasis on preventive, community, environmental, occupational, and social interventions. This shifting of priorities will require a combination of government interventions with popular participation in which the populations affected by the health programs should play a major role in their governance. Just one example: occupational medicine. This branch of medicine is primarily controlled by management rather than labor. Most occupational doctors are paid by management, and their work shows it. We must reverse this situation, as has been done in other Western countries, and give a major voice to the workers and their unions in the governance of their occupational health services. There is plenty of evidence that workers pay far more attention to their health and safety than bosses do. The NHP will emphasize promotion of occupational health and safety services to protect the life and health of our workers and farmers. Also, the NHP will require that firms employing more than 20 people have a major role in the development of occupational health and safety policies in their work place. Such firms will have to provide occupational health and safety services under the directorship of a health and safety board in which the employee representatives will have a majority.

6. All citizens and residents will have a free choice of provider.

7. The NHP will guarantee quality of care by establishing federal norms and standards of good health care to be followed by providers that receive funds from the NHP. Moreover, the National Health Boards, as well as the State and Local Health Boards, will have, among their planning responsibilities, the task of evaluating the health care given by the providers and assuring their high standards of quality.

8. The NHP will mandate the establishment in each health care institution (such as hospitals, nursing homes, and group practices) and each local authority of a patient advocate(s) who will be appointed by the local Health Board and who will have responsibility for responding to and acting upon the grievances and concerns of patients. The Boards of these institutions will act upon the grievances and complaints brought to the Boards by the patient advocate(s).

Effects of the Jackson National Health Program

On Patients. The NHP will assure everyone in the United States the right to comprehensive health care. Each person will receive an NHP identification card entitling him or her to all necessary medical care without copayments or deductibles. The card will be usable at any fee-for-service practitioner and at any institution receiving a global budget. Patients opting for capitated care in an HMO will receive nonemergency care only through that HMO, though they will be able to transfer to the fee-for-service option after a 30-day waiting period. Patients and potential patients—citizens and residents of the United States—will be the ones to benefit most from the Jackson National Health Program. They will have full access to all types of medical care, including acute, rehabilitative, chronic, long-term, and home care; mental health and dental care; prescription drugs and medical supplies; and preventive and public health measures. The Jackson NHP will be fully comprehensive and universal; everyone will be covered. People will receive care according to their needs rather than according to their ability to pay or their bargaining strength.

1. The elderly will stop worrying about becoming bankrupt because they need long-term care, or any other form of care.

2. The poor will get all the care they need without the indignities of having to pass means tests.

3. Workers will stop worrying about being able to pay the ever-growing premiums, copayments, and deductibles. They will also stop worrying about losing health insurance when they change or lose a job.

4. Farmers will stop worrying about being able to pay all the family's bills.

5. Mothers and fathers will stop worrying about insufficient coverage to protect their children.

6. AIDS patients will stop worrying about how to pay their bills and being discriminated against because of their conditions.

All Americans will benefit from the Jackson NHP. This program will provide health security and will empower all our people in solidarity.

On Unions. Labor will benefit extensively from the Jackson NHP. As in Canada and the overwhelming majority of industrialized nations, labor unions will not have to bargain for health care benefits, enabling them to focus on other work-related issues. One of the reasons the Canadian United Auto Workers (UAW) split from the U.S. UAW was the need of Canadian labor (whose health benefits are already covered by the Canadian national health system) to focus on other issues more important to them, while the U.S. UAW still must focus its bargaining power on the achievement of health benefits. Also, the Jackson NHP will emphasize occupational health and safety at the workplace. It will mandate employer-provided occupational health and safety services to employees.

Unions will continue to influence their health trust funds and the self-managed employer-employee health trust funds. These trust funds will become administrative agencies for the NHP and will be regulated by the NHP.

On Corporations and Employers. Under the Jackson NHP, employers will be able to control the costs of health care more easily than under current arrangements. The NHP will control the growth of health expenditures far better than under current arrangements. Therefore, the employers' contributions will stop increasing at the current high rates. Employers will continue to influence their self-managed trust funds, which will become administrative agencies for the NHP, subject to NHP regulations.

On Practitioners. Physicians will freely choose fee-for-service and/or salaried practice. Fee-for-service practitioners will be reimbursed for the care of anyone not enrolled in an HMO. Since financial barriers to care will be eliminated, the number of ambulatory visits are likely to increase, at least initially. Physicians will be able to practice at any hospital willing to grant them privileges. The entrepreneurial aspects of medical practice—the problems as well as the possibilities—will be greatly limited. Doctors will concentrate on medicine; every patient will be fully insured, and billing greatly simplified; physicians will be able to increase their incomes only by providing more patient care.

Bureaucratic interference in clinical decision-making will sharply diminish. Cost containment will be achieved through controls on overall spending made possible by the NHP's role as a monopsony payer, and through limiting pecuniary incentives, obviating the need for the kind of detailed administrative supervision characteristic of the diagnosis related group (DRG) program and similar schemes. Indeed, there is much less administrative intrusion in day-to-day clinical practice in Canada (and most other countries with NHPs) than in the United States.

Billing will involve imprinting the patient's NHP identification card on a billing slip, checking the box appropriate for the complexity of the encounter, and sending the slip (or a computer disc or tape) to the physician payment board. This simplified billing arrangement will save thousands of dollars per practitioner annually in office expense.

Practitioners in HMOs and institutions will be salaried, and insulated from the financial consequences of clinical decisions. Since savings on patient care will no longer be used for institutional expansion or profits, pressure to skimp on care will be largely eliminated.

Physicians will have a free choice of practice settings. Neither the choice of patients served nor the management of a given patient will be constrained by the patient's financial position or by bureaucratic dictum. Based on the Canadian experience, we expect average physician income to change little, though differentials between specialties might well be attenuated.

On Other Health Workers. For nurses and other clinical personnel, the burden of paperwork associated with reimbursement will be lightened; otherwise their day-to-day work will change little. The jobs of many administrative personnel and insurance company employees will be eliminated, necessitating a major effort at job placement and retraining. We advocate that many of these displaced workers be retrained and deployed in expanded programs of public health, health promotion and education, and home care, and as support personnel to free nurses for clinical tasks. The current system has too many administrators and too few care givers.

On Hospitals. Hospitals' revenues will become stable and predictable. As in the case of ambulatory care, there will probably be an increased demand for hospital services, at least initially. The costs of this increased care will be offset by savings from the abolition of billing and many other administrative tasks. More than half of the current hospital bureaucracy will be eliminated, and the remaining administrators can focus on facilitating clinical care and planning for future health needs, rather than on financial matters.

The capital budget requests of hospitals wishing to expand or modernize will be weighed against other priorities for health care investment. Hospitals will neither grow because they are profitable nor fail because of unpaid bills—though regional health planning will undoubtedly mandate that some expand and others close or be put to other uses.

On the Insurance Industry. The greatest impact will be on the insurance industry: it will diminish considerably in size. The NHP will oversee a retraining and job placement program for insurance company and hospital billing personnel.

Transition from Current Systems

The transition to the full establishment of the NHP is expected to take six years. During this period, programs will be introduced in demonstration states, with changes that will mimic existing expenditure patterns and minimize economic disruption. These changes will include (*a*) some modifications of pending legislation enabling the integration of these new programs into the NHP; (*b*) the coordination and integration of different federal and federal-state health programs; (*c*) changes in current private arrangements, stimulated by the federal government; and (*d*) development of a new federal-state-local partnership. Among these changes, the key and most important ones include:

1. The expansion of health care coverage to all employees through mandatory employer-provided comprehensive coverage of all employees. The Jackson Campaign supports the Kennedy-Weicker employer-mandated coverage proposal as a necessary step toward the establishment of an NHP.

2. The gradual transfer of the payments made by employers-employees from the group insurance or self-managed trust funds to the NHP Trust Fund. After six years, the NHP will contract directly with all the providers. The corporate contributions through earmarked taxes will be set so that the total collections equal the previous year's statewide total employer expenditures for health care, adjusted for inflation. Employers obligated by preexisting contracts to provide employee health coverage could credit the cost of those benefits toward their NHP tax liability.

3. The Jackson Campaign supports the pending Catastrophic Health Care Bill, and Senator Pepper's newly proposed program. The Jackson Campaign favors further expansion of this program to provide comprehensive long-term care. (See Jackson's campaign position paper on long-term care.) Under the Jackson NHP, Medicare funds will be integrated into the NHP Trust Fund, and federal administration of Medicare will be integrated into the NHP. Medicaid will be eliminated. Federal and state Medicaid funds will be allocated to the NHP Trust Fund. Since billing and eligibility determination will be eliminated, the contribution of each program will be based on the previous year's expenditures, adjusted for inflation.

4. After one year, individuals will stop paying premiums, copayments, and deductibles to insurance companies and fees to providers. Instead, they will pay earmarked health taxes levied to an amount lower than the health spending currently derived from individuals' insurance premiums and out-of-pocket costs. It is critical that all funds flow through the NHP. Such single-source (monopsony) payment has been the

cornerstone of successful cost containment and health planning in the Canadian system. At the establishment of the NHP, individuals will be provided with American Health Care Cards allowing free access to the health care providers of their choice.

5. The federal government, in collaboration with the state and local governments, will establish a nationwide planning, regulatory, and evaluation group that will assure the avoidance of waste and duplication of services, and the identification of still unmet needs and resources that should be developed.

6. Within three years, the federal government, with assistance from state and local governments, will establish patient advocates to defend the interests of patients in institutions receiving federal funds.

7. The federal government, with assistance from state and local governments, will take the necessary steps to change the present nonrepresentative and nonaccountable executive boards of institutions receiving federal funds.

8. The President will appoint and the U.S. Congress approve a National Commission to direct the six-year transition from current arrangements to a fully developed NHP.

9. The President will appoint and the U.S. Congress approve the establishment of the National Board of the NHP. The governors of the 50 states will appoint and the state legislatures approve the establishment of the State Boards of the NHP. The mayors and county executive officers and city and county councils will approve the city and county boards of the NHP.

The Need for Change

These are the steps necessary to guarantee that health is a human right in the United States. The Jackson NHP will strengthen the positive features of our system and reduce and even eliminate the negative features. This program can and should be established. People want it, and it is the right thing to do.

Needless to say, many arguments will be made against the establishment of such a program. One will be that the changes it calls for are too sweeping. To this argument we must answer that we cannot afford to continue in the patchwork way we have followed in the past. The problems that we face are enormous, and our people are hurting. We have tried the gradual approach, and it has failed. Twenty years after the establishment of Medicare—the program that was supposed to solve the major health care problems of our elderly—elders still pay the same percentage of their annual income for medical care. We need to change direction. We need to address the roots of the problem and dare to change. Actually, the changes proposed here have been proposed before. Back in 1969, Senator Kennedy and Congressman Griffith put forward a proposal for the establishment of a National Health Program that called for federal administration of the NHP and for the elimination of private insurance. (This proposal was similar to the Jackson National Health Program.) Later on, the Kennedy-Griffith proposal was changed to the Kennedy-Mills proposal, which was less comprehensive and allowed a role for the private insurance companies. This proposal was opposed by the Nixon Administration, which preferred to leave the existing funding arrangements unchanged. Nixon proposed to cover the uninsured by mandating all employers to offer coverage to all employees and by expanding Medicaid to increase coverage of the poor.

It speaks of how much to the right the political establishment of this country has moved that the current major Democratic proposal for covering the uninsured— Senator Kennedy's proposal—is similar to the Nixon proposal of 1974, and that what Candidate Dukakis is calling for in his plank is also a modification of the Nixon proposal. We need to change direction and raise again our people's hope and expectations. We can and should do better. Americans want it and deserve it.

Differences Between the Dukakis and the Jackson National Health Proposals

Dukakis's Campaign did not ask for a National Health Program until after the Michigan primary defeat. Since then, the Dukakis Campaign has called for a Universal Health Program. As CBS News underlined, Dukakis is trying to steal the health issue from Jackson by also calling for health care for all. Unfortunately, however, Dukakis stole the slogan but not the content of Jackson's major health proposal.

Dukakis's position paper on health asks for the "need to work towards the creation of Universal Health Care Coverage for all Americans." How? Dukakis refers to the need to mandate employer-provided health benefits for employees, as well as to expand Medicaid for the poor and Medicare for the elderly. Dukakis frequently cites his proposals for a Universal Health Care Program in Massachusetts as a model for the country.

These proposals will be an improvement over the current situation. But they will be dramatically insufficient to solve the major problems that Americans face, i.e., high costs and limited coverage of health benefits. The major flaws of the Dukakis program are the following:

1. Dukakis's program is not universal. It will still leave millions of Americans uninsured and underinsured. Individuals who are not employed or who work less than 17 hours a week, and who also cannot benefit from Medicaid, will remain uncovered. Also, the Dukakis Massachusetts Health Insurance Bill will not cover workers who work less than 20 hours a week or less than five months a year (which excludes the majority of migrant farm workers), employees of employers who hire less than five workers (one-third of the uninsured workers), or workers' dependents. Under Jackson's program, all Americans and U.S. residents will be covered.

2. Dukakis's program is not comprehensive. It excludes payment for preventive care services, long-term care, rehabilitation, home care, occupational health services, prescription drugs, and medical devices. The Dukakis Massachusetts Health Insurance Bill does not cover these benefits either. Jackson's program covers all these health benefits.

3. Dukakis's program continues to rely on copayments, deductibles, high premiums, and large fees. Under the Dukakis Massachusetts Health Insurance Bill, a worker with dependents could end up paying over $3,500 a year in deductibles and copayments. To that amount, the worker will have to add from 20 to 50 percent of the insurance premium—a lot of money that many working families cannot afford. Under the Jackson program, people will not have to pay premiums, copayments, deductibles, or fees.

4. Dukakis's program will continue to rely for the insurance of Americans primarily on the more than 1,500 U.S. insurance companies. Under the Dukakis national proposal, we will continue to waste $70 billion each year in excess billing and

administrative costs. Also, it will be unable to control the huge growth of health care costs. Medical costs are sky high in Massachusetts—hospital costs, for example, are 25 to 30 percent above the national average. Hospital profits have increased in Massachusetts from $63 million in 1981 to $127 million in 1986. Meanwhile, out-of-pocket expenses of people in Massachusetts have increased. Under the Jackson Administration, medical care costs will be far better controlled, profits will be significantly reduced, and direct and out-of-pocket expenses will be eliminated.

5. Dukakis's program relies heavily on the private insurance companies for the solution of major problems of lack of coverage, for example, long-term care. Today, 50 percent of our elders (and their families) who need extensive long-term care services are driven into poverty within 13 weeks. At the cost of $1,000 per week, a stay in a nursing home can easily cost $50,000, well beyond the means of our families. Private insurance, however, covers less than 2 percent of long-term care, and it is expected to cover only 5 percent by the year 2000. The premiums are prohibitive, and only the wealthy can afford them. The private insurance companies have failed in solving the long-term care problem. And yet the Dukakis program plans to encourage more active involvement of the private insurance companies in long-term care. Under the Jackson program, long-term care will be part of the NHP and will be federally funded. Our elders and their families will not have to worry about exhausting their benefits.

6. The Dukakis program leaves control of funds to the private sector, leaving the insurance companies largely unregulated. Under Jackson's NHP, the federal government will control funding, the private sector will be strongly regulated, and the role of the insurance companies will be enormously reduced.

7. The Dukakis program indicates that all those who are not covered by the employer-mandated coverage may have access to private group insurance. A state trust fund will subsidize that part of the premium, an amount that will depend on family size and income. This policy does not assure that everyone who needs coverage will get it. Basically, it is a handsome subsidy to the private insurance companies. For the people, it means an enormous expansion of the means test to the whole population. Moreover, the approximately $1,900 that the Massachusetts Trust Fund will provide as maximum subsidy for a family of four will, in 1992 (the year the state program is supposed to start), be dramatically insufficient to cover the premium for that family. Under the Jackson program, people will stop paying premiums.

8. The Dukakis program is highly technocratic. It does not leave room for patient, consumer, labor, and community participation. The Jackson program calls for patient advocates to defend the rights of patients and calls upon democratic and community participation.

APPENDIX

Canadian versus U.S. Medical Care[1]

Canada and the United States have taken two distinct and nearly opposite approaches in delivering health care. In the United States, which has the highest health care budget in the world, good health has become a function of free market economics.

---

[1] This section is an expanded and modified version of a text originally prepared by Tom Johnson.

According to the Health Care Finance Administration, in the 1980s, "private industry, followed by government, began to challenge the social perception of health care as a right rather than as part of a total consumption market basket." Accessibility to health care is clearly tied to the ability to pay in the United States. In Canada, however, health care as a right for all is firmly ingrained. In 1966, the Canadian Medical Care Act (Medicare) introduced federal funding into a health care system that is administered by the provinces. In order to receive matching federal tax dollars, the provincial health programs must adhere to five health care principles: (*a*) comprehensive coverage; (*b*) universal application of the program; (*c*) ability to transfer coverage to other provinces; (*d*) speedy accessibility to the system; and (*e*) public nonprofit administration. In 1984, the Canadian Parliament passed the Canada Health Act, holding back federal funding for provinces that allow doctors to "extra-bill" above normal negotiated rates or charge user fees for special services. Presently, only two provinces continue to allow extra-billing.

The United States spent about $500 billion in 1987 on health services. That is about 11.2 percent of our GNP, a 5.6 percent increase over 1986. Health costs consistently outrace the cost of living in the United States. Though health costs are increasing in Canada, the Canadian health care budget for 1985 was 8.6 percent of the GNP, about 20 percent less than in the United States. Dollar for dollar, Canada's universal system, which is 80 percent publicly owned and operated, is more efficient and less inflationary than ours, 60 percent of which is financed and administered by the private sector. Ironically, Canada spends relatively more on public health and capital expenditures but one-third as much on administration.

Canadians also save in other areas, some of which are matters of contention. In 1985, Canada spent less than half of what we spend on research. Some observers suggest this is because the publicly administered system is unable to absorb high-technology advances quickly enough. Others suggest that too much high-technology medicine is overpriced, limited in use, and ineffective. Canadian physicians receive about 80 to 85 percent of the income of their U.S. counterparts. Doomsayers have suggested that this would lead to a doctor shortage, but the desertion has not yet happened. Provincial medical societies are calling for an increase in the size of medical schools, where tuition costs less than a tenth of what is charged in the United States. Also, Canadian doctors pay only about 10 percent of what U.S. physicians dole out for malpractice insurance.

Additionally, since all Canadians are automatically insured in the health system, it is impossible for them to be denied proper medical treatment. Meanwhile, in the United States, 38 million people are uninsured, and millions, including the elderly, are underinsured.

Ironically, the publicly administered Canadian program greatly reduces the paperwork that chokes our system. In the United States, a hospital or doctor bills a patient, who then attempts to recover the costs from a public or private insurer (if she or he is insured). In Canada, doctors and hospitals directly bill the province to reimburse fees that have been set by the government through negotiation with representatives of the medical profession. And Canada spends virtually nothing on the advertising and marketing of basic medical services. In the United States, the recent trend toward underutilized hospital beds has led to multi-million dollar advertising campaigns in which hospitals are merchandised like fast-food outlets.

However, the final, most important measures of effectiveness are quality of care and public health. Generally, infant mortality and life expectancy rates are the common indicators of a nation's medical well being. Canada, which trailed the United States until it passed the NHP, now leads in both categories. For example, in 1982, the infant mortality rate in the United States was 20 percent greater than Canada's—11.5 deaths per 1,000 live births compared with 9.1. Canada's citizens outlive their southern neighbors by more than a year on the average, about 1.5 percent. As for quality, U.S. certifying agencies readily accept Canadian medical credentials as equal to ours, and there are constant and frequent exchanges of medical information and techniques between the two nations.

Notes on Sources of Data

The methods of estimating administrative costs are detailed elsewhere by Himmelstein and Woolhandler (1). Estimates have been updated using the latest figures and projections for health spending provided by the National Center for Health Statistics. Estimates of lives saved by universal access to care are based on the $78 million federally funded Rand Corporation Health Insurance Experiment. The method of extrapolation from the Rand data is also detailed elsewhere (2). Estimates of current employer benefit costs are based on data from the Employee Benefits Research Institute.

The figures for total spending and government spending under the existing system were provided by the Office of the Actuary, Health Care Financing Administration. Estimates of corporate and individual spending were derived by assuming that the proportion of costs borne by each of these groups at present (corporate share 25 percent, individual share 35 percent) would remain unchanged in 1989 and thereafter. Estimates of cost savings under an NHP are derived from Rand Corporation data on increased utilization of health services with the abolition of financial barriers to care, and the savings on administration and billing that have been realized under the Canadian NHP. The estimates of costs to corporations and individuals under an NHP are based on the assumption that increased corporate taxes to fund an NHP would exactly offset savings on employee benefits, while increases in individual taxes would make up the remaining costs of the program.

Statistics on the U.S. medical care system were compiled primarily from *The Need for a National Health Program* (3), *The Health of America's Children* (4), and *Medical Care Chart Book* (5); on international health expenditure, primarily from Navarro (6); and on U.S. popular opinion on medical care, primarily from Navarro (7, 8).

REFERENCES

1. Himmelstein, D. U., and Woolhandler, S. Cost without benefit: Administrative waste in U.S. medicine. *N. Engl. J. Med.* 314: 441–445, 1986.
2. Himmelstein, D. U., and Woolhandler, S. Free care, cholestyramine, and health policy. *N. Engl. J. Med.* 311: 1511–1514, 1984.
3. *The Need for a National Health Program.* Report of the National Health Commission of the National Rainbow Coalition, 1987.
4. *The Health of America's Children.* Children's Defense Fund, 1988.

5. *Medical Care Chart Book*. Health Administration Press, Ann Arbor, Mich., 1986.
6. Navarro, V. The public/private mix in the funding and delivery of health services: An international survey. *Am. J. Public Health* 75: 1318–1320, 1985.
7. Navarro, V. Where is the popular mandate? *N. Engl. J. Med.* 13(1), 1983.
8. Navarro, V. In defense of American people: Americans are not schizophrenic. *Int. J. Health Serv.* 15(3): 515–519, 1985.

SECTION V

Some False Solutions

The Relevance of the U.S. Experience to the Reforms in the British National Health Service: The Case of General Practitioner Fund Holding

Vicente Navarro

A primary purpose of the health care reforms proposed by the British government is the introduction of market forces in the allocation of medical care resources, giving patients a greater choice of medical care providers. As indicated in the White Paper on the British government's proposals, some desirable outcomes of these reforms are an increased sensitivity of the health care system to consumer needs and an enlargement of the private sector role, which would allow greater efficiency and responsiveness to market forces (1).

A key component of these reforms is the establishment of General Practitioner Fund Holding schemes (GPFHS), in which general practices with lists of not less than 11,000 persons can be given the responsibility of managing the budget for a large range of designated services, including general practice services, hospital and consultant services for elective care, diagnostics and investigations ordered or performed by general practitioners (GPs) or consultants, all drugs dispensed by the GPs, all outpatient services provided by the hospital-based consultants and auxiliary staff, and administrative expenses incurred in the management of the Fund Holding plan. These GPFHS are similar to provider-sponsored health maintenance organizations (HMOs) in the United States. This similarity is not coincidental. The architects of the GPFHS have explicitly referred to the experience of the provider-sponsored HMOs as the source of inspiration for their proposals on reform of general practice in the United Kingdom. In both schemes, the providers organize as a group practice and receive a payment that covers the provision of a wide array of health benefits, a health benefits coverage that is not

Originally published in the International Journal of Health Services, 21(3): 381–387, 1991.

comprehensive in the United States but would be almost comprehensive in the United Kingdom.

Considering the enormous influence of the HMO model on the design of the proposed GPFHS, it is very surprising that almost nothing has appeared in the British literature on the experience of HMOs and its relevance to the GPFHS. The only exception is a report published by the King's Fund Institute (KFI Report), which touches primarily on how the management systems in HMOs operate and how they may be adapted to the proposed GPFHS (2); it only briefly notes the advantages and disadvantages of the HMO type of funding and organization of health services compared with current general practice. The purpose of this article is to analyze the empirical information published in the United States and see whether it confirms or refutes some of the key assumptions made in the White Paper. Indeed, the key components of the GPFHS have been in existence in the United States for a long time. British readers may benefit from knowledge of the U.S. experience and may be more able to judge whether introduction of GPFHS will or will not improve general practice in the National Health Service (NHS).

First assumption: The HMO type of practice is better able to respond to people's needs than are current GP arrangements. The White Paper defines as an objective of the health care reforms the improvement of the health system's ability to respond to patients' needs. The definition of patients' needs, however, is a complex one. Still, there is a wide consensus that patients' and potential patients' satisfaction with a health care system is of great importance in evaluating how people perceive the system as meeting their needs. The published information from polls shows that the level of satisfaction with the health care system is higher in the United Kingdom than in the United States. The percentage of people who feel that the health care system needs to be completely rebuilt is much larger in the United States (29 percent) than in the United Kingdom (17 percent) (3). Also, the percentage of people who are satisfied with visits to physicians is lower in the United States (54 percent) than in the United Kingdom (63 percent). Similar differentials appear in people's satisfaction with hospital stays; the percentage of people satisfied is lower in the United States (57 percent) than in Great Britain (67 percent). In the light of these findings, it is not surprising that more Americans prefer the British NHS (29 percent) than British prefer the U.S. system (12 percent). The overwhelming majority of British people (80 percent) prefer the NHS (poll results published in 4). No comparable studies have been published comparing satisfaction of American enrollees in HMOs or provider-sponsored HMOs with British satisfaction with their GP arrangements. The White Paper assumes that substituting an HMO type of practice for current GP arrangements would improve people's satisfaction. The available evidence, however, questions this assumption. Enrollees' satisfaction with HMOs in the United States is lower than people's satisfaction with their primary care arrangement in the United Kingdom. The rate of turnover of people enrolled in HMOs is much higher than that in GP practices. The most complete study of disenrollment in HMOs, done in Massachusetts, shows an annual disenrollment of 281 persons per 1,000 enrollees, far larger than the disenrollment of patients from their GPs in the United Kingdom, estimated to be 50 persons per 1,000 enrollees (5, 6). The majority of British people (75 percent) are satisfied with their GPs, and the overwhelming majority oppose the changes in the NHS advocated by the British government. The future of the NHS is the second most important concern (after law and order) for British citizens (7).

Second assumption: Entrepreneurship in medicine is good for patients. The White Paper emphasizes the need to change the ethics, culture, and practice of medicine to encourage entrepreneurship: physicians should become entrepreneurs; clinical and financial divisions should be closely linked. The NHS is criticized in the White Paper and in the KFI Report for not offering that linkage. Physicians, like any other entrepreneurs, should accept financial risks as a consequence of clinical decision-making. The White Paper suggests, for example, that GPs should be given control of the funds for pharmacies, and left to take care of savings on that front, since this is an area where significant savings can occur. The KFI Report comments: "Some of the biggest savings might accrue in pharmacy since it is an area where the GP exerts a high level of direct control" (2, p. 19). The KFI Report goes even further than the White Paper on the point of linking financial gain to clinical practice. The White Paper advocates that financial gains accrued by physicians should go to bettering their working conditions, physical facilities, secretarial assistance, and productivity bonuses, but not to bettering their basic income. The KFI Report disagrees with that limitation, encouraging the reformers not to feel constrained on that point: GPs' financial gains should also be allowed to enrich their basic income; savings could "be returned directly to the GPs in the form of added salary" (2, p. 19).

The uniqueness of these British reforms is not that they encourage entrepreneurship in primary care, but rather that they aim at making GPs themselves entrepreneurs. The White Paper advocates an HMO controlled by physicians. In other words, not only do the White Paper and the KFI Report want to make the NHS into a business, they want to make businesspersons of physicians; they claim that this would mean better care for patients. No evidence is provided by either document to support this assumption. In fact, the U.S. experience shows that business culture and practice in medicine and the business attitudes of physicians work against the patient. It is the patient, not the physician, who is at risk when financial decisions are linked to clinical decisions. In the United States, very few medical businesses owned and controlled by physicians go bankrupt, but millions of patients (both in and outside HMOs) are dissatisfied with physicians' practices and have sued their doctors for malpractice. Indeed, the prescribing practices of physicians who control the budgets of pharmacies (as will be the case in the GPFHS) have forced even the American Medical Association to question the ethics of this type of linkage between financial gain and clinical practice.

Dissatisfaction with medical treatment is much more prevalent among HMO enrollees and the U.S. public than among patients in the NHS. Physician malpractice suits are more common among HMO physicians than among GPs in the United Kingdom. Thirty-seven percent of U.S. physicians have been sued by their patients. This is the outcome of business practices. Business culture leads to distrust between patients and physicians, in which a confrontation exists between the entrepreneur and the subject of that entrepreneurship (8). A patient's realization that the clinical decisions of the physician are influenced by financial considerations establishes an element of distrust. The physician, aware of that distrust, practices a defensive medicine aimed at protecting himself or herself against a legal suit. In the United States, the costs of defensive medicine are 3.5 times the costs of insurance malpractice premiums. This level of confrontation is much less in the United Kingdom. Consequently, the average annual fee for malpractice insurance in 1989 was nine times higher in the United States than in the United Kingdom (9).

Yet another example of the effect of linking financial and clinical decisions has been the negative impact of diagnosis related group (DRG) payments on the quality of care. Evidence has surfaced that providers have changed their practices to favor some DRGs over others, to unduly shorten the length of hospital stay for certain DRGs, and to reduce necessary tests. Gay and Kronenfeld have shown that DRGs have promoted premature discharges in response to economic considerations; as they put it, "Compression of service markets and retrenchment in services were associated with less profitable DRGs and cohorts, while expansion of service/markets occurred for more profitable DRGs and cohorts" (10). Another recent report on the impact of DRGs on quality of care indicates that "more patients—up from 10.3 to 14.7 percent—were unstable when sent home. Patients who leave the hospital with one or more instabilities are more than one and a half times more likely to die within 90 days of discharge" (11). These studies show that there are indeed risks in adding entrepreneurship to medical practice—risks to the patient rather than the provider.

Third assumption: Market-based primary care is more efficient than the nonmarket system in the United Kingdom. The U.S. experience does not support this assumption. By whatever indicators of efficiency one chooses, the NHS is much more efficient than the U.S. health care system (or better, nonsystem). The United States spends more on health care, in absolute and percentage terms, than any other country (11.6 percent of gross national product in the United States versus 6.88 percent in the United Kingdom in 1989). Nevertheless, the United States still has major problems of increasing costs and lacking or limited health benefits coverage, problems not faced by the United Kingdom or any other comparable industrialized nation. Seventeen percent of the U.S. population does not have any health benefits coverage whatsoever. In a 1990 poll, 75 percent of Americans reported having problems in paying for the care they and their families received, and 25 percent indicated that these payments represented a financial difficulty (12). The administrative costs of running the market-oriented system are staggering: 25.1 percent of U.S. health dollars go to administration (13). Compared with this, the NHS is a model of simplicity and efficiency, with administrative costs of only 7 percent.

This unfavorable comparison between the U.S. and the U.K. health care systems remains even when comparing the NHS with HMOs. The average enrollee in an HMO pays far more in out-of-pocket expenses, premiums, and taxes for health care than does the average person in the United Kingdom—and gets much less. The level of coverage in the United Kingdom is almost comprehensive; the level of coverage in HMOs is not. Very few HMOs, for example, cover long-term care. And the administrative costs are much higher in HMOs than in the NHS. It has been reported that administrative overhead costs are well above 10 percent of revenues for most HMOs; average administrative expenses were 11.7 percent in 1988. Provider-sponsored HMOs had the highest administrative expenses (12.6 percent) (14). The U.S. experience raises doubts that the introduction of a market-driven system, organized around HMOs, will improve the efficiency of the NHS. The administrative costs would increase enormously with the increasing number of economic transactions and regulations. Bureaucratization and interference in clinical practice would similarly expand. U.S. medicine, including the

HMOs, is more bureaucratic, has higher administrative costs, and interferes more aggressively with clinical practice than medicine in any other industrialized nation. The further encouragement of competition in the United States in the 1980s worsened rather than improved this situation. Administrative expenditures have been the highest growth sector in medicine, quintupling since 1980. From 1980 to 1986, increases in administrative costs were more than double the rate of overall health cost increases (15). In 1986, physicians' offices had more personnel involved in administrative chores (1.7 persons per physician) than in medical care (1 per physician). The overhead and administrative expenses of medical practice in the United States are 50 percent of all revenues, compared with 29 percent in Great Britain. Himmelstein and Woolhandler (16) have estimated that if the United States had a health system like that in the United Kingdom, it would save $38 billion in administrative expenses alone. In the United States, the strengthening of market forces during the 1980s also meant a reduction in health care benefits. Eighteen percent of the U.S. population (under 65 years of age) have seen their health benefits reduced (12). Also, the share of employer contributions to the payment of employees' premiums has declined from 80 to 69 percent, with the employee paying the difference (17). People are paying more and getting less coverage.

Fourth assumption: The expansion and strengthening of the private sector is an efficient and equitable means of encouraging competition and raising revenues. The White Paper does not touch on the negative side of expanding the private sector, such as the regressive nature of private funding, the impoverishment of the public sector that accompanies reliance on the private sector, and the growing inequities that would occur with the expansion of that sector. Most private sources of revenues, premiums, and out-of-pocket expenses, including user fees, are highly regressive. The White Paper is silent about user fees, but the KFI Report advocates them: "We recognize that the NHS prides itself on having almost no user fees. Based on considerable health services research in the United States, we suspect that this has contributed to consumers requesting services that are not needed. . . . It would be worth exploring the effects of budget-holders' charging a modest per visit copayment (say, £3–£5) for the non-poor. This might decrease inappropriate use as well as provide extra resources for use in improving services" (2). Health services research in the United States does not support the claim that user fees have beneficial effects on the patient and the system. Studies in both Canada and the United States (not mentioned in the KFI report) show that user fees discourage utilization, to the detriment of patient care (18–21). Also, the Canadian experience shows that the extra expenses needed to administer copayments, deductibles, and fees consume large proportions of the extra revenues raised by such forms of payment. After retaining such forms of payment for a few years, all Canadian provinces dropped them as inefficient, unnecessary, and medically unwise.

U.S. experience shows that reliance on the private sector impoverishes the public sector. Witness, for example, the nursing shortage in the United States. There is a shortage of nurses throughout the U.S. health system, but it is much more acute in the public than in the private sector, due in part to the absorption of nurses by the private sector. Moreover, those who benefit most from the private sector are the better-off, whose interest in and support of the public sector consequently diminishes. This lessening of support from those with the most political muscle further impoverishes the public sector. A similar fate has befallen the U.S. public school system: the existence of private schools led to the weakening of public schools. In societies where the overwhelming majority of the population uses the public schools, as in Sweden, the overall public school system is much better than in societies where private and public schools coexist.

In the United Kingdom, the private sector has been, for the most part, *within* the public sector. Private and nonprivate medicine has meant better amenities and shorter waiting lists for private patients attended in the public hospitals. It is analogous to people taking first- or second-class seats, all using the same plane. The Labour Party is committed to eliminating private beds in public hospitals, yet one could say that under current arrangements at least everyone flies in the same plane; a certain amount of social solidarity is maintained. But the White Paper and the KFI Report advocate an HMO type of practice that will lead to the development of two different types of HMOs, one for the better-off and one for the worse-off. There will be two types of planes: first-class planes and second-class planes. In the United States, we already know the consequences of this. The disparities in medical care are large. HMOs catering to poor patients provide worse care, and are themselves worse off, than those catering to the nonpoor. Both the White Paper and the KFI Report are, of course, aware of this reality, and they try to cope with it by acknowledging the necessity to "correct the level of capitation to favor the lower social classes." Such corrections have been tried unsuccessfully in the United States (either by increasing Medicare payments or by providing vouchers). Correcting these disparities requires far more than financial incentives to the providers.

The most effective and most equitable way of raising much-needed revenues is not through the private sector but through the public one, by changing government priorities and/or by raising taxes. There is active popular support for both types of intervention. The majority of people in the United Kingdom believe that the government should spend far more on health care (and much less on defense), and 75 percent are willing to pay higher taxes if they are assured that these extra revenues would be spent in the health sector. Polls show that people are hostile to user fees and support instead higher government revenues on health. The primary concern of the public and of providers is the underfunding of the NHS (7).

In summary, the U.S. experience seems to lead to a conclusion opposite to that reached by the NHS reformers. Changes in the NHS may indeed be necessary. There is evidence that people want to see changes; 52 percent of British people want to see fundamental changes to make the system work better (3). But the U.S. experience should be a warning to health reformers that those changes should not necessarily be toward a U.S.-style system (in which an even larger percentage of Americans—60 percent—want fundamental changes), but away from it.

REFERENCES

1. *Working for Patients. The Health Service: Caring for the 1990s.* White Paper. Her Majesty's Stationery Office, London, 1989.
2. Weiner, J. P., and Ferris, D. M. *GP Budget Holding in the UK: Lessons from America.* Research Report No. 7. King's Fund Institute, London, 1990.

3. Blendon, R. J., et al. Satisfaction with health systems in ten nations. *Health Aff.*, Summer 1990, p. 188.
4. Blendon, R. J. Three systems: A comparative survey. *Health Management Q.*, First Quarter, 1989.
5. Shimsak, D. G., et al. An analysis of HMO disenrollment data. *GHAA J. 8*(1): 13–22, Summer 1987.
6. Leavey, R., and Wilkin, D. H. Consumerism and general practice. *Br. Med. J.* 298: 1128–1129, 1989.
7. Jacobs, E., and Worcester, R. *We British: Britain under the Moriscope*, p. 50. Weidenfeld & Nicolson, London, 1990.
8. Lee, P. R., and Etaeredge, L. Clinical freedom: Two lessons for the UK from US experience with privatisation of health care. *Lancet* 4: 263–265, 1989.
9. Coyte, P. C., Dewees, D. N., and Trebilcock, M. J. Medical malpractice. *N. Engl. J. Med.* January 10, 1991, p. 89.
10. Gay, E. G., and Kronenfeld, J. J. Regulation, retrenchment—the DRG experience: Problems from changing reimbursement practice. *Soc. Sci. Med.* 31: 1103, 1990.
11. Kahn, K. L., et al. The effects of the DRG-based prospective payment system on quality of care for hospitalized medicare patients. *JAMA* 264: 1953–1955, 1990.
12. *Los Angeles Times* Poll No. 212: Health Care in the United States. Roper Center for Public Opinion Research, Storrs, Conn., March 1990.
13. Woolhandler, S., and Himmelstein, D. U. To Save a Penny Two Are Spent: The Deteriorating Administrative Efficiency of US Health Care. Unpublished paper. Center for Health Policy, Harvard University, 1990.
14. Palsbo, S. J., and Gold, M. R. *HMO Industry Profile: Vol. 3. Financial Performance, 1988.* Group Health Association of America, 1990.
15. Reinhardt, U. The medical B factor: Bureaucracy in action. *Washington Post*, August 9, 1988.
16. Himmelstein, D., and Woolhandler, S. Cost without benefit: Administrative waste in US medicine. *N. Engl. J. Med.* 314: 441–445, 1986.
17. Leist, K. R., Freeland, M. S., and Waldo, D. R. Health spending and ability to pay: Business, individuals, and government. *Health Care Financing Rev.* 3: 10–12, 1989.
18. McDonald, A. D., et al. Effects of Quebec Medicare on physician consultation for selected symptoms. *N. Engl. J. Med.* 291: 649–652, 1974.
19. Beck, R. G., and Horne, J. M., et al. Utilization of publicly insured health services in Saskatchewan before, during and after copayment. *Medical Care* 18: 787–806, 1980.
20. Brook, R. H., et al. Does free care improve adults' health? Results from a controlled trial. *N. Engl. J. Med.* 309: 1426–1434, 1983.
21. Siu, A. L., et al. Inappropriate use of hospitals in a randomized trial of health insurance plans. *N. Engl. J. Med.* 315: 1259–1266, 1986.

CHAPTER 14

The West German
Health Care System: A Critique

Vicente Navarro

*Several leading health policy staff of the AFL-CIO and major unions met with the Board of
Physicians for a National Health Program (PNHP) in May 1990. They described the active
discussions currently ongoing within the AFL-CIO Health Care Committee, which is composed of
14 international union presidents and sets AFL-CIO policy on health care issues. Some union
presidents reportedly favored a single-payer, Canadian-style approach, while others apparently
preferred a proposal modeled after the West German system, which preserves a major role for
insurance companies. The PNHP Board was emphatic in its preference for the single-payer
approach. Board member Dr. Vicente Navarro wrote the following letter to the union presidents
on the AFL-CIO Health Care Committee detailing his critique of the West German approach.*

As a member of the Executive Board of Physicians for a National Health Program
(PNHP), I have had the opportunity to follow the splendid role the AFL-CIO has played
in this country in the task of making sure that access to health care in time of need is a
human right in America. God bless labor.

Because of the great influence the AFL-CIO will have in shaping national health
program legislation, and also because of my great respect and warmth for the AFL-CIO,
I feel obliged to share with the AFL-CIO Health Committee my profound reservations
about some of the advice you have received regarding the type of national health
program the country may need. PNHP has been told that some of your consultants have
advised your committee that the West German health insurance scheme is preferable to
the Canadian program. The primary reason for my concern is that the West German
system—in the words of Dr. Fritz Beske, Director of the Institute of Health Systems
Research in Kiel, West Germany—is one of the most complicated and complex systems
in Europe (1). The roots of its complexity are based in its system of funding. Such
complexities are well known to us in the United States. As you know, our current
predicament of high costs and limited health benefits coverage is due in part to the more
than 1500 insurance companies contracting with nearly a million providers of different
types of care. In West Germany, there are over 1200 health insurance companies (the

Published in the *International Journal of Health Services*, 21(3): 565–571, 1991. This is a slightly modified
version of the letter published in *PNHP Newsletter*, July 1990.

Germans call them sickness insurance funds) for a population one quarter the size of ours. West Germany has a far greater density of insurance organizations than the United States! These payers can be private insurers or autonomous sickness insurance funds; only the latter offer community ratings.

These sickness insurance funds (SIF) contract with sickness funds physicians' associations (Kassenärztliche Vereinigung, or KV), controlled by the medical profession, for payment and delivery of health services. Physicians are paid by KVs on a fee-for-service basis. The physician-controlled KVs are enormously powerful, and not only pay physicians but often own hospitals as well. Not surprisingly, physicians' incomes are the highest in continental Europe. On average, a German physician makes six times the wage of a production worker (compared with a fourfold difference in the United States and Canada) (2). Also, because of physicians' dominance in the funding and delivery system, German pharmacy costs are the second highest (after France) in Europe (18 percent of all health expenditures, compared with 10 percent in Canada and 9 percent in the United States) (3, p. 71). The close relationship between the medical profession and the pharmaceutical industry in West Germany has been the subject of an extensive bibliography. The medical profession is united at both the regional and national levels by the German Medical Association (GMA). All practicing physicians must be members of this association. The GMA is extremely powerful, and its voice is highly influential in the KVs. Part of its power results from Germany's being governed for most of the last 80 years by conservative forces close to the medical profession (as well as to the employers' associations). For most of the post–World War II period, Germany has been governed by Christian Democrats—the party of business and the medical profession. Social Democrats—the party of labor—have been in power for only a few years during this period, though not in the majority. From 1967 to 1969, they governed in coalition with Christian Democrats, and from 1969 to 1982, in coalition with the Liberal Party (a right-of-center party).[1]

The physician-controlled KVs contract with the SIFs to be paid for the delivery of services. SIFs are financed by employer–employee contributions, with employers and employees each paying 50 percent. Bismarck established the SIFs in 1888 in response to pressure from labor, led by the Social Democratic Party (one of the larger labor parties in Europe at that time), because he was afraid of what could happen in Germany—in neighboring France, workers had taken over Paris and established the Paris commune. Bismarck was very explicit about what he intended to do when he established the SIFs. The primary objective was to placate the rebellious working class and to break its solidarity. To achieve this objective, he established the SIFs by trades. (For a brief historical view of how Germany and other countries developed their health insurance funds, see 4.) Railroad workers, for example, had different SIFs and benefits from construction workers. These SIFs were jointly administered by representatives of employers and employees, under the supervision of the state. This is how SIFs are

[1] There are many references documenting the linkages between the medical profession, the employers' associations, the KVs, and the Christian Democratic Party. Most of these references have not been translated into English. The best-known author in this field is Professor Hans-Ulrich Deppe, Professor of Medical Sociology at Frankfurt University, Federal Republic of Germany.

structured today. Individuals and their families must enroll in SIFs according to their income and/or occupation.

Each SIF is completely autonomous and self-financed. There is no transfer of monies among them. The level of benefits depends on the SIF. Blue-collar workers, for example, belong to different SIFs from white-collar workers. In addition to the minimum package of benefits assured to everyone, white-collar workers have benefits (such as preventive cancer-screening programs) not available to blue-collar workers. This situation, besides undermining labor solidarity, is profoundly unfair, since blue-collar workers are at greater risk of getting cancer. Benefits also vary depending on the workers' occupations and the regions where they live. SIFs in wealthy areas with low unemployment and high-wage labor have more resources—and better benefits—than those in poor areas with high unemployment and low-wage labor.

The nonprofit autonomous SIFs cover close to 90 percent of the population; 6 to 8 percent is covered by private insurance companies. Private insurers provide approximately 20 percent of physicians' income, and since they pay more than the SIFs, physicians are more attentive to their private patients.

The German system is therefore a two-class system. Private insurance takes care of the top 6 to 8 percent, and the SIFs take care of everyone else—or almost everyone else, since 2 percent of the population (in U.S. terms, this would be equivalent to four million people) does not have any form of coverage, public or private. Moreover, because of the enormous diversity of autonomous SIFs, second-class citizens—the 90 percent of Germans insured by the SIFs—have different types of benefits depending on where they live and what type of job they hold. The German health insurance system is highly stratified, dividing society rather than uniting it, and lacking in social solidarity.

Some unions have supported this system since it gives them a say in running the SIFs. The increasing costs of care, however, have caused serious doubts about the wisdom of keeping this arrangement. I am consultant to the Social Policy Committee of the European Parliament and also to the International Metalworkers' Union. In this capacity, I have had many opportunities to speak with German trade unionists about their health insurance system. They have had enough of the current arrangement and want to change it. They would prefer a single-payer system that allows better control of benefits coverage and costs and promotes greater social solidarity.

Another outcome of having the 1200 or so SIFs is that they are not in a strong position to impose their terms on the medical profession and providers and on the KVs, which are, as I mentioned, in a very powerful position. This is analogous to the situation in the United States. A further consequence of the large number of SIFs is that, as in the United States, administrative costs are very high. The only study that has compared these costs among different countries shows that the administrative costs of the SIFs, including the costs of collecting and disbursing health insurance services, were higher in West Germany (6.0 percent of all medical care expenditures) than the equivalent costs in the United States (4.7 percent) or Canada (1.7 percent) (3, p. 84). This study did not include the administrative costs and overheads for hospitals and physicians, which are much higher in West Germany than in Canada. If the United States had a system like the Canadian one, we could save over $24 billion just in hospital billing, while a German-style system would save at most $2.4 billion.

The poor administrative control over providers explains why the rate of growth of health expenditures for the period 1970–75 was 20 percent per year, the largest in Europe and one of the largest in the world! (1, p. 237). That growth forced the SIFs and the regional governments to take some steps, the most important of which was to establish caps for physician payments; i.e., the SIFs limited the overall amount they pay to KVs for physician reimbursement. Also, the regional governments established more stringent controls over the development of hospitals and hospital services by requiring that all capital expenditures be approved (and/or funded) by them (5). These and other measures have been responsible for a decline in the rate of growth of expenditures. The rate of annual growth of health expenditures for the period 1985–90 is estimated to be 9.8 percent, compared with 11.8 percent in Canada and 11.8 percent in the United States (estimated from annual reports of the federal government of the Federal Republic of Germany for the years 1985–90; see also 6). Contributing to this decline has been a decrease in the West German population. During the period 1985–87, the population decreased at a rate of 0.1 percent per year, while the Canadian and U.S. populations increased by 1 percent per year.

The decline in the rate of growth of health expenditures has occurred primarily by limiting payments to the KVs. The KVs, which operate somewhat as medically controlled HMOs, have responded to these cuts in revenue by reducing services to patients and increasing patients' copayments and deductibles for hospitalization. The average duration of a visit to a general practitioner in West Germany is nine minutes, compared with 14 minutes in the United States and 15 minutes in Canada (7). As in the United States, medical costs have been growing, and the numbers of uninsured have increased. As mentioned before, 2 percent of West Germans do not have any form of health benefits coverage (5, p. 73). In a recent international survey (still unpublished) of peoples' satisfaction with their health care system, the West German system did not have great popular support. The Canadian people were the most pleased with their health care system.

West German health indicators are not very good. Infant mortality (nine deaths per 1000 live births) is worse than in Canada (eight deaths per 1000 live births), although better than in the United States (ten deaths per 1000 live births). Life expectancy is shorter (75 years) than in either Canada (77 years) or the United States (76 years). Life expectancy at ages 40, 60, and 80 is significantly worse in Germany than in the United States, with Canada's statistics being the best for every age group for both sexes. Canada also has better health indicators than West Germany or the United States. A very important point in evaluating Canada's national health program is that prior to the program's establishment, Canada's health indicators were even worse than those of the United States (8). Since the national health program was established, Canada's health indicators have improved much faster than—and have surpassed—those in the United States. This has not been the case with West Germany.

I have provided some references that document the points made in this letter, in case the AFL-CIO Health Committee wants to get further information on these topics (see also 9, 10). The conclusion from this extensive information is that the West German system is not a good one for labor. Labor pays 50 percent of the employer–employee contribution, a far larger percentage than in most European countries. This situation is again due to the power of the employer vis-à-vis labor; the employers have strong political clout in the Christian Democratic Party. In spite of the large labor contributions, workers, besides receiving different benefits depending on their trade, still have to pay hospital copayments, coinsurance, and complementary costs. The worker does not get a good deal. Moreover, the German health care system does not provide much employment. German hospitals employ less than half as many workers per hospital bed as U.S. hospitals (1.2 versus 2.75), with Canada being only slightly below the U.S. level. Germany has 60 percent fewer nurses per capita than the United States and half as many as Canada.

If the choice is between the Canadian and the West German plans, the best system for labor would be the Canadian one. This system is not perfect; far from it. Many things need improvement, in the areas of cost controls, community participation, and quality control, to mention only three. Quebec has some interesting improvements in all these areas. Still, much needs to be done. The critical advantage of the Canadian over the West German and U.S. schemes is the single-payer system whereby the federal and provincial governments can use their financial muscle to establish their terms and priorities over the providers. Of course, the health care system that finally emerges in the United States will be based on our own history and traditions. But it is important to learn from other countries. And I believe the Canadian system has the most to offer.

I understand that one of your consultants who is advocating the German model is Dr. Uwe Reinhardt. Frankly, I am most concerned that the committee relies on the advice of an individual well known in this country for his anti-labor positions. A well-known Reagan supporter (he came to the Johns Hopkins University and publicly indicated his support for Reagan in 1980 and 1984), he tried to disassociate himself from Reagan's disastrous economic policies in a recent article in the *New Republic*. But his anti-labor position has not changed one bit. His answer (which appeared in the *Wall Street Journal* and in *Health Affairs*) to employers' concerns about the negative impact of the growing cost of health benefits on the international competitiveness of U.S. business was that the health benefits provided by employers are far too generous. Let me quote directly: "American business, rather than the public sector, has been and continues to be the main source of health care cost inflation in this country. It is business that sets the high price and utilization standards in health care and thus the system's high expenditures. By the standards of American business, the benefit packages and prices offered by Medicare and Medicaid are downright lean. While the Reagan (and now the Bush) administration and Congress have sought to tighten their control over health care costs during the 1980s, American business had *expanded* its benefit packages! Partly as a result of that expansion, for example, the nation's psychiatric hospitals now look to American business as the latest richly laden economic frontier" (11). In other words, according to Reinhardt, the problem is that businesses chose to expand benefits rather than reduce them as the federal government did.

In another article, also published in *Health Affairs*, he explains that the business community has responded too easily to labor pressure by granting "excessive" health benefits packages (12). His advice to corporate America is that instead of passing the cost of those benefits to the consumer by raising prices, it should cut wages. Incidentally, he also advocates taxing health benefits. In the same article, Reinhardt also advocates further cuts in public expenditures in the health sector, on the basis that such public funds are unproductive. I sent a reply to *Health Affairs*, stressing that U.S. public expenditures in health are much lower (4 percent of the gross domestic product) than those of any other country. Those expenditures are critical investments in human capital, and Sweden, which has the largest government health expenditures (and social expenditures in general), also has the highest productivity, lowest unemployment, and largest economic growth.

Frankly, it concerns me that labor would rely on Reinhardt's advice. His pen works full-time for the powerful of this country.

I hope that you will give PNHP a chance to present our position to the members of your committee. A paper prepared by Drs. Himmelstein and Woolhandler and published in the *New England Journal of Medicine* represents our position (13).

In conclusion, I again thank labor for its enormous historical role in improving the health and well-being of all our people. It was the AFL-CIO, after all, that put the Canadian model on the political map back in the early 1970s. At that time, the AFL-CIO supported the Kennedy–Griffith Proposal (very similar to the proposal advocated by PNHP), while, on the other side of the political spectrum, Nixon was supporting employer-mandated coverage. Almost 20 years later, the AFL-CIO seems to have given up on the Canadian model, and now supports employer-mandated coverage. I am aware, of course, that this change responds to the widely held perception that political institutions have moved further to the right and that the Kennedy–Griffith proposal no longer seems feasible. Frankly, I disagree with that perception. Many of us in PNHP have worked for more than 25 years toward a universal and comprehensive health benefits program. Never before have we seen so many forces favorable to the establishment of such a program. Seventy-eight percent of Americans want a national health program, and, when offered a choice between the U.S., Canadian, and U.K. systems, the majority support the Canadian model. People want major changes in the system of funding and organizing their health care.

Even among physicians, the second-largest medical association in this country—the American College of Physicians—has called for major reorganization of health care. At its recent congress, the College called for a system that comes remarkably close to the Canadian model. In your own area, employers are beginning to realize that this may be the proper road. In recent testimony before the Executive Board of PNHP, the Director of Benefits for Chrysler expressed great sympathy for our efforts. He predicted that Ford would soon come to this same position. All these factors were unthinkable 20 years ago when the AFL-CIO was asking for the Kennedy–Griffith proposal. Because of these developments, I would encourage the AFL-CIO to strongly support a system that mandates universal and comprehensive coverage at a cost the country can afford.

REFERENCES

1. Beske, F. Expenditures and attempts at cost containment in the statutory health insurance system of the Federal Republic of Germany. In *The Public/Private Mix for Health: The Relevance and Effects of Change*, edited by G. McLachlan and A. Maynard. Nuffield Provincial Hospitals Trust, 1982.
2. Organization for Economic Cooperation and Development. *Expenditures of Health Under Economic Constraints*, Table 13. Report of the Directorate for Social Affairs. Washington, D.C., 1984.

3. Maxwell, R. J. *Health and Wealth. An International Study of Health Care Spending.* Lexington Books, Lexington, Mass., 1981.
4. Navarro, V. Why some countries have national health insurance, others have national health services, and the US has neither. *Soc. Sci. Med.* 28: 887–898, 1989.
5. Kirkman-Liff, B. Physician payment and cost-containment strategies in West Germany. *J. Health Polit. Policy Law* 15: 69–100, 1990.
6. Schieber, G. J., and Poullier, J-P. Overview of international comparisons of health care expenditures. *Health Care Financing Rev.*, Annual Suppl. 1989, p. 6.
7. Sandier, S. Health services utilization and physicians' income trends. *Health Care Financing Rev.*, Annual Suppl. 1989, p. 38.
8. UNICEF. *The State of the World's Children 1989*, p. 95. Oxford University Press, New York, 1989.
9. Navarro, V. The public/private mix in the funding and delivery of health services: An international survey. *Am. J. Public Health* 75: 1318, 1985.
10. Navarro, V. A national health program is necessary. *Challenge*, May/June 1989, p. 36.
11. Reinhardt, U. Assessing the health of a nation. *Health Aff.*, Summer 1989, p. 12.
12. Reinhardt, U. Health care spending and American competitiveness. *Health Aff.*, Winter 1989, p. 10.
13. Himmelstein, D. U., and Woolhandler, S. A national health program for the United States: A physician's proposal. *N. Engl. J. Med.* 320: 103, 1989.

SECTION VI

The Solution for the United States

CHAPTER 15

Free Care: A Quantitative Analysis of Health and Cost Effects of a National Health Program for the United States

Steffie Woolhandler and David U. Himmelstein

The United States is the only developed country other than South Africa that fails to guarantee all citizens access to medical care. Virtually everyone in the United States must pay at least some portion of their health care bills. Fifteen percent of Americans have no health insurance at some time during the year (1). An additional 10 percent have insurance so inadequate that a major illness would lead to financial ruin (2), and illness causes one-half of personal bankruptcies.

As a result many people are unable to obtain needed medical care. In 1982 a million people were denied services when they were ill because they could not pay (3). Many more forego preventive care such as immunizations, well baby visits, Pap tests, hypertension control, mammography, and prenatal check-ups (4, 5). Both common sense and experimental evidence indicate that eliminating the gaps in coverage would improve health (6–12).

However, recent health policy initiatives have focused on cost containment through measures that impede access: restricting eligibility for coverage, charging patients higher co-payments, and instituting bureaucratic controls to ration services (13–15). As a result the numbers of the uninsured and underinsured have increased sharply; the proportion of health costs paid out-of-pocket has begun to rise after more than 50 years of steady decline (16); and health indices for minorities and the poor have stagnated or even deteriorated (16, 17). Meanwhile the costs of health care bureaucracy have grown rapidly (13), and administrative intervention in clinical practice has been encouraged by reforms such as the Medicare diagnosis related group (DRG) program (18). Ironically, the rationing of care has been accompanied by a growing surplus of health resources (19). Hospital occupancy rates are at an all time low (20),

Originally published in the International Journal of Health Services, 18(3): 393–399, 1988.

and a growing number of physicians (21) vie for a shrinking number of paying patients. In contrast to policies that ration services through decreased coverage and increased administrative oversight, providing universal, publicly funded medical care through a national health program (NHP) would allow considerable savings on billing, administration, and other ancillary costs (13, 14). Such a program would allow fuller use of the growing surplus of medical facilities and personnel. In addition, evidence from Canada and other countries suggests that bureaucratic intervention in clinical practice would actually decrease with an NHP.

In this article we use findings from several recent studies to analyze the health and cost effects of instituting an NHP. We conclude that providing universal free care and eliminating billing could save between 47,000 and 106,000 lives per year and decrease total health care costs, without affecting net provider incomes.

THE ANALYTIC MODELS

Calculating the Health Effects of a National Health Program

We calculated the health effects of instituting an NHP in two different ways based on data from two studies: The Rand Health Insurance Experiment (Rand HIE) (6-9, 22, 23), and Hadley's examination of geographic variation in health spending and death rates (24). The Rand HIE randomly assigned 2005 families to differing health insurance plans and measured the health and cost outcomes over a mean follow-up of 3.6 years. Several plans required co-payments (as do most U.S. health insurance policies), while a free care plan provided complete coverage at no cost (as would an NHP). Since health outcomes were similar in the various co-payment groups, the Rand researchers aggregated them for most comparisons to the free care families. Differences between the co-payment and free care groups can be used to estimate the effects of an NHP on health and the utilization of health care.

The Rand study excluded the subpopulations with the highest expected death rates: the elderly, neonates, and the chronically ill. Thus there were few deaths among study participants and little chance of finding statistically significant differences in mortality. The study observed decreases in death rates associated with free care for both adults [co-payment groups 1.1 percent versus free care group 0.9 percent (6)] and children [co-payment groups 0.4 percent versus free care group 0 percent (22)]. These differences were not statistically significant, but would be of great public health significance if they were in fact attributable to the differences in health insurance plans rather than random variation.

Because the Rand HIE had insufficient statistical power to assess differences in death rates, the researchers calculated the risk of dying in subsequent years for each adult based on blood pressure, smoking habits, weight, and serum cholesterol. For the 25 percent of adults at highest risk at entry to the study, free care reduced the risk of dying by 10 percent, a statistically significant decrease of the same magnitude as the observed improvements in death rates (6). Because the calculated risk of dying was the most reliable estimate of mortality differences in the Rand HIE, we based our first calculation of the health effect of instituting an NHP on this figure.

Hadley's study of health and health spending in 400 county groups throughout the United States yielded an independent estimate of the health benefits of increased utilization (24). He found that more health spending is associated with lower death rates (after correction for confounding variables such as age, sex, race, income, education, and smoking), and developed regression equations that describe the magnitude of this effect. A 10 percent increase in health spending was associated with a 1.57 percent decrease in mortality rates, a relationship that was very similar for each of the age, sex, and race groups examined. We used this equation along with the Rand estimate of increased utilization due to the introduction of free care to derive a second estimate of the health outcomes of an NHP.

Calculating the Cost of a National Health Program

Families provided free care in the Rand HIE had more ambulatory visits, more hospital adminissions, and higher medical expenses than families with co-payment insurance plans. Those enrolled in the plans with highest co-payments used the least services.

The Rand study free care plan closely approximates coverage under an NHP. However, none of the experimental co-payment plans was equivalent to the average U.S. health insurance coverage. The Rand researchers noted that U.S. average per capita health expenditure adjusted for comparability to their data was within the range of expenditures observed in the experimental co-payment groups (7). Per capita spending for the free care group exceeded the adjusted U.S. average figure by 14.6 percent (7). Therefore, for our calculations we assume that instituting an NHP would increase health care utilization by 14.6 percent.

While this figure reasonably approximates the increased utilization expected in an NHP, costs are unlikely to rise as sharply for two reasons. First, the excess "costs" reported in the Rand study represent charges to insurers rather than the actual expense for hospitals and physicians to provide additional services. Since the United States has a surplus of medical facilities and personnel, additional services could be provided at low cost if existing resources were more fully used. For example, the average U.S. hospital has 180 beds, of which 114 are occupied. If hospital occupancy increased 14.6 percent as predicted by Rand, 131 beds would be filled. Fixed hospital costs (e.g., buildings, equipment, heat, round-the-clock staffing of laboratories, etc.) currently billed to 114 patients would instead be distributed among 131 patients, and average per diem costs would fall.

Hence the actual expense of added care is less than the charges measured in the Rand study; how much less varies from hospital to hospital. Moreover, the precise figure is often hotly debated when health maintenance organizations, preferred provider organizations, etc. negotiate discounts from hospitals in exchange for referring patients to fill otherwise empty beds. Two large and careful studies estimated the marginal costs of hospital care at 55 (25) and 74 (26) percent of charges. We employed the midpoint of these figures for our estimate that the ratio of actual expense to charges for these added hospital services is 64.5 percent. Similarly, the impending surplus of physicians, each with "fixed" costs such as office overhead, malpractice insurance, and repayment of educational loans, means that additional physician services could be obtained at a lower cost per service without lowering average net physician compensation per service. We assume that the marginal cost-to-charge ratio for physician services is also 64.5 percent, implying that about three-quarters of current professional expenses represent "fixed costs" (27).

A second reason why costs under an NHP would be lower than those measured in the Rand HIE is that free care, if universal, would simplify or eliminate billing and reduce many administrative and ancillary costs. The Rand experiment could not demonstrate these savings because free care was not universal. Savings on administration and billing would range from 8.2 to 10.8 percent of health spending, depending on payment methods under an NHP (13). Additional savings under an NHP on marketing and hospital and nursing home profits would total 2.5 percent of health spending (14). For our analysis we assume that administrative and ancillary savings in an NHP would be 10.8 percent of current health spending.

Therefore, in order to estimate the projected costs of instituting universal free care, we adjusted the utilization increase demonstrated in the Rand study (14.6 percent) for the expense-to-charge ratio (64.5 percent), and administrative savings inherent in a universal system (10.8 percent), according to the formula:

Percent change in health costs with an NHP =
$$100 \times \left([1 - 0.108] \, [1 + (0.645 \times 0.146)] - 1 \right)$$

RESULTS

Projecting the Rand HIE figure for risk of dying to the U.S. population as a whole yields an estimate of 0.45 deaths averted by free care per 1000 person years (28), about 106,000 deaths per year. This estimate is based on the conservative assumptions that free care has no health benefit for the 75 percent of the population at lower risk, and that the highest risk quartile of the groups excluded from the Rand HIE (the elderly, neonates, and the chronically ill) would receive no greater benefit from free care than did the study population.

Hadley's results suggest that free care would save about 47,000 lives each year. This figure is based on the Rand HIE finding that free care caused a 14.6 percent increase in spending, the 1984 U.S. death rate of 866.8 per 100,000 (16), and the U.S. population of 236,200,000 (29).

An NHP would cost $10.2 billion per year less than our current health care system. The Rand HIE found a 14.6 percent increase in health care charges in the free care group compared with families with typical U.S. health insurance coverage. Adjusting this figure for the expense-to-charge ratio of 64.5 percent and administrative and ancillary savings of 10.8 percent yields an estimated net cost savings of 2.4 percent with an NHP. Based on 1985 health care spending of $425 billion, $35.7 billion spent for additional services would be more than offset by savings of $45.9 billion on administration and other ancillary costs.

DISCUSSION

A national health program providing universal, comprehensive free care would save between 47,000 and 106,000 lives and $10.2 billion each year. In striking contrast, more conventional policy proposals aspire only to minimize the health damage that seems an unavoidable concomitant of cost containment. Thus debate over DRG reimbursement centers on the potential for harm, e.g., premature discharges, disincentives for adopting new technologies, and the "dumping" of unprofitable physicians, services, or patients. Virtually no one claims that such policies improve health. Moreover, recent data show that health care costs continue to rise rapidly (30). We fear that cost control through DRG-like strategies will require ever greater administrative intrusion into clinical practice and/or ever widening gaps in insurance coverage.

Cost savings from an NHP depend on universal entitlement to free care, which would simplify administration by eliminating the need to determine eligibility for services, apportion hospital costs to individual patients, collect bills, sell insurance, etc. Such simplification would threaten insurance companies and bureaucrats currently paid for these tasks, as well as for-profit providers whose profits would be constrained. These are powerful foes. On the other hand the majority of the American people support an NHP (31), as do most physicians (32). In addition, corporations facing stiff international competition and rapidly rising health insurance bills may welcome an NHP that would contain costs and transfer part of the burden of financing care to firms not currently providing health benefits (33). Active physician advocacy for an NHP could be crucial in forging an effective coalition and shaping the resulting health system to assure diversity and quality.

Experience in Canada and Britain supports our forecast of lower costs and mortality rates under an NHP. In both countries, institution of universal free care was followed by a sharp drop in death rates and relatively stable health costs while U.S. costs were skyrocketing (34–36). The Canadian example also demonstrates that an NHP need not constrain patients' or physicians' freedom of choice. Indeed, there is probably less bureaucratic control of medical practice in Canada than in the United States, where day-to-day clinical decisions are increasingly dictated by government regulations and corporate financial imperatives (37).

Our estimates of improvements in mortality and cost under an NHP may understate the potential benefits. Our cost estimate incorporates a substantial increase in provider incomes due to greater volume of services without change in net compensation per service. We ignored the financial benefits of higher patient earnings and productivity resulting from improved health due to free care. We conservatively assumed that the elderly, neonates, and the chronically ill receive no greater benefits from free care than less vulnerable groups. We also excluded benefits that might arise from improved preventive services made possible by the more organized framework of an NHP (38). Finally, our analysis did not take account of possible decreases in morbidity and greater patient satisfaction with free care.

In addition to the two studies already cited, a wealth of data has shown that removing barriers to medical care is life saving. Perhaps the most striking was the demonstration by Lurie and associates (10, 11) that termination of health insurance for ambulatory diabetics and hypertensives led to a rise in blood pressure and a fourfold increase in death rates within one year.

The Hypertension Detection and Follow-up Program also documented the benefits of free medical care (39, 40). This massive population-based, randomized trial compared "community standard care" with a program of free hypertension care including intensive outreach, convenient clinic hours, and subsidized transportation to the clinics. Death rates in the intervention group were 17 percent lower for all causes of death, not only for hypertension (39). These differences were heavily concentrated among blacks (40), whose access to care was almost surely compromised in the "community standard" group. These findings are remarkably similar to the results of the Rand study.

The fashionable nihilism of the 1970s that dismissed medical care as useless (41, 42) is now untenable. A variety of studies confirm the obvious: requiring payment for care is a barrier to access; this barrier is greatest for the poor and sick, who as a result forego potentially lifesaving care. Conversely, universal free care under an NHP would save lives and money.

REFERENCES

1. Rowland, D., and Davis, K. Uninsured and underserved: Inequities in health care in the U.S. *Milbank Mem. Fund Q.* 61: 149-176, 1983.
2. Farley, P. J. Who are the underinsured? *Milbank Mem. Fund Q.* 63: 476-503, 1985.
3. *Updated Report on Access to Health Care for the American People.* Robert Wood Johnson Foundation, Princeton, N.J., 1983.
4. Aday, L. A., and Andersen, R. M. The national profile of access to medical care: Where do we stand? *Am. J. Public Health* 74: 1331-1339, 1984.
5. Butler, J. A., et al. Medical care use and expenditure among children and youth in the U.S.: Analysis of a national probability sample. *Pediatrics* 76: 495-507, 1985.
6. Brook, R. H., et al. Does free care improve adults' health? Results from a randomized controlled trial. *N. Engl. J. Med.* 309: 1426-1434, 1983.
7. Newhouse, J. P., et al. Some interim results from a controlled trial of cost sharing in health insurance. *N. Engl. J. Med.* 305: 1501-1507, 1981.
8. O'Grady, K. F., et al. The impact of cost sharing on emergency department use. *N. Engl. J. Med.* 313: 484-490, 1985.
9. Keeler, E. B., et al. How free care reduced hypertension in the Health Insurance Experiment. *JAMA* 254: 1926-1931, 1985.
10. Lurie, N., et al. Termination of Medi-Cal—does it affect health? *N. Engl. J. Med.* 311: 480-484, 1984.
11. Lurie, N., et al. Termination of Medi-Cal benefits. A follow-up one year later. *N. Engl. J. Med.* 314: 1266-1268, 1986.
12. Himmelstein, D. U., and Woolhandler, S. Pitfalls of private medicine: Health care in the USA. *Lancet* 2: 391-394, 1984.
13. Himmelstein, D. U., and Woolhandler, S. Cost without benefit: Administrative waste in U.S. health care. *N. Engl. J. Med.* 314: 441-445, 1986.
14. Himmelstein, D. U., and Woolhandler, S. Socialized medicine: A solution to the cost crisis in health care in the United States. *Int. J. Health Serv.* 16: 339-354, 1986.
15. Hewitt Associates. *Salaried Employee Benefits Provided by Major U.S. Employers: A Comparison Study, 1979 Through 1984.* Hewitt Associates, Lincolnshire, Ill., 1985.
16. National Center for Health Statistics. *Health, United States, 1985.* DHHS Publication No. (PHS) 86-1232. Public Health Service. U.S. Government Printing Office, Washington, D.C., December 1985.
17. Swick, T. Medical travails of America's poor and underinsured. *American College of Physicians Observer* 6(6): 1, 24, 1986.
18. Burnum, J. F. The unfortunate case of Dr. Z: How to succeed in medical practice in 1984. *N. Engl. J. Med.* 310: 729-730, 1984.
19. Reinhart, U. Economics, ethics and the American health care system. *The New Physician,* October 1985, pp. 20-42.
20. Hospital occupancy rate hits a record low at 63.6%. *Mod. Healthcare,* April 25, 1986, p. 11.
21. Iglehart, J. K. The future supply of physicians. *N. Engl. J. Med.* 314: 860-864, 1986.
22. Valdez, R. B., et al. Consequences of cost-sharing for children's health. *Pediatrics* 75: 956-961, 1985.
23. Leibowitz, A., et al. Effect of cost-sharing on use of medical services by children: Interim results from a randomized controlled trial. *Pediatrics* 75: 942-951, 1985.

24. Hadley, J. *More Medical Care, Better Health?* The Urban Institute, Washington, D.C., 1982.
25. Ingbar, M. L., and Taylor, L. P. *Hospital Costs in Massachusetts.* Harvard University Press, Cambridge, Mass., 1968.
26. Lave, J. R., and Lave, L. B. Hospital cost function analysis: Implications for cost controls. In *Hospital Cost Containment: Selected Notes for Future Policy*, edited by M. Zubkoff, I. E. Raskin, and R. S. Hanft. Prodist, New York, 1978.
27. Reynolds, R. A., and Duann, D. J. (eds.). *Socioeconomic Characteristics of Medical Practice.* American Medical Association, Chicago, 1985.
28. Himmelstein, D. U., and Woolhandler, S. Free care, cholestyramine, and health policy. *N. Engl. J. Med.* 311: 1511–1514, 1984.
29. U.S. Bureau of the Census. *Statistical Abstract of the United States: 1986*, Ed. 106. Washington, D.C., 1985.
30. Merrill, J. C., and Wassermann, R. J. Growth in national expenditures: Additional analyses. *Health Affairs* 4(4): 91–98, 1985.
31. Navarro, V. Where is the popular mandate? *N. Engl. J. Med.* 307: 1516–1518, 1982.
32. Colombotos, J., and Kirchner, C. *Physicians and Social Change.* Oxford University Press, New York, 1986.
33. Iglehart, J. K. Report of the ninth Duke University Medical Center Private Sector Conference. *N. Engl. J. Med.* 311: 204–208, 1984.
34. *Compendium of Health Statistics.* Office of Health Economics, London, 1984.
35. Maxwell, R. *Health and Wealth: An International Study of Healthcare Spending.* Lexington Books, Lexington, Mass., 1981.
36. Roemer, R., and Roemer, M. I. *Health Manpower Policy Under National Health Insurance — The Canadian Experience.* DHEW Publication No. (HRA) 77-37. Health Resources Administration, Hyattsville, Md., 1977.
37. Iglehart, J. K. Canada's health care system. *N. Engl. J. Med.* 315: 202–208, 778–784, 1986.
38. Terris, M. A cost-effective national health program. *J. Public Health Policy* 4: 252–258, 1983.
39. Hypertension Detection and Follow-up Program Cooperative Group. Five-year findings of the Hypertension Detection and Follow-up Program: I. Reduction in mortality of persons with high blood pressure, including mild hypertension. *JAMA* 242: 2562–2571, 1979.
40. Hypertension Detection and Follow-up Program Cooperative Group. Five-year findings of the Hypertension Detection and Follow-up Program: II. Mortality by race-sex and age. *JAMA* 242: 2572–2577, 1979.
41. Illich, I. *Medical Nemesis: The Expropriation of Health.* Bantam, New York, 1977.
42. Fuchs, V. R. *Who Shall Live? Health, Economics, and Social Choice.* Basic Books, New York, 1974.

CHAPTER 16

Socialized Medicine: A Solution to the Cost Crisis in Health Care in the United States

David U. Himmelstein and Steffie Woolhandler

Supporters of a national health service for the United States have argued that universal free access to care is a human right, that equal access would improve the health of the oppressed, and that a unified public system would provide a framework for more rational resource allocation and the promotion of prevention (1-4). However, advocacy of a national health program has been muted in recent years because of the perception that such reform would fuel health care cost inflation. There has been remarkable unanimity among U.S. health policy "experts" that the extension of health benefits is impossible given the current imperative to control costs. In this paper we argue that this seemingly irreconcilable contradiction between cost control and equity is phony, and that nationalization of the health care system would save both lives and money. The obstacles to a national health service are political, not economic.

The widespread belief in the United States that a national health program would increase costs is at odds with the experience of our closest linguistic and geographic neighbors. Both the British National Health Service and the Canadian national health insurance system have successfully contained costs. Health care consumes 6 percent of gross national product in Britain, 8 percent in Canada, and nearly 11 percent in the United States (5-7). While the savings in Britain attributable to rationing of care have received considerable attention (8) (there is no more rationing in Canada than in the United States), the economies on non-clinical expenditures in both Britain and Canada have been ignored. Contrary to stereotypes, these government-sponsored programs are

Originally published in the International Journal of Health Services, 16(3): 339–354, 1986. Some of this material was reprinted from the New England Journal of Medicine, 314: 441–445, 1986, with permission.

much less bureaucratized than private U.S. health care. National health programs abolish the need for much of the administrative apparatus of health care, and decrease spending for profits and marketing (4). We have analyzed the administrative savings that could be realized from instituting a Canadian-style national health insurance program or a national health service similar to that in Britain, and the potential savings from additional reforms to curtail spending for profits, marketing and litigation. We have based our calculations on 1983 data unless otherwise indicated. Our analysis suggests that nationalization of the health sector would achieve economies in non-clinical areas which would more than offset the costs of providing universal free access to care.

ADMINISTRATIVE COSTS

Many observers have noted the growing size and influence of the health bureaucracy in the United States (9,10). Between 1970 and 1982, the number of health care administrators increased 171 percent. In contrast, the number of physicians and total health care personnel increased 48 percent and 57 percent, respectively (11,12). The bureaucratization of medical care is also reflected in rapidly rising costs of health insurance overhead, hospital and nursing home administration, and doctors' office expenses (13-16). As detailed below and in Table 1, we estimate that administrative costs totaled $77.7 billion in 1983—22 percent of health spending.

The 1500 private U.S. health insurers received $110.5 billion in premiums and paid out $100 billion in benefits (17). The "overhead" of $10.5 billion paid for processing bills, marketing, building and furnishing insurance company offices, and profits for the commercial insurers. In addition the administrative costs of the Medicaid and Medicare programs were $2.9 billion (17). Other government and private health programs incurred central administrative costs of $2.2 billion (17). Total net costs for health insurance and program administration were $15.6 billion (17).

Hospital administration costs are more difficult to quantify since the line between administrative and medical tasks is often blurred, and many personnel classified as clinical for accounting purposes perform some administrative work. For instance, internists in one academic department of medicine spend 18 percent of their time on administration (18), and social workers at many hospitals devote considerable effort to insurance and reimbursement problems. Even excluding this administrative work of clinical personnel, vast amounts of money and human talent are committed to non-clinical tasks such as billing, marketing, cost accounting, and institutional planning. In California, administration and accounting constitute 18.3 percent of hospital costs (18 percent in voluntary hospitals and 19 percent in for-profit hospitals) (19,20). Similar figures have been reported for hospitals in Florida and Texas (21). We estimate that nationwide, hospital administration and accounting cost $26.9 billion in 1983 (18.3 percent of the $147.2 billion spent for hospital care).

Nursing home administration accounted for 14.4 percent of total costs in California's long-term care facilities (22,23), and a similar proportion of costs in Texas nursing homes (24). Projecting the California figure to the $28.8 billion spent

Table 1

Expenditures for administration in 1983 and projected savings from adoption
of national health insurance or national health service[a]

Category of expenditure	Actual cost ($billion)	Projected savings, NHI ($billion)	Projected savings, NHS ($billion)
Program administration and insurance overhead	15.6	6.7	6.4
Hospital administration	26.9	15.2	18.5
Nursing home administration	4.1	1.1	2.5
Physician's overhead	31.1	6.2	11.0
Total	77.7	29.2	38.4

[a]NHI = national health insurance, NHS = national health service. See Appendix for calculation
of projected savings.

nationally for nursing home care yields estimated annual nursing home administrative
costs of $4.1 billion.

Physicians incurred professional expenses of $31.1 billion in 1983, 45 percent of
their gross income (15). The proportion of professional expense devoted to office
administration is substantial. Secretarial and clerical staff make up 47 percent of
non-physician personnel employed in doctors' offices, and much of their time is
spent on administrative tasks such as patient and third party billing (13).

Spending for each of the above administrative categories has increased more rapidly
than overall health spending. Between 1965 and 1983, insurance overhead costs rose at
an annual rate of 13.8 percent, compared to the health care cost inflation rate of 12.6
percent, and this difference was most striking in the latest year (16.4 versus 10.3
percent) (14). The costs of hospital administration have risen more rapidly than have
other hospital costs (16). At a major northeastern teaching hospital, the proportion of
total expenditures devoted to administration has doubled over the past 55 years (25).
The number of office clerical personnel per office-based physician rose 14 percent
between 1975 and 1981 (13), and professional expenses increased from 37 percent to
45 percent of gross physician income between 1970 and 1983 (15). Since the volume
of services and insurance claims has increased only modestly, most of the increase in
administrative cost is due to a rapid rise in cost per service or claim (despite computer-
ization), or the addition of new administrative tasks.

ADMINISTRATIVE WASTE

While the delivery of care to 234 million Americans requires considerable administrative effort, the $77.7 billion spent annually for bureaucracy seems astonishingly large. Is it all necessary? Much of the expense is mandated by the current reimbursement system, which requires that charges for each of the 1.6 billion hospital admissions and physician visits each year be attributed to individual patients. Additional expense results from hospitals' and insurers' efforts to gain financially by identifying and marketing lucrative services (26).

Nationalization of health services could generate substantial savings by eliminating the entire private health insurance industry, much of hospital and nursing home bureaucracy, and some of doctors' office expenses. Canada's universal health insurance system is administered by the provincial governments, gives each hospital a single annual lump sum to cover operating expenses (7), and pays doctors on a fee-for-service basis. Capital spending is tightly controlled, binding fee schedules are negotiated between government and physicians, and competing private insurance programs are banned. A Canadian hospital has virtually no billing department and little of the detailed internal accounting structure needed to attribute costs and charges to individual patients and physicians. Physicians' billing is simplified by the unified insurance system. The overhead of the universal public insurance programs averages 2.5 percent of premium income (27), one-quarter of private U.S. insurers' overhead. Administration accounts for 8 percent of hospital spending, and insurance overhead and hospital administration together consume 6 percent of total health resources (28). Canadian physicians' professional expenses amount to 36 percent of gross income (27,29).

The British National Health Service (NHS) owns most hospitals, pays physicians on a salaried or capitation basis, and has no insurance overhead. Administrative costs amount to 5.7 percent of hospital expenses, central administration consumes 2.6 percent of total spending, and together these categories account for 6 percent of health spending (5,30). Physicians' professional expenses average 29 percent of gross income (31).

Estimation of the costs of nursing home administration under national health insurance or a national health service is difficult. In much of Canada nursing home care is reimbursed in a manner similar to that in the United States, i.e., by private insurance or "out-of-pocket" payments. The proportion spent for administration in this private system (10.5 percent) is higher than in Canada's acute care hospitals (32). In the British NHS, long-term and acute-care facilities are more integrated than in the United States, and statistics for both are usually reported in a single category. For our projections we assumed that British nursing homes, like British hospitals, devote 5.7 percent of spending to administration.

We calculated potential administrative savings by projecting the proportion of spending for administration in Canada and Britain to U.S. health expenditures. The details of these calculations are presented in the Appendix. Based on these international comparisons, administrative savings of $29.2 billion, 8.2 percent of health spending, could be realized by adopting a Canadian-style national health insurance program in the United States. $38.4 billion, 10.1 percent of total health spending, could be saved by following Britain's lead and instituting a national health service (Table 1).

PROFITS

Health care profits accrue to owners of for-profit hospitals, nursing homes, and other health institutions; to pharmaceutical and medical equipment manufacturers; to health facility construction firms; and to financial institutions involved in health care capital acquisition and construction. The profits of health-related industries have soared in the past three decades. After-tax profits averaging 7.6 percent over the last five years place health care third among the 42 U.S. industry groups (33). Profits represent health spending in excess of the costs of care, and no clear evidence suggests that profits are associated with improved quality of care. Indeed, the scant empirical evidence comparing proprietary and not-for-profit hospitals and nursing homes supports the opposite conclusion (34,35). Similarly, claims of greater efficiency in the for-profit health sector are not supported by current data. Private insurance plans have much higher overhead than do government insurance programs (17,36,37). For-profit hospitals economize on clinical personnel and services but have higher total per diem costs because of greater expenditures for administrative and ancillary services (20,21,38–41).

The pursuit of profit also diminishes the cost effectiveness of the health care system as a whole by basing resource allocation primarily on financial considerations. The profit-maximizing behavior of medical enterprises often conflicts with the cost-minimizing interests of society. Potentially cost-effective services offering scant financial reward such as immunization programs, prenatal care for the poor, and non-pharmacologic treatment of borderline hypertension are markedly underdeveloped. Meanwhile vast resources are devoted to lucrative but unproven services such as executive stress tests, weight loss clinics, and coronary artery surgery for asymptomatic patients without left main disease. Pharmaceutical firms squander enormous sums promoting "me-too" formulations of popular drugs, while eschewing vaccines or "orphan" drugs for uncommon illnesses (42–44). Similarly, the option of home-based renal dialysis is unavailable in many areas, forcing all dialysis patients into institution-based treatment, which is twice as expensive (and more profitable) (45).

Profits for the various sectors of the health industry are shown in Table 2. Estimates for pharmaceutical firms and hospitals were obtained from standard published sources (46,47). Since national data on nursing home profits are unavailable, we based our estimates on the 5.6-percent profit rate of California's nursing homes (22) projected to the $28.8 billion spent nationally for nursing home care. Most corporations prominent in health care capital financing, construction, equipment manufacture, and supply also engage in non-health care business and do not report health care related profits separately. We therefore estimated profits for these sectors from figures for revenues (17,48–50), outstanding debt (51), and average profit rates for health related industries (33,50,52).

Adopting the British model of nationalization or a Canadian-style tightly controlled public insurance system in the United States would largely eliminate the profits of health care providers ($2.8 billion) and financial institutions ($2.1 billion). Broader

Table 2

Expenditures for profits in 1983, and projected savings from adoption of
national health insurance, national health service, or nationalization of
all health-related industries[a]

Sector of health industry	Actual profit ($billion)	Projected savings, NHI ($billion)	Projected savings, NHS ($billion)	Projected savings, NHRI ($billion)
Health institutions	2.8	2.8	2.8	2.8
Financial institutions	2.1	2.1	2.1	2.1
Hospital construction	0.2	0	0	0.2
Medical equipment and supplies	2.8	0	0	2.8
Pharmaceuticals	5.6	0	0	5.6
Total	13.5	4.9	4.9	13.5

[a]NHI = national health insurance, NHS = national health service, NHRI = nationalization of all
health-related industries. See text for calculations and data sources.

reform could curtail profits in the drug ($5.6 billion (46)), medical equipment ($2.8
billion), and hospital construction ($0.2 billion) industries. Thus potential savings
from eliminating health care profits range from $4.9 billion to $13.5 billion in 1983,
depending on whether nationalization were limited to health providers or were
extended to suppliers and construction as well (Table 2).

PHYSICIANS' INCOMES

Another area of potential savings is physicians' incomes, which have increased
sharply relative to average wages. In 1941, U.S. doctors earned 3.5 times as much as
an average worker. This ratio had climbed to 4.2 in 1951 and 5.5 in 1983, when
physicians' incomes averaged $106,300 (12,15,53). We are unaware of any evidence
that quality of care has improved as a result, and 70 percent of Americans believe
physicians are overpaid (54). Current reimbursement mechanisms skew the distribution of physician services toward financial rather than health needs (3), and have
reinforced income disparities between primary care and procedure-oriented specialties.

The impact of a national health program on physician incomes would depend on
the fee or salary scale. In 1982, the average Canadian physician earned $97,000
(Canadian dollars), 4.8 times the average wage, and disparities among specialties were
considerably smaller than in the United States (29). Inter-specialty financial
inequalities are also smaller in Britain, where in 1980 the average physician earned 2.3
times the average male worker's wage (55). If U.S. doctors' incomes (relative to
average wages) were reduced to the level found in Canada or England, doctors would
be paid an average of $93,400 or $53,700, respectively. This would represent total
savings of $4.6 billion or $18.6 billion.

MARKETING

U.S. drug companies spend approximately $2 billion annually for advertising and "detailing" (56). Some have argued that such marketing adversely affects physicians' prescribing habits (57), and no health benefit has ever been demonstrated. Similar arguments apply to advertising for medical equipment and supplies. Marketing expenses for these categories are substantial, but are not included in our calculations because reliable estimates of aggregate expenditures are unavailable.

Advertising by hospitals, Health Maintenance Organizations (HMOs), and other health providers has increased dramatically in recent years (26). Hospital industry sources estimate that advertising and marketing account for one percent of total not-for-profit hospital spending, and between three and five percent of for-profit hospital spending (58). Based on these figures, provider marketing cost at least $1.9 billion in 1983. This estimate excludes marketing expenditures by HMOs and other non-hospital providers since reliable data on these expenditures are unavailable.

Total marketing and advertising costs exceeded $3.9 billion in 1983. If reimbursement under a national health program excluded compensation for marketing costs, at least this much would be saved.

LEGAL WASTE

The legal profession has become increasingly entangled in health care, and the legal complexity of medical practice and administration now requires many hospitals to retain full-time legal counsel (59). Malpractice litigation and so-called defensive medicine (e.g., excessive diagnostic testing) also consume considerable physician time and expense (60), with malpractice premiums alone costing $2.1 billion in 1983 (61). The effect of malpractice litigation on the quality of care is uncertain (62). At best, litigation seems an inefficient and capricious method of health care quality assurance. Between 66 and 80 percent of malpractice premiums are consumed by legal costs and insurance overhead (62,63). While 8 percent of physicians are sued annually, fewer than 300 verdicts favorable to plaintiffs result each year (61). Even assuming that many more cases are settled before trial, it is clear that the financial benefits of the massive malpractice expenditures accrue to lawyers and a tiny minority of injured patients.

While malpractice claims are much less frequent in Canada and Britain than in the United States, it is unclear whether this is a result of differences in health care or reflects a more general litigiousness of U.S. society. However, a national no-fault compensation system for iatrogenic damage or error modeled after the Swedish "malpractice" system (64) or the accident compensation system in New Zealand (65) would undoubtedly compensate injured patients more evenly and reduce legal fees. While projection of Swedish experience to the United States suggests that substantial savings in malpractice costs could be realized, such extrapolation is complex and probably not warranted. However, considerable savings would result from the abolition of incentives for "defensive medicine", estimated to cost between 15 and 100 billion dollars annually (66). Based on the lower figure and assuming that 15 percent of this potential saving has already been included in our calculation of

Table 3

Expenditures for medically irrelevant services in 1983, and projected savings
from adoption of national health insurance, national health service, or
nationalization of all health-related industries[a]

Category of expenditure	Actual cost ($billion)	Projected savings, NHI ($billion)	Projected savings, NHS ($billion)	Projected savings, NHRI ($billion)
Health administration and insurance overhead	77.7	29.2	38.4	38.4
Profits	13.5	4.9	4.9	13.5
Physicians' incomes	38.2	4.6	18.6	18.6
Marketing	3.9	3.9	3.9	3.9
Defensive medicine	12.8	0	0	12.8
Total	146.1	42.6	65.8	87.2

[a]NHI = national health insurance, NHS = national health service, NHRI = nationalization of all health-related industries.

administrative costs and profits, legal reform might be expected to yield yearly savings of at least $12.8 billion, 3.6 percent of health spending.

In summary, the total potential savings from curtailing medically irrelevant expenditures are shown in Table 3. These savings range from 12.0 to 24.5 percent of health spending ($42.6 to $87.2 billion in 1983), depending on whether national health insurance, a national health service, or complete nationalization of health related industries were undertaken, and depending on the level of physicians' incomes.

DISCUSSION

One quarter of health spending ($87.2 billion in 1983) is wasted on aspects of care without demonstrated health benefit: excess administration, profits, high physician incomes, marketing, and defensive medicine. Curtailing these aspects of care through structural reform of the health care system would yield substantial savings without resort to rationing or further bureaucratic constraint on patients, health workers, or physicians. The potential savings we have identified are greater than those envisaged by any cost control program seriously entertained in Washington, and exceed the likely cost of extra services needed to provide universal free access to care.

We have almost certainly underestimated potential savings. Our estimates are based on the assumption that administrative costs would be reduced to the same proportion of total health spending as in Canada or Britain. Since both countries spend much less for health care than the United States, calculations based on the amount (rather than proportion) spent for administration would yield estimates of savings between $25 and $30 billion higher (even after correction for wage differentials between the United States, Britain, and Canada). In addition, our estimate of U.S. administrative costs excludes administrative costs for clinics, federal hospitals, and union and employer health benefit programs, and the administrative work of clinical personnel. Potential savings in legal and compensation costs with a no-fault malpractice system were likewise excluded. Finally, we omitted the large potential savings from changes in medical practice likely to occur after the abolition of financial incentives for providers. Past reimbursement practices have rewarded and undoubtedly stimulated excessive interventions, superfluous medical services and products, and the duplication of health institutions, while discouraging population-based prevention. The elimination of pecuniary interests in health care might result in substantial reductions in unnecessary services and further savings through adequate funding of prevention (67).

Much of the data on which this analysis is based are well substantiated, but in a few areas there is a paucity of reliable information. Remarkably little research has been undertaken on the costs and benefits of health administration, and the comparability of cost estimates for the United States, Britain, and Canada is uncertain. Similarly, our estimates of profits and marketing expenses for health-related industries are imprecise. However, it is undeniable that large sums are consumed by entrepreneurial activities, and that U.S. administrative and insurance overhead costs could be considerably reduced by adopting a health system similar to that of Canada or Britain. Indeed, the Shriners Hospitals in the United States (charitable institutions that do not bill for services) claim that administrative overhead accounts for only two percent of total spending. Overall, while the exact amount wasted on excess administration, profits, marketing, defensive medicine, and exhorbitant physician incomes is open to question, there can be little doubt that it is substantial.

Canada and Britain also provide evidence that a national health program need not compromise quality of care. The standards of care and availability of high technology services are strikingly similar in Canada and the United States. While underfunding of the British NHS has caused rationing of some costly services, the improved availability of routine care has apparently offset shortcomings in high technology services relative to the United States. Prior to instituting universal free access to care, both Canada and Britain had age-adjusted mortality rates higher than those in the United States. In both, the introduction of free care was followed within a decade by a sharp decline in mortality to current levels, slightly lower than U.S. levels (5,68,69). Moreover, neither innovation nor research appear to have suffered, and both health care systems enjoy enthusiastic public support (70,71).

The wasteful expenditures that we have identified are deeply rooted in the current U.S. reimbursement system. Differential access to care based on ability to pay necessitates the herculean administrative task of attributing each charge and payment to an individual patient. Reliance on market forces for the allocation of health resources compels health institutions to engage in marketing and to construct bureaucratic sieves to separate lucrative from unprofitable patients, services, and physicians. Indeed, the lowest-cost hospitals and those serving inner city areas with the greatest medical needs have been at highest risk of financial failure (72,73). Finally, reimbursement rates have virtually assured profits for entrepreneurs with access to private capital and with a willingness to tailor services to meet financial needs.

The abolition of billing would at a single stroke eliminate the need for the entire health insurance industry and much of doctors' office and hospital administration.

Distribution of funds based on health needs rather than market forces would excise spending on marketing. Proscribing pecuniary gain from health care would make additional funds available for health services and research. Abandoning litigation in favor of no-fault compensation could direct remuneration to victims of medical errors rather than to attorneys and laboratories.

In contrast, health policy reforms that leave intact these basic structures can attain savings only by limiting the volume of clinical services or the wages of health workers. Most "mainstream" health policy debate has concentrated on the optimal means of rationing care (74,75). Cost effectiveness analysis is usually advocated as a way of minimizing the ill effects of such rationing (76,77). Unfortunately, analysts have based their calculations on current costs (or charges), which include large sums wasted on bureaucracy, marketing, profits, high physician incomes, and defensive medicine. Since the proportion of total costs wasted varies widely from one service to another, curtailing wasteful expenditures would radically alter the relative cost effectiveness of clinical practices. Hence the cost effectiveness approach is based on the assumption that the structure of the health care system will remain essentially unchanged, and implicitly ignores the potential for savings through structural reform. Moreover, rationing based on cost effectiveness analysis requires the collection of detailed financial data, the growth of administrative control, and further bureaucratic hypertrophy. While clinical epidemiologists and economists have used cost effectiveness analysis to dissect extravagances from bargains in medical practice, government and industry have applied the blunter instruments of prospective payment systems (which give providers financial incentives to limit care) and reductions in both the number of people with health insurance and the comprehensiveness of coverage (78–80).

All of these approaches ignore the inefficiencies inherent in the private provision of health care. Indeed, most recent reforms have involved hiring more administrators to assure the delivery of less care, and have actually encouraged entrepreneurialism and bureaucratization while exacerbating inequalities in health care and health (81–83). Consequently the costs of administration and entrepreneurialism are rising at an accelerating rate (84). Between 1983 and 1984, hospital profits more than doubled (85) and insurance overhead and central administration costs rose 22.4 percent compared to a 9 percent increase in total health spending (86). One major cost control effort, the Medicare Diagnosis Related Group (DRG) program, has resulted in the creation of a new federal enforcement bureaucracy costing tens of millions of dollars (87), elimination of more than 150,000 hospital jobs (88), addition of at least 6000 new fiscal personnel (89,90), a "blizzard of new paperwork" (89), purchase of hundreds of millions of dollars of administrative computer equipment (91) and "outlier insurance" (92), and the threat of premature discharges, slow adoption of useful new technologies, and undercare for the most seriously ill (93,94). All such programs have eliminated some wheat of needed care along with the chaff of excess services.

The political obstacles to our proposed radical reforms are formidable but not insurmountable. Both the British National Health Service and Canadian national health insurance program are immensely popular (70,71). Opinion polls in the United States indicate strong public support for an egalitarian national health program, even if this program entailed paying higher taxes (95). In contrast, enthusiasm has been notably lacking among politicians and physicians. Policy makers have been reluctant to back reforms that challenge both tradition and powerful private interests, while doctors have viewed a national health program as a threat to clinical independence.

Recent developments may prod physicians to reevaluate their long-standing opposition to a national health program. The stark contrast between unevaluated profligacy in administration and detailed financial scrutiny of clinical practice illuminates the incipient relationship between bureaucrats and clinicians. Administration is being transmogrified from the servant of medicine to its master, from a handful of support personnel facilitating patient care to a vast apparatus increasingly influential in medical decision making. Each new "reform" deposits yet another layer of administrators with the power to say "no" but not "yes." In this context, the potential threat to physicians' clinical freedom from a national health program pales in comparison to the reality of growing bureaucratic control. Many physicians may prefer the public accountability of a locally controlled universal health system, and even some modest income reductions, to the ascendancy of entrepreneurialism, litigiousness, and bureaucracy.

Radical critics of U.S. health care have focused on inequalities in health care and have convincingly argued that universal free access to care would improve health. Unfortunately, few have exposed the waste inherent in the health industry under capitalism, and the bourgeois claim that the "free market" in health care engenders efficiency has rarely been challenged. As a result, advocates of socialized medicine have confronted skyrocketing costs as an obstacle rather than an opportunity. Our analysis demonstrates that socialized medicine would save both lives and money. Far from exacerbating the health care cost crisis, universal and equal access to health care would solve it.

It is striking that despite overwhelming evidence to the contrary most experts believe that cost control and equality in health care are in contradiction. The 22 percent of health spending devoted to administration and the billions of dollars spent for marketing and profits are virtually unmentioned in the voluminous health policy literature. This stunning epidemic of selective ignorance suggests a profound ideological bias that prevents the serious consideration of nationalization of the health industry. In our view this bias is a reflection of the capitalist class's opposition to nationalization. Capitalists within the health sector are dismayed at the prospect of socialized medicine because it would directly threaten their profits. For the rest of the capitalist class, the fact that most people have health insurance only when they are employed provides an important lever that weakens the ability of workers to withhold their labor (96). Concern for profit and political control rather than worry over the cost of care lies at the heart of opposition to socialized medicine. The facade of contradiction between equity and cost control hides a very real conflict between capital and labor.

Socialized medicine can solve the cost crisis at the expense of bureaucrats and barristers, entrepreneurs and actuaries. We think many will find this a more attractive solution than the preservation of a private system that protects profit and privilege, while waste coexists with want.

APPENDIX

Administrative savings from adopting national health insurance were calculated as follows:

Potential health insurance overhead and central program administration savings = [(insurance overhead and program administration as percent of total health spending, U.S.) - (insurance overhead and program administration as percent of total health spending, Canada)] × (total health spending, U.S.)
$$= (0.044 - 0.025) \times \$355.4 \text{ billion} = \$6.7 \text{ billion}$$
Potential hospital administration savings = [(percent of hospital spending for administration, U.S.) - (percent of hospital spending for administration, Canada)] × (total hospital spending, U.S.)
$$= (0.183 - 0.08) \times \$147.2 \text{ billion} = \$15.2 \text{ billion}$$
Potential savings on doctors' office administration = [(professional expenses as percent of physicians' gross income, U.S.) - (professional expenses as percent of physicians gross income, Canada)] × (physicians' gross incomes, U.S.)
$$= (0.45 - 0.36) \times \$69 \text{ billion} = \$6.2 \text{ billion}$$
Potential nursing home administration savings = [(percent of nursing home spending for administration, U.S.) - (percent of nursing home spending for administration, Canada)] × (total nursing home spending, U.S.)
$$= (0.144 - 0.105) \times \$28.8 \text{ billion} = \$1.1 \text{ billion}$$

Administrative savings from adopting a national health service or from complete nationalization of all health related industries were calculated as follows:

Potential health insurance overhead and central program administration savings = [(insurance overhead and program administration as percent of total health spending, U.S.) - (insurance overhead and program administration as percent of total health spending, Britain)] × (total health spending, U.S.)
$$= (0.044 - 0.026) \times \$355.4 \text{ billion} = \$6.4 \text{ billion.}$$
Potential hospital administration savings = [(percent of hospital spending for administration, U.S.) - (percent of hospital spending for administration, Britain)] × (total hospital spending, U.S.)
$$= (0.183 - 0.057) \times \$147.2 \text{ billion} = \$18.5 \text{ billion.}$$
Potential savings on doctors' office administration = [(professional expenses as percent of physicians' gross income, U.S.) - (professional expenses as percent of physicians gross income, Britain)] × (physicians' gross incomes, U.S.)
$$= (0.45 - 0.29) \times \$69 \text{ billion} = \$11.0 \text{ billion.}$$
Potential nursing home administration savings = [(percent of nursing home spending for administration, U.S.) - (percent of nursing home spending for administration, Canada)] × (total nursing home spending, U.S.)
$$= (0.144 - 0.057) \times \$28.8 \text{ billion} = \$2.5 \text{ billion.}$$

Acknowledgments — We thank government statisticians in London, Ottawa, Washington, D.C., Texas, and California without whose work and assistance this and other economic analyses of health care systems would not be possible. Drs. David Bor and Howard Waitzkin provided advice and inspiration. Drs. Mary Bassett, David Berger, Mark Nelson, and Steven Shea made valuable comments on early drafts of the manuscript. The opinions expressed and any errors are solely those of the authors.

REFERENCES

1. Terris, M., et al. The case for a national health service. *Am. J. Public Health* 67: 1183–1185, 1977.
2. Dellums, R. The United States Health Service. *Congressional Record* vol. 129, no. 79, June 7, 1983.
3. Himmelstein, D. U., and Woolhandler, S. Pitfalls of private medicine: health care in the USA. *Lancet* ii: 391–394, 1984.
4. Waitzkin, H. *The Second Sickness: Contradictions of Capitalist Health Care.* Free Press, New York, 1983.
5. Office of Health Economics. *Compendium of Health Statistics.* London, 1984.
6. Health and Welfare Canada. *National Health Expenditures in Canada 1970–1982.* Department of National Health and Welfare, Ottawa, 1984.
7. Detsky, A. S., Stacey, S. R., and Bombardier, C. The effectiveness of a regulatory strategy in containing hospital costs: the Ontario experience, 1967–1981. *N. Engl. J. Med.* 309: 151–159, 1983.
8. Aaron, H. J., and Schwartz, W. B. *The Painful Prescription: Rationing Hospital Care.* The Brookings Institution, Washington, D.C., 1984.
9. Alper, P. R. The new language of hospital management. *N. Engl. J. Med.* 311: 1249–1251, 1984.
10. Morone, J. A., and Dunham, A. B. The waning of professional dominance: DRGs and the hospitals. *Health Affairs* 3(1): 73–87, 1984.
11. National Center for Health Statistics. *Health United States 1979.* Department of Health, Education, and Welfare Publication No. (PHS) 80-1232, Hyattsville, Maryland, 1980.
12. Bureau of the Census. *Statistical Abstract of the United States 1984*, p. 109, Washington, D.C., 1983.
13. Reynolds, R. A., and Abram, J. B. (eds.). *Socioeconomic Characteristics of Medical Practice.* American Medical Association, Chicago, 1983.
14. Crozier, D. A. National medical care spending. *Health Affairs* 3(3):108–120, 1984.
15. Reynolds, R. A., and Ohsfeldt, R. L. (eds.). *Socioeconomic Characteristics of Medical Practice 1984.* American Medical Association, Chicago, 1984.
16. Alper, P. R. What price management? (letter) *N. Engl. J. Med.* 312: 448, 1985.
17. Gibson, R. M., et al. National Health Expenditures, 1983. *Health Care Financing Rev.* 6(2): 1–29, 1984.
18. Chin, D., et al. The relationship of faculty academic activity to financing sources in a department of medicine. *N. Engl. J. Med.* 312: 1029–1034, 1985.
19. California Health Facilities Commission. *Aggregate Hospital Financial Data for California: Report Periods Ending June 30, 1982-June 29, 1983.* California Health Facilities Commission Report No. II-84-7, Sacramento, 1984.
20. Pattison, R. Personal communication, 1985.
21. Lewin and Associates. *Studies in the Comparative Performance of Investor-owned and Not-for-profit Hospitals*, vol. IV. Washington, D.C., 1981.
22. Pape, C. G. (ed.). *Aggregate Long-term Care Facility Financial Data.* California Health Facilities Commission, Sacramento, 1985.
23. Gerould, P. Personal communication, 1985.
24. Hart, G. (ed.). *1983 Cost Report Data.* Texas Department of Human Resources Office of Programs Budget and Statistics, Economic Analysis Division, Cost Finding Section, Texas Medicaid SNF/ICF Program, Austin, 1985.
25. Bor, D., Himmelstein, D. U., and Woolhandler, S. Unpublished data.
26. Yanish, D. Hospitals spending more money on advertising, market research. *Modern Healthcare* March 5, 1985, pp. 49–50.

27. Rehmer, L. Director, Health Information Division, Health and Welfare Canada. Personal communication, 1985.

28. Administrative and Supportive Services (Internal report). Health Information Division, Information Systems Directorate, Policy, Planning and Information Branch, Health and Welfare Canada, Ottawa, 1981.

29. Health Information Division. *Estimates of Physicians' Earnings, 1973-1982.* Policy, Planning and Information Branch, Department of National Health and Welfare, Ottawa, 1983.

30. Deitch, R. The NHS debate: Mr. Kinnock leads attack. *Lancet* ii: 1092-1093, 1983.

31. Maynard, A. *Health Care in the European Community*, p. 203. University of Pittsburgh Press, Pittsburgh, 1975.

32. Dowler, J. Institutional Statistics Section, Statistics Canada. Personal communication, 1985.

33. Anonymous. Annual report on American industry. *Forbes*, January 12, 1985, p. 260.

34. Vladek, B. C. *Unloving Care: the Nursing Home Tragedy.* Basic Books, New York, 1980.

35. Williams, R. L. Measuring the effectiveness of perinatal medical care. *Med. Care* 17: 95-110, 1979.

36. Health Insurance Association of America. *Source Book of Health Insurance Data: 1984 Update.* Washington, D.C., 1984.

37. Donahue, R. J. Health premiums set record in 1984. *National Underwriter* 89(22): 28, 1985.

38. Pattison, R. V., and Katz, H. M. Investor-owned and not-for-profit hospital: a comparison based on California data. *N. Engl. J. Med.* 309: 347-353, 1983.

39. Schlesinger, M., and Dorwart, R. Ownership and mental-health services: a reappraisal of the shift toward privately owned facilities. *N. Engl. J. Med.* 311: 959-965, 1984.

40. American Hospital Association. *Hospital Statistics: 1984 Edition.* American Hospital Association, Chicago, 1984.

41. Watt, M. J., et al. The comparative performance of investor-owned chain and not-for-profit hospitals. *N. Engl. J. Med.* 314: 89-96, 1986.

42. Glenn, K. The great American vaccine shortage. *Washington Report on Medicine and Health* January 14, 1985.

43. Asbury, C. H. Medical drugs of limited commercial interest: profit alone is a better pill. *Int. J. Health Serv.* 11: 451-462, 1981.

44. Ashbrook, T. Malaria vaccine: orphan drug of the 80s? *Boston Globe*, April 25, 1983, pp. 35-36.

45. Roberts, S. D., Maxwell, D. R., and Gross, T. L. Cost-effective care of end-stage renal disease: a billion dollar question. *Ann. Intern. Med.* 92: 243-248, 1980.

46. Bureau of the Census. *Quarterly Financial Report for Manufacturing, Mining, and Trade Corporations, Fourth Quarter 1983.* U.S. Department of Commerce Publication No. QFR-83-4, Washington, D.C., 1984.

47. Federation of American Hospitals. *Statistical Profile of the Investor-owned Hospital Industry, 1983.* Washington, D.C., 1984.

48. Punch, L. Healthcare construction boom continued to show vigor in 1984. *Modern Healthcare*, March 1, 1985, pp. 63-88.

49. Hale, A. B., and Hale, A. B. (eds.). *The Medical and Healthcare Marketplace Guide: a Comprehensive Industrial Guide to the U.S. Medical and Healthcare Marketplace*, 3rd ed. The International Bio-Medical Information Service, Miami, 1983, with quarterly updates through March 31, 1984.

50. Office of Technology Assessment. *Federal Policies and the Medical Device Industry.* U.S. Congress, Office of Technology Assessment, OTA-H-230, Washington, D.C., 1984.

51. Wood, S. P., American Hospital Association, Division of Hospital Planning and Finance. Personal communication, 1985.

52. Buchanan, R. J. The financial status of the new medical-industrial complex. *Inquiry* 19: 308-316, 1982.

53. Bureau of the Census. *Historical Statistics of the United States Colonial Times to 1970: Bicentennial Edition*, Part 1. Washington, D.C., 1975.

54. Ross, C. E., and Lauritsen, J. Public opinion about doctors' pay. *Am. J. Public Health* 75: 668-670, 1985.

55. Harrison, A., and Gretton, J. (eds.). *Health Care UK 1984: an Economic, Social and Policy Audit.* Chartered Institute of Public Finance and Accountancy, London, 1984.

56. Portman, R. A new strategy for promotional spending. *Pharmaceutical Executive*, April, 1983, pp. 42-45.

57. Avorn, J., Chen, M., and Hartley, R. Scientific versus commercial sources of influence on the prescribing behavior of physicians. *Am. J. Med.* 73: 4-8, 1982.

58. Super, K. Hospitals will favor hard sell in advertising, experts predict. *Modern Healthcare*, January 3, 1986, pp. 74–76.
59. Wallace, C. Role of hospital legal departments debated at health lawyers' forum. *Modern Healthcare*, November 1, 1984, p. 106.
60. Zuckerman, S. Medical malpractice: claims, legal costs, and the practice of defensive medicine. *Health Affairs* 3(3): 128–133, 1984.
61. Glenn, K. Malpractice insurance: affordability crisis? *Washington Report on Medicine and Health* December 10, 1984.
62. Annas, G. J., Katz, B. F., and Trakimas, R. G. Medical malpractice litigation under national health insurance: essential or expendable? *Duke Law Journal* 6: 1335–1373, 1975.
63. Danzon, P. M. *Medical Malpractice: Theory, Evidence, and Public Policy*, p. 187. Harvard, Cambridge, Mass., 1985.
64. Cooper, J. K. Sweden's no fault patient injury insurance. *N. Engl. J. Med.* 294: 1268–1270, 1976.
65. Smith, R. Compensation: making the best of a bad job. *World Health Forum* 4(1): 51–56, 1983.
66. Glenn, K. Legislators prescribe malpractice reforms. *Washington Report on Medicine and Health* April 30, 1984.
67. Terris, M. A cost-effective national health program. (Editorial) *J. Public Health Policy* 4: 252–258, 1983.
68. Maxwell, R. J. *Health and Wealth: an International Study of Health Care Spending.* Lexington, Toronto, 1981.
69. Roemer, R., and Roemer, M. I. *Health Manpower Policy Under National Health Insurance— the Canadian Experience.* Health Resources Administration, Department of Health, Education, and Welfare Publication No. (HRA) 77-37. Hyattsville, Maryland, 1977.
70. Gill, D. G. *The British National Health Service: a Sociologist's Perspective*, p. 124. Public Health Service, Washington, D.C., 1980.
71. Canadian House of Commons. *Report of the Special Committee on the Federal-Provincial Fiscal Arrangements (Breau Committee).* The Queen's Printer, Ottawa, 1980.
72. Sager, A. Why urban voluntary hospitals close. *Health Services Research* 18: 451–475, 1983.
73. Hadley, J., Mullner, R., and Feder, J. The financially distressed hospital. *N. Engl. J. Med.* 307: 1283–1287, 1982.
74. Fuchs, V. R. The rationing of medical care. *N. Engl. J. Med.* 311: 1572–1573, 1984.
75. Evans, R. W. Health care technology and the inevitability of resource allocation and rationing decisions. *J.A.M.A.* 294: 2047–2053, 1983.
76. Bloom, B. S., and Luft, H. S. (eds.). *Cost Benefit, Cost Effectiveness, and Other Decision-making Techniques in Health Care Resource Allocation.* Biomedical Information Corporation, New York, 1983.
77. McNeil, B. J., and Pauker, S. G. Decision analysis for public health: principles and illustrations. *Annu. Rev. Public Health* 5: 135–161, 1984.
78. Anonymous. Manufacturers reducing health benefits. *Health Lawyers News Report* 11: 7, September 1983.
79. Melia, E. P., et al. Competition in the health care marketplace: a beginning in California. *N. Engl. J. Med.* 308: 788–792, 1983.
80. Iglehart, J. K. Medicare begins prospective payment of hospitals. *N. Engl. J. Med.* 308: 1428–1432, 1983.
81. Waitzkin, H. Two-class medicine returns to the United States: impact of Medi-Cal reform. *Lancet* ii: 1144–1146, 1984.
82. Schoen, C. Medicaid and the poor: Medicaid myths and reality and the impact of recent legislative changes. *Bull. N.Y. Acad. Med.* 60: 54–65, 1984.
83. Lurie, N., et al. Termination of Medi-Cal: does it affect health? *N. Engl. J. Med.* 311: 480–484, 1984.
84. Anonymous. Earnings up for most providers, suppliers. *Modern Healthcare* August 2, 1985, p. 20.
85. Anonymous, IG report: hospital profits soared in 1985. *Washington Actions on Health* December 2, 1985, p. 7.
86. Anderson, G. F. National medical care spending. *Health Affairs* 4(3): 100–107, 1985.
87. Health Care Financing Administration. Unpublished data.
88. Davis, K., et al. Is cost containment working? *Health Affairs* 4(3): 81–94, 1985.
89. Baldwin, M. F., and Facklemann, K. A. Blizzard of paperwork, new rules are burying PROs and hospitals. *Modern Healthcare* January 3, 1986, pp. 46–54.

90. Anonymous. Hospitals' PPS paperwork forcing personnel additions. *Modern Healthcare* November 15, 1984, p. 16.
91. Jackson, B., and Jensen, J. Hospitals turn to new software, hardware to cope with DRGs. *Modern Healthcare* September 1984, pp. 109–112.
92. Anonymous. NorthStar offering outlier insurance. *Modern Healthcare* February 15, 1985, p. 32.
93. Glenn, K. DRGs and quality of care. *Washington Report on Medicine and Health* January 7, 1985.
94. Anonymous. Medicare patients leaving hospitals sooner, sicker. *Modern Healthcare* March 15, 1985, p. 28.
95. Navarro, V. Where is the popular mandate? *N. Engl. J. Med.* 307: 1516–1518, 1982.
96. Himmelstein, D. U., and Woolhandler, S. Medicine as industry: the health sector in the U.S. *Monthly Review* 35(11): 13–25, 1984.

Contributors

THOMAS BODENHEIMER is a practicing internist in San Francisco and an assistant clinical professor at the University of California, San Francisco. He received his A.B. and M.D. degrees from Harvard University and an M.P.H. from the University of California, Berkeley. Dr. Bodenheimer is coauthor of three books: *Billions for Bandaids* (1972); *Closing the Doors on the Poor: The Dismantling of California's County Hospitals* (1975); and *Rollback! Right-wing Power in U.S. Foreign Policy* (South End Press, 1989). He has also written numerous articles on health policy, and is active in Physicians for a National Health Program.

ROBERT M. BRANDON is executive director of Citizens Fund, Washington, D.C.

TIM BRIGHTBILL is a contributing editor for *HealthWeek,* a biweekly news magazine covering the health care industry. He has written for several other health care trade publications and previously served as managing editor of *Hospital Materials Management.* He received his bachelor's degree from Northwestern University, Evanston, Illinois.

DAVID U. HIMMELSTEIN is associate professor of medicine at Harvard Medical School and chief of the division of Social and Community Medicine at Cambridge Hospital, Cambridge, Massachusetts. He received his M.D. from Columbia University and completed internal medicine training at Highland Hospital in Oakland, California. He was a founder of Physicians for a National Health Program, and he serves as the Co-Director of the Center for National Health Program Studies at The Cambridge Hospital/Harvard Medical School.

VICENTE NAVARRO is professor of health, sociology, and policy studies at The Johns Hopkins University. He is advisor to several governments and international agencies, as well as to labor organizations in many countries. A founder and past president of the International Association of Health Policy and the founder and editor-in-chief of the *International Journal of Health Services,* he has written extensively on sociology, political sociology, and the political economy of medical and social services. Dr. Navarro is the author of *Medicine Under Capitalism; Social Security and Medicine in the U.S.S.R.; Class Struggle, the State and Medicine: An Historical and Contemporary Analysis of the Medical Sector in Great Britain;* and *Crisis, Health, and Medicine.* He is editor of the collections *Health and Medical Care in the U.S.: A Critical Analysis; Imperialism, Health and Medicine;* and (with D. Berman) *Health and Work Under Capitalism: An International Perspective.* He was health advisor to the Jesse Jackson 1988 Campaign and a member of the Democratic Party Platform Committee.

MICHAEL PODHORZER is education director of Citizens Fund, Washington, D.C.

THOMAS H. POLLAK is research director of Citizens Fund, Washington, D.C.

STEFFIE WOOLHANDLER is an assistant professor of medicine at Harvard Medical School, an adjunct associate professor of public health at Boston University, and the Director of Inpatient Services at Cambridge Hospital, Cambridge, Massachusetts. She received her M.D. from Louisiana State University, New Orleans, and her M.P.H. from the University of California, Berkeley. She completed an internal medicine residency at Cambridge Hospital. Dr. Woolhandler was a founder of Physicians for a National Health Program, and she serves as the Co-Director of the Center for National Health Program Studies at The Cambridge Hospital/Harvard Medical School.

Index

Page numbers in italics indicate figures; those followed by "t" indicate tables.